CHSP
HUNGARIAN STUDIES SERIES
NO. 1

EDITORS
Peter Pastor
Ivan Sanders

András Gerő EMPEROR FRANCIS JOSEPH,
KING OF THE HUNGARIANS

Translated from the Hungarian by
James Patterson and *Enikő Koncz*

Social Science Monographs, Boulder, Colorado

 Center for Hungarian Studies and
Publications, Inc., Wayne, New Jersey

Distributed by Columbia University Press, New York
2001

EAST EUROPEAN MONOGRAPHS
NO. DLXVI

Center for Hungarian Studies and Publications, Inc.
47 Cecilia Drive, Wayne, New Jersey 07470–4649
E-mail: pastorp@mail.montclair.edu

Library of Congress Card Number 00–134924
ISBN 0–88033–464–9

Printed in the United States of America

To my mother, who was born five years
after the death of Francis Joseph

CONTENTS

PREFACE

Readers looking for a romantic life of Francis Joseph will be disappointed by this book, for two reasons: first, the life of Francis Joseph was not romantic, and secondly, this book does not seek to tell the king's life story. It is concerned with something quite different, namely, how relations between the Hungarian people and Francis Joseph developed, and why they turned out the way they did. Needless to say, this cannot be said to be unrelated to the personal life of Francis Joseph, and in this sense. therefore, this book is a biography. However, it is much more a book about Hungarian history: how could it be otherwise, given that the lives of Francis Joseph and the Hungarian people were intertwined for more than sixty years? Their liaison did not begin as a love match, but it was consummated in 1867 by a legal act. Subsequently, however, it proved impossible to obtain a divorce. The only way out was death, whether in bed or in battle, each to his own, on the way to the Hungarian royal throne....

ON THE WAY TO THE ROYAL HUNGARIAN THRONE: THE FIRST 37 YEARS

It was as if on 8 June 1867 the full pomp of the Middle Ages had been revived for a day: Pest and Buda were preparing for a coronation. The Holy Crown had last been lawfully bestowed on a monarch thirty-two years before, when the man who was now to be crowned was only a five-year-old child. His future wife had yet to be born. Together, they were the stars of their day: thirty-seven-year-old Francis Joseph and thirty-nine-year-old Elizabeth of Wittelsbach. The politician Ferenc Pulszky recalls that it was a fine, sunny day, while according to writer Mór Jókai, the whole city was up and about as early as five o'clock in the morning. And in all probability it was so, because when preparations get under way for such a colorful spectacle, there must also be an audience. Of course, not everyone was invited: in accordance with the strict rules of the "medieval world view," not everyone was allowed to take up a position at the principal locations. And yet the ordinary citizen was also well advised to wipe the sleep from his eyes, in the knowledge that the coronation procession would be something well worth getting up for. He could also look forward—with a bit of luck—to catching one of the silver or even gold coins which were customarily thrown into the crowd on such occasions. If the money gained in this fashion was not spent, it was likely to become a cherished family heirloom. Ordinary folk also knew that, in the evening, a grand feast would be held free of charge at the Vérmező parade grounds, where the bill for the ox roasting and the wine would be met by the noble monarch.

True, one did not have to rise early for that, but there would be so much to see beforehand. Invited guests would assemble in the Church of Our Lady (Matthias Church) between 6:00 and 6:30 in the morning, sitting in stands constructed especially for the purpose. This was also the assembly place for those aristocrats who were unable to ride—those who were more at home in the saddle had other things to do—ladies of the court, diplomats, and, last but not least, the delegation of the Imperial Diet and members of the Hungarian Parliament. The latter came over from Pest, from the House of Representatives on Sándor Street, where they had already been in session at 5:30 A.M.

Church dignitaries lined up at the church gate to await the royal couple. The coronation procession left for the church from the royal palace at 7 A.M. sharp, marking the official commencement of a series of events which would last throughout the day. These events would have two novel features: first, it was the first time that both king and queen had been crowned on the same day, and secondly, it was the first time that part of the coronation had taken place in Pest. These were seemingly small changes, but they were by no means insignificant: the choice of Pest as a venue marked a kind of informal recognition for it as the country's political center, location of the Parliament. Since Pest had been declared the seat of the Parliament by law in 1848, the fact that part of the coronation festivities were held there symbolized the continuity of the reforms of 1848. Also, Elizabeth was very much a favorite of the Hungarian people. Her adoring public did not want to see her reduced to a mere spectator, and so they managed to make room for her in a ceremony of medieval origin. We shall have much more to say later on about why this was done.

Certainly, both innovations gave expression to national feelings and national will. ["And albeit it is still long to go before the spectacle's end."] The citizens could see from the outset that the struggles of the last few decades had not been in vain because even the Habsburg monarch felt compelled to respect the nation's wishes. True, as already mentioned, this manifested itself in seemingly small matters—but awareness of the fact was far more important than the fact itself.

The procession moved slowly towards Matthias Church. In front walked two postilions, and at the rear walked half-a-company of infantry and a company of hussars, enclosing—in accordance with a strict choreography—the participants of the procession arranged in twenty-six groups, including equestrian aristocrats. In the twelfth row was Count Gyula Andrássy, who would have an important role to play later on. Nineteenth was Francis Joseph himself, on horseback, dressed in a Hungarian general's uniform, with a shako on his head, and adorned with medals. On either side of him walked the dignitaries of Pest and Buda, with their heads uncovered. In the twentieth row came Elizabeth. She was dressed in Hungarian style, wearing a Hungarian headdress, riding in an eight-horse carriage. Both sides of the road were lined with soldiers, the cheering crowd swelling behind them. Inside the church, the king and queen retreated to the chapel for a short time. While they did so, part of their entourage occupied their seats. Then another procession got under way, this time somewhat shorter, the column comprising no more than fourteen groups, enclosed by twelve members of the Royal Guard. It seems that Francis Joseph—and Count Antal Szapáry, who conducted the ceremony—were not superstitious, since they walked in the thirteenth row. Francis Joseph was followed by Elizabeth, already wearing the so-called "house-crown" (házikorona) on her head. Then came the coronation insignia: cross, sword, scepter, and orb. Count Andrássy carried the crown. Draped all around were the national flags of the medieval Hungarian kingdom: Bulgaria, Serbia, Galicia, Dalmatia, Slovakia [Tótország], and finally the symbols of Cumania, Lodomeria, Transylvania, Croatia, and Bosnia. (Who would have thought that the Bosnian flag would later become the basis for a territorial claim to Bosnia?) At the center stood the raised throne, approached by three steps. A chair stood on the lowest step of the altar. While the audience was seating itself, Francis Joseph sat down. Waiting for everyone to find their place, he knelt down on the cushion on the floor and then made an oath, declaring—in Hungarian—that he would preserve peace and justice. Then he proceeded to put on the cloak of Saint Stephen at the altar and received Saint Stephen's sword from Archbishop János Simor. He gestured in front of him with the sword in his right hand, and then to his right and left. Then the sword was slipped back into its sheath. Francis Joseph knelt down on the top step of the altar. He was now only moments away from becoming the lawful king of Hungary.

Chapter One

A WELL BROUGHT UP YOUNG MAN, WHO MIGHT EVEN BE-COME HEIR TO THE THRONE

Contemporary censorship was careful not to allow press coverage to stir up too much excitement among Hungary's still relatively small reading public. Political information was thoroughly sifted in order to direct readers' attention to reports about what ought to be the supreme object of their loyalty, the royal family. One such report was published in the 25 August 1830 issue of *Hazai és Külföldi Tudósítások* (Hungarian and International Reports). It read as follows:

Her Imperial Highness the Archduchess Sophia, spouse of His Royal Highness the Archduke Francis Charles, went into labor on 18 August at the imperial and royal palace of Schönbrunn, and at 9:15 A.M., with God's grace, gave birth to an archduke, a happy event which was signaled to the people of the capital with a twenty-one-gun salute. The christening of the baby archduke took place at a splendid ceremony at noon next day at the Ceremonial Hall of Schönbrunn Palace. The sacred Christian rite was celebrated by His Grace the Bishop Firmián. His Imperial and Royal Highness held the infant archduke under the baptismal water himself as the godfather, and the baby was then named Charles Francis Joseph. According to medical reports dated 20 August, both Her Imperial and Royal Highness the Archduchess Sophia, and the baby archduke are in good health.

Loyal readers could finish reading the newspaper with a sense of satisfaction. The family tree of the beloved royal family had been extended by yet another tiny branch. It was unlikely, however, that any reader would have excitedly rushed around to his neighbors to tell them the blissful news, unless he had the gift of prophecy. More typically, people would have read between the lines and would probably have gathered what was behind such reports. To readers of this kind these passages communicated the following: the birth of a son—especially in a royal family—always carries greater significance than the birth of a daughter, especially if the newborn boy could one day become the heir to the throne. However, the report clearly indicated that there was no possibility of direct succession. If there had been, then not a twenty-one-gun but a one-hundred-and-one-gun salute would have been duly given.

Theoretically, of course, the newborn child could indeed one day become king. Very many coincidences were required for that to happen, however. First of all, the ruling monarch was still alive, and when he died he would be followed on the throne by his eldest son, Ferdinand. If Ferdinand died childless, his eldest brother, Francis Charles, the father of the newborn child, would inherit the throne. Only after his father could little Francis Joseph accede to the throne. It was nevertheless only right that the godfather should be the monarch himself, even if the likelihood of the baby becoming Hungarian king was small. Readers who were a little more closely acquainted with the circumstances of the royal family—and were able to see into the future—would probably not have agreed that Francis Joseph's chances were so slim. Observers with an acute sense for both the political and the personal would perhaps have commented that, while they did not dispute the soundness of the argument, at the same time, Francis I of Austria, the present ruler, was an old man; his eldest son, Ferdinand, was a half-wit and, moreover, rumor had it that his potency left a lot to be desired. It was all too plausible that, due to his mental state, he would be unable to assume the throne or forced to renounce his right of succession. But even if that did not happen, it was almost certain that he would be succeeded by his brother, as Ferdinand was not expected to father a child. And as soon as Francis Charles became king, the Holy Crown would surely, as night follows day, go to Francis Joseph at some point, in which case the twenty-one cannon shots would have been worth every bit as much as one-hundred-and-one. But even readers with an acute sense for both politics and personal matters could not have guessed when their prediction might become reality. That was indeed still an unmarked grain among the sands of time.

And the secret probably interested no one in Hungary. Active readers with an interest in politics were curious about something totally different in 1830. For instance, the activities of Count István Széchenyi and one of his highly controversial works, *Credit*. Some praised it, seeing in it a manifestation of the long-awaited national renewal, while others condemned it, considering it inflammatory. As the almighty Chancellor Klemens Metternich put it: "The government loves clarity, but it shuns the fire from which light emanates."

Only one person was really interested in the secret: Sophia, the mother. She had obviously weighed up carefully how accurate the conclusions of our well-informed reader might be. In addition, she knew things which no one else could have known: she was aware of her own willpower and, at the same time, the weakness of her husband's will. Being intimately acquainted with the true situation she had every reason to believe that she had indeed given birth to a future ruler, and that by exerting influence on her husband she would be able to help her child's star to rise. Her plans cannot be called too ambitious, as they were based on the objective analysis of the situation. But of course even she must have had her doubts about when things would actually begin to go her way. The family statute of the Habsburg dynasty had been the work of decades and it was still not complete. One of the things it regulated was when an archduke comes of age, that is, when he can start ruling without a regent. She could have no knowledge either of future political developments which—statutory regulations notwithstanding—would determine the right time when her intentions could turn into reality.

One thing she knew she would insist on: to give her son an upbringing befitting a future monarch. Matters of education generally had to be decided by the head of the family, however, and under the family rules of the Habsburg dynasty this was the privilege of the monarch, who until his death in 1835, was Francis I to be succeeded by Ferdinand. Although Ferdinand was feeble-minded, the principle of legitimacy demanded that he succeed to the throne. This principle was jealously guarded by the man who was really in charge, Chancellor Metternich. His power had, if anything, increased as a result of the monarch's incapacity. It allowed the chancellor to make decisions in the name of the emperor and king. Metternich was well aware that the young archduke had a good chance of assuming the throne one day. It would be he or—should destiny warrant it—one of his brothers (Maximilian was born in 1832, Charles Louis in 1833, Maria Anna Caroline, who died at the age of five, in 1835, and Louis Victor in 1842). A decision had to be made about the upbringing of the archdukes. But how should one raise heirs to the throne? What should they be taught, and what was probably even more important, in what spirit?

Their education was to be governed by a set of rules. One of these was that the children would have a chief tutor, a so-called "ajó," while each child would have his own personal tutor. The activities of teachers of individual subjects were coordinated within a more general framework; rules determined how the youngsters spent their day, and prescribed timetables. Education combined with vocational training started at the age of five or six. As Francis Joseph was the firstborn, his "ajó" and tutor were appointed at roughly the same time, in the persons of Count Henrik Bombelles and Count Sándor Coronini-Cronberg. Both also held military rank. Childhood—at least for the archdukes—basically ended at the age of six. They had to live according to a regulated pattern, and work hard to complete a broad curriculum. The personality of Francis Joseph enabled him to submit to the rule of duty and order with relative ease, however. According to some an idealized image presented of him in memoirs, he was a lover of order even as a very small child. For example, he is supposed to have tidied up his toys from the age of eighteen months without having to be asked. The fundamental principle underlying the rigorous curriculum had been formulated in the late eighteenth century: all things relating to the intellectual and material world must be conveyed to the young student, who was expected to learn the grammar-school curriculum by the age of fifteen. History, literature, aesthetics, metaphysics, logic, and physics were but part of a long list of disciplines to be studied. The details were not so important: the main thing was to give high-quality and versatile vocational training to the potential heir to the throne. Learning languages was a high priority. As the Habsburgs were traditionally good at languages, this should not have been difficult for the young archduke. His language training was made even easier by the fact that the children of Czech, Polish, and Hungarian aristocrats were among his playmates. This "hands-on" experience could not replace regular lessons of course. The curriculum included Hungarian, alongside Czech, Polish, French, and Latin: the different social orders expected the future monarch to understand and speak the languages of their realm.

They started to make their demands in this regard more emphatic as the 1830s and 1840s saw the advance of the Hungarian language in Hungary. From 1840 all laws had to be written in two columns, one in Latin and one in Hungarian, and in 1844 Hungarian became Hungary's official language. However, the Habsburg dynasty included the Hungarian language in the curriculum of the archdukes not because they were under pressure from the legislature to do so, but rather out of enlightened self-interest. They knew well that political resistance could more easily be broken if the monarch spoke with his subjects in their mother tongue. Francis Joseph knew some Hungarian anyway since at the age of five he had had a Hungarian nanny—for the period of a year—named Mari Aczél. She was selected on the recommendation of Gábor Döbrentei, a well-connected writer with a strong commitment to Hungarian language and culture. He must also have learned some Hungarian words from his playmates Dénes Széchenyi and the two Erdődy brothers, Ferenc and Tamás. Francis Joseph started taking regular Hungarian lessons in 1837 at the age of seven, studying it for three and a half hours every week. From the age of ten he was taught Hungarian by Canon Pál Nemeskéri Kiss, who adopted a very unusual approach. As he also taught Latin and Greek to Francis Joseph, he simply added the geography and history of Hungary to his Latin exercises. When his pupil reached a certain level of proficiency, the canon taught him Hungarian by way of giving him an insight into contemporary Hungarian belles-lettres. Francis Joseph read the novel *The Village Notary* by József Eötvös, which was not only good reading but also furnished him with some knowledge of the world. His tutor had a deep respect for István Széchenyi, so he also "sneaked" into the curriculum the sophisticated views of the Hungarian count. In order to be able to follow Széchenyi's writings one had to have a sound knowledge of Hungarian as Széchenyi's style, though highly expressive, used rather complicated syntax. Francis Joseph was assigned to translate extracts from Széchenyi's *Political Program* from German back into Hungarian. The young student continued to perfect his proficiency as he grew up. In the early stages he struggled with the difference between object and subject, and the general use of noun suffixes. Nevertheless, by 1847 Pál Nemeskéri Kiss expressed satisfaction with his pupil's progress, saying that although his Hungarian was not yet perfect, it was already reliable.

We can trust Nemeskéri's judgment, as he was a skilled pedagogue with great experience (he was fifty-five in 1847). In 1830 he authored a manual on teaching methodology, and in the mid-1830s he published two Hungarian grammars. In addition, he had a point of reference in judging his pupil's ability, as in the 1840s he also tutored Francis Joseph's two younger brothers. Until 1847 the young archduke had little chance to practice his Hungarian, however. He visited Hungary—with his two younger brothers—for the first time in September 1843. This trip was the idea of his "ajó" and it lasted for only five days. Count Bombelles decided after a bathing holiday in Ischl to take his young pupils and show them around the Transdanubia region of Hungary.

Details of this trip were reported by the newspaper *Pesti Hírlap*, edited by Lajos Kossuth, and Francis Joseph took notes himself. We therefore have the opportunity to compare how adults and a thirteen-year-old child saw each other. The traveling party arrived in Hungary on 13 September. They lunched at the Körmend castle of Fülöp Batthyány, then in the evening went to see László Festetich in Keszthely. Having visited the sights of this town they rode to Sümeg in their carriage on 14 September, where they stayed at the residence of the Bishop of Veszprém. They were shown around by important dignitaries, including high commissioner Gábor Döbrentei (who had recommended the archduke's Hungarian nanny). Then, surrounded by a large crowd, they rode uphill to the Sümeg castle ruins, where they were awaited by the poet Sándor Kisfaludy who was required to make an appearance especially for the occasion. Clearly it was Döbrentei's idea to summon the poet to the scene, as this allowed him to present the Hungarian poetic genius to the offspring of the Habsburg dynasty in a Romantic setting, befitting Kisfaludy's art. The news report concluded with great satisfaction that Francis Joseph had demonstrated an impeccable knowledge of Hungarian when he discoursed with this great master of the language. In Sümeg the royal party saw Nemeskéri who was visiting his mother there. The news reporter found out that the archdukes' attention was most drawn to a salt grinder, corn flour, and corn cake that they saw at this house. They had never seen a salt grinder before, did not know that corn flour was the food of poor people, and had never tasted corn cake either. But now they did, and they liked it. During the rest of the journey they visited Sárvár, Szombathely, Kőszeg, Horpács, Esterháza, Cenk, Sopron, Fraknó and Kismarton. They were back in Schönbrunn on 18 September.

Francis Joseph saw these same events with a different eye. His notes make no mention of his having met Sándor Kisfaludy at all. It seems that the idea merely reflected Döbrentei's own taste, and did little to interest the thirteen-year-old child. He does not mention Nemeskéri either, whom he met regularly anyway. It seems that the question of poverty did not make a deep impression on Francis Joseph either. His attention was much more captivated by the scenery. His notes give a detailed account of the unique features of the Austrian and Transdanubian landscapes, with remarks about architecture and the way people dressed. Since the royal party had reached Keszthely late in the evening, Francis Joseph caught a glimpse of Lake Balaton only when he got up in the morning. What a magnificent sight it was! The lake, the vineyards, the villages. He writes about the lake at length and with enthusiasm. His imagination was engaged most of all by the Bakony Hills, and what the life of swineherds and the world of the Bakony outlaws might be like. He also mentions having breakfasted at Széchenyi's palace. His susceptibility to the beauty of the landscape tells us something about Francis Joseph's personality. He was also very good at drawing. His drawings are characterized by a great attention to detail. These childhood creations show an artist with little imagination but with a keen power of observation. Visual memory was another one of his strengths.

Politics was of no concern on this trip, at least not directly. Indirectly, the intention was to create an impression that, together with an emphasis on the need to speak Hungarian, would make the young members of the Habsburg dynasty "more Hungarian." Clearly, there was an advantage in telling an increasingly nationally minded public that the future of the empire—and Hungary within it—would be vested in a man who embraced Hungarian culture and understood how Hungarians felt, and would perhaps come to understand one day that nation's political aspirations. These hopes were not clearly articulated, yet they were a logical derivative of the 1840s, which were becoming increasingly impregnated by ideals of national identity. Bleak reality, however, did not support these hopes, at least not for the time being: at the age of thirteen Francis Joseph showed no receptivity to Hungarian culture, and although he knew perfectly well how to behave among Hungarians, he resisted attempts to make him "more Hungarian." Nevertheless Hungarian public opinion, which remained oblivious to the fact that a child can respond to the impressions he encounters only within the limitations of his own abilities, did not lose hope for a better future, insisting that slowly but surely, the archduke would get to like Hungary and want to visit it more often. And then he would be able to fulfill the needs of the Hungarian people. Another hope was that, as part of his education, especially his undergraduate studies, Francis Joseph would get to know Hungary's system of public law and acquire a detailed knowledge of Hungarian history. In short, knowledge of the Hungarian language, personal experience, and background understanding would make him more open-minded towards Hungary.

Following the visit in September 1843, Francis Joseph visited Hungary on two more occasions before early 1847. In 1846 he went hunting in the Lake Fertő region, and on another occasion, in January 1847, he came to attend Palatine Joseph's funeral. In his notes made on the latter visit Francis Joseph expresses delight at the sight of Pest with its many construction sites. By the age of seventeen Francis Joseph had seen little of Hungary, and what little he had seen, he thought merely interesting. He had had no official engagements in Hungary. The archduke's actions neither refuted nor confirmed the hopes of the Hungarian public. His first public appearance before the Hungarian people, when it came, would therefore have great political significance.

The possibility that he would acquire a significant knowledge of Hungary through his education still remained. In 1845, at the age of fifteen, Francis Joseph completed his grammar school studies. The government decided to take the archduke's further education into its own hands. A higher education program was devised on the orders of Metternich. Much emphasis was placed at this stage on developing rationally formulated guidelines to govern the actions of a future Habsburg monarch.

Let us begin by describing how Francis Joseph's education continued, especially as it largely defined his personality and attitude to the world. His military studies were the most important. Military education had always been part of any archduke's education, but the situation of Francis Joseph was exceptional. Military training, or the military "ethos," played an extraordinarily important role in Francis Joseph's upbringing. Three factors deepened his commitment to the army and instilled a military spirit in him. One was his mother, Sophia, who believed that the principal support of the monarch was the army, so she made a special effort to give her son the best military training possible.

The historian Dávid Angyal has pointed out that Sophia's aspirations did not meet with unanimous approval. Some courtiers—for example, General Heinrich Jaroslav Clam-Martinitz, adjutant general to Ferdinand V—opposed the plans of Francis Joseph's ambitious mother. They believed that a religious education centered upon moral teachings would serve as a more suitable foundation for the strenuous art of ruling, and that too much emphasis on military education would only divert the future monarch's attention from governing the empire in an ethical fashion. Sophia had to bow to the arguments of those with more political power than herself, though retreat did not mean surrender. When formulating her own arguments she made reference to past experience: Maria Theresa herself had put much emphasis on the military education of her sons. Therefore the debate was not so much about the need for a military education at all as about its extent.

However, Sophia's arguments and political influence alone could not have ensured that her son would be educated up in a predominantly military spirit. A similar inclination was needed in the child— an interest in, even a passion for, a military career. Francis Joseph's love of precision and order, his peculiar lack of imagination as demonstrated by his drawings, and his preference for transparency in relationships based on subordination and rule, predisposed him to take pleasure in the acquisition of a military outlook.

But even that would not have been enough. There also had to be someone to take charge of his military education; one who had the talent and personality to influence this impressionable archduke. From the age of six the archduke took part in military exercises for two hours every week. This did not, however, take up a significant part of his education as a whole. The turning point came in 1843, when Francis Joseph was entering adolescence, and wore tails for the first time at a court ball in January. His regular military training began in the same year, and his military studies made such a deep impression on him that on formal occasions he would henceforth always don a military uniform in preference to tails. In May 1843, Colonel Franz Hauslab became his tutor in military studies, and he was responsible for developing a full educational program for Francis Joseph in this subject. In the same year the monarch made Francis Joseph colonel in chief—as was customary for archdukes, thereby making him the proud commander of Dragoon Company 11. Francis Joseph led his regiment in a parade for the first time at the age of fourteen. The proud regimental commander marched ahead of his soldiers, although technically he had still not been awarded officer rank.

Under Hauslab's scheme Francis Joseph's military education had two main aspects. On the one hand, he was taught about service in the infantry and the artillery. In both corps he started off as an ordinary recruit, gradually climbing the ladder. To begin with he was given only a couple of soldiers to command, then a platoon, a battalion, a battery, and finally an entire regiment. After having gained experience in the three main corps he had to learn about the various technical divisions, for example, the work of sappers and pontoneers. He had to learn to use the spade and pickax, always as required by the corps in question. Field training went hand in hand with theoretical training. Hauslab himself taught only a few subjects, while other officers taught their respective subjects within the framework of his plan and under his supervision. Among the subjects which the young Francis Joseph was required to study we might mention fortifications, applied tactics, comparative weapons studies, practical implementation of army service rules, military drawing, and other technical studies. Francis Joseph had the most difficulty, at least at the beginning, with horseback riding, although he eventually became an excellent horseman in the capable hands of a Hungarian captain, András Gáspár. (Gáspár later became a general in the Hungarian national army and was pardoned after the defeat of the War of Liberation of 1848–49.)

Hauslab was fifty years old when he was put in charge of Francis Joseph's military education. He had the necessary experience, having been the tutor of Archduke Albrecht. His carefully devised and thorough training plan was intended to turn his young student into a versatile field officer in the space of four years. The fifth year was to be devoted to military history and strategy, studies considered at the time essential for commanding an entire army or larger divisions. Francis Joseph's training was sufficiently comprehensive to entitle him to the rank of general. He could have risen to a general straight from being an officer.

The fifth year of military training was to be the fateful year 1848. When in 1845 discussions were held concerning how to proceed with our hero's upbringing, no one even thought of interrupting the carefully planned course of military training which had begun in 1843. There were signs that Francis Joseph, influenced by his mother, his own inclinations, and Hauslab's teaching methods, was increasingly drawn towards the military life, but it was also rightly assumed that he would benefit from having his intellectual horizons widened. These higher studies were planned to last for three years with a curriculum including the humanities, law and political science, civil and penal law, statistics, politics, and ecclesiastical law. Two special subjects were to be included in the last two years, Hungarian private and public law, and the tutor was selected well in advance. A court counselor called Fejes was appointed to this position which had so much significance for the Hungarian people. The counselor would probably have introduced his student to the intricacies of Hungarian law in a conservative spirit, but when the time came, in 1848, Metternich decided that he would teach some of the subjects himself. It was not the first time he had undertaken such a task: he had given lessons to the reigning monarch, Ferdinand V, and to Francis Charles, Francis Joseph's father.

He chose a subject which in his opinion was a combination of an art and a science. It was called governance. Starting from October 1847, every Sunday Francis Joseph went to the Chancellery, accompanied by Bombelles, his "ajó," and Metternich's son, to listen attentively and respectfully to the elderly Chancellor for a couple of hours. Metternich talked about his life and political experience in a remarkably informal style. There was a lot for him to talk about: he had been an important influence in matters of state in the Habsburg empire since 1808, and since 1815 on the future of Europe as a whole. We do not know the details of what Metternich told his young student. But he must have repeatedly mentioned two things. One was the frequently voiced opinion of the old chancellor that the foundation of good governance was the distinction between governance and public administration. The monarch's role was not simply to approve and seal with his signature the submissions made by various offices of state. On the contrary, it was the monarch's role to take the initiative and to keep the bureaucratic machine in motion, since it was prone to becoming clumsily overbureaucratized. Metternich warned him against excessive leniency, and from freemasons and secret societies, which could cause a great deal of mischief. He also indulged in historicizing, and portrayed the French Revolution as the embodiment of all things evil: not just because of the amount of bloodshed and the number of victims it had claimed, but above all because in his eyes the French Revolution illustrated the anarchy which can result when the "will of the people" supercedes the rule of the monarch. According to Metternich, the dynasty and the state were one and the same.

For Francis Joseph, Metternich's teachings constituted an authoritative and practical confirmation of all that he had previously been taught. During his scripture lessons, he was taught (and the same was repeated by his university professor in the humanities, the titular Abbot Joseph Rauscher, whom Francis Joseph was later to appoint Archbishop of Vienna) that world order was founded on religious ethics. Being a Habsburg and therefore a Catholic, his religion meant a great deal to him. These religio-ethical principles in their turn confirmed what he had been taught in politics. As a coursebook written specifically for him put it, almost in the spirit of the Middle Ages (that is, free of the influence of the French Enlightenment and liberalism), the prince's crown and law come from God. The prince should not be expected to sacrifice himself for his people, or to surrender his rights, as he has been selected by God to be the first among his people. In religio-ethical terms, the prince's power is limited only by one thing: he must not sacrifice the blood and possessions of his subjects purely for his own entertainment. This teaching would probably not have had such a profound effect had Francis Joseph not breathed in the same message at home and at court. He never heard anything else either from his mother or from his high and majestic relatives. In addition, if we consider his strong attraction for the autocratic command structure and clear discipline of the army, there can be no doubt that, in his view, there was no room for the nation, only for subjects. Furthermore, there were no rights apart from the single right bestowed by God: the right of the prince.

In the mind of the adolescent Francis Joseph, the vision emerged of an ideal state in which the monarch ruled, the government executed his orders, and the people obeyed. The question arises of course concerning the relationship between his slowly crystallizing but firmly defined views and reality: would experience support or challenge his ideas?

For the time being he did not have to worry about such things. All he had to do was study. He could spend the rest of his time engaged in his favorite activities. He was not so much of a theater buff as his father, but he did occasionally "pay homage to Thalia's shrine." He was able to fulfill any ambitions he might have as an amateur actor at home with his brothers and other relatives. They would often set up tableaux vivants and stage the occasional play. Whenever a play had

an amoroso part in it, that was most likely be played by the archduke.
He was also a keen hunter, for which he had ample opportunity. At
court balls or family parties he always danced. He drew less, but his
visual memory did not suffer as a result; he invariably noted the slightest changes in his surroundings.

Chapter Two

A ROYAL ARCHDUKE ATTIRED IN THE HUNGARIAN TRICOLOR

The noise of politics was unable to penetrate the archduke's cushioned world, which was made up of little else but study, family, and leisure. Events in the wider family did of course cause ripples. As already mentioned, Francis Joseph went to Hungary to attend the funeral of Palatine Joseph. But he felt little of the rough and tumble of politics—nor was he supposed to. He never thought, and he had no way of guessing, that his first public appearance in Hungary would be linked to this funeral. The country needed a new palatine, which was the highest Hungarian public office after the kingship. In the king's absence the palatine substituted for the monarch with all his powers, and while the monarch was under age, the palatine acted as regent. By custom, if not by law, one of the Habsburg archdukes was generally appointed the palatine and traditionally would also become the lord lieutenant of Pest County. At the county assembly of Pest County Lajos Kossuth made a recommendation: he proposed the son of the late palatine, Archduke Stephan. The inaugurating ceremony for the lord lieutenant was to take place on 16 October 1847. The inaugurating speech was to be made on the king's behalf by Archduke Albrecht, but due to a death in the family, he had to cancel. The organizers were running out of time and so they had to decide quickly; the monarch chose Francis Joseph to step in.

Archduke Stephan enjoyed exceptional popularity at the time. His father, the late palatine, had been a much liked figure, but Stephan inspired particular affection by giving more than five hundred speeches in Hungarian during his nationwide preinauguration tour, and on the occasion of his birthday (14 September) made an oath in Arad to love the fatherland [Hungary]. In 1847, Archduke Stephan won himself undivided and enthusiastic loyalty in Hungary—especially in the key opposition counties—by wearing the colors of the national tricolor and speaking in Hungarian. The vague wish to have a Habsburg with pro-Hungarian sentiments seemed to have found embodiment. Francis Joseph, who was seventeen years old at the time, found himself in the middle of a general meeting which was full of enthusiasm and loyalty in opposition. And Francis Joseph had studied his role well. The speech was written for him by two experienced and staunch conservative Hungarian aristocrats, loyal to the court, Count György Apponyi and László Szőgyény-Marich. All he had to do was to read it, which he accomplished in a fine voice, loud and well articulated (he had practiced the speech with Nemeskéri, his language teacher). Written in accordance with Ferdinand V's instructions, the speech was delivered by Francis Joseph as follows:

> This splendid-looking officer [that is, the officer performing the inauguration ceremony—A. G.] has given me the opportunity to enter my beloved Hungary at a moment when—as is the wish of His Majesty, our father—it is facing the prospect of a blissful future, and because I may witness both the love of the people, which Your Majesty [Archduke Stephan—A. G.) has inherited from your father of glorious memory—and which, due to your own radiant character, you have strengthened even further—and also the trust of the people, which Your Majesty has already earned by your high virtues and patriotic enthusiasm, and which I see will guarantee a joyful future, not only for the county, but also for our beloved homeland....As far as my own person is concerned, I shall celebrate both today, when I have been able to publicly express my faithful love for Your Majesty and my strong affection for the Hungarian nation.

These words uttered by Francis Joseph gave way to a great ovation. According to the historian Sándor Márki the speech was a success

because Hungarians were enthralled by the idea of two Habsburgs trying to outdo each other in showing their patriotic (that is, pro-
Hungarian) feelings. They thought or at least hoped, that they were
witnessing the birth of a pro-Hungarian monarchy under the Habsburg
scepter. Loyal over-enthusiasts and those who could not see beyond
appearances probably did believe that this had come to pass, and took
ephemeral words for reality. Nemeskéri interpreted the abundant con-
gratulations, in which he himself participated, as a sign that everyone
attending the function took the view that the nation had not had such a
glorious day for three hundred years.

In fact, in an address made three weeks later in memory of the
recently deceased Pál Nemeskéri Kiss, honorary member of the
Academy of Sciences, who was at once language teacher, censor, and
the noted literary scholar, Ferenc Toldy expressed this view as follows: "Francis Joseph, like a certain great hero of antiquity, 'came,
saw and conquered,' not with the weapons of war, but with those of
the heart." He reminded those present of the scene at a General
Assembly meeting when Francis Joseph ("upon whom our gaze
became steadily fixed") delivered a speech. He then reminded them

> of this voice, upon whose utterance complete silence overcame a
> crowd of thousands of people; and his words, no, his oration was
> uttered with so much personal dignity, with such serious aware-
> ness of the importance of the moment, and knowledge of our
> melodious language, with such stylish and truly masterful formu-
> lation of the underlying thoughts, that we were rendered children
> by our rapture; what is more, our deep emotions [caused] our
> hearts to tremble, and the honeydew of joy descended on our
> eyes. The joyful murmur of thousands upon thousands of lips
> conveyed how infinite the love of this nation can be, and that
> those who are charged with the destiny of our people have found
> the key to their power! This day was a great event in the thou-
> sand-year history of the homeland; this day was the finest reward
> for groans uttered in vain, and thousands of tears shed by patri-
> ots; this day was the token of a new and more fortunate era; a new
> betrothal between king and nation.

A conservative speech-writer, Szőgyény-Marich, expressed himself more reservedly about Francis Joseph's speech: "The fact that he uttered it with a perfect Hungarian accent, and above all his delightful affability, charmed everyone." The Viennese court was also satisfied. Széchenyi, however, entered in his diary somewhat more skeptical comments: "Alas, two young Austrian archdukes learn a couple of Hungarian words by heart, and the faithful Hungarian people are willing to let their heads spin!" After all, why were Hungarians so enthusiastic and why was this enthusiasm greeted in Vienna with so much satisfaction? Some of the causes of this sudden burst of enthusiasm in the Hungarian people were already mentioned. Naturally, the degree of enthusiasm varied: needless to say, the least moved were those who linked the national cause with far-reaching liberal reforms. They knew perfectly well that the application of a thin tricolored veneer would serve only to arouse emotional support while failing to offer substantive reforms. Moreover, this was precisely the aim of conservative speech writers, who knew that this was the way to weaken the influence of those seeking to curtail the powers of the Habsburg ruler in favor of increased national sovereignty. They were seeking to create a public mood free of any significant opposition; when emotionally charged, grievances are powerless against a properly functioning administration.

Others obviously believed—and not without reason—that the time had come to seize the opportunity and to present the court's "compliance" as a sign of a willingness to "turn over a new leaf," despite the fact that it had found expression only in gestures; the appearance had therefore to be created that something was really happening.

In the final analysis, the public's reaction was in large part motivated by its loyalty, which at this time could still be combined, at least on the surface, with an emotionally popular national theme. Everyone had reason to be happy, although not everyone was enthusiastic. Vienna had reason to be happy, as it believed that the conservative approach had been vindicated: the reform opposition had lost ground, and the popularity of the two archdukes was transporting the national-liberal grievances of the Hungarians into the "harbor" of loyalty to the court and maintenance of the status quo. The opposition believed that the Habsburgs had "retreated" somewhat from absolutism. Members of the loyal "semi-opposition" had reason to be happy because they believed that their loyalty could be reconciled with their opposition, just as they could emotionally identify with the political power holders. Only the future would confirm or deny these rather differently motivated feelings of optimism.

At the age of seventeen, Francis Joseph was not overexcited by the notion of his own greatness. He was prevented from doing so by the vague suspicion that his learning of the speech "on the spot," and his "stepping-in" at the last minute were no more than instruments used to promote a higher objective—the consolidation of the rule of the dynasty. He did not even fully understand why the Hungarians had been so enthusiastic. In fact, the whole business of being a palatine must have been rather odd for him; all the more because both he and those who appointed him must have known perfectly well that the status of palatine was not recognized by the Statutes of the dynasty, their supreme rule, and therefore had little practical relevance.

The Statutes created a uniform framework for existing common law based on precedent, and laid down in writing the rules governing the dynasty, and the rights and duties of family members. It was advisable for family members to familiarize themselves with the content of the Statutes because they also laid down the rules governing the remuneration of the different members of the Habsburg family, determining the size of both their allowance and their dowry, and the eligibility requirements pertaining to Habsburg marriages. (It will become apparent that, as a ruler, Francis Joseph implacably enforced these same rules in the case of his own son, and interfered in the personal life of heir-to-the-throne Francis Ferdinand.)

The idea of the Statutes had been originally suggested by Emperor Francis I in 1829. He believed that the mental retardation of the heir to the throne, Ferdinand, called for regulations which would ensure the survival of the dynasty, and a legal document which would to guarantee the unchallengeable legitimacy of their rule. Work on this document did not proceed rapidly, and was finally completed only in 1838. The Statutes, comprising six chapters and sixty-one articles, were signed by Ferdinand on 3 February 1839, and they were to be binding on all Habsburgs. Refusal to acknowledge them entailed exclusion from the family, and even loss of the right to bear the Habsburg-Lotharingian name. On exclusion, family members would also be stripped of all their entitlements.

The Statutes were not debated by any representative body of the different social estates and were never made public. A number of Chancellery officials and court councilors did participate in the wording of the document, but only those with unreserved loyalty to the sovereign. Given that the whole point of the Statutes was to consolidate the absolutist nature of the dynasty and the unity of the empire based on it without the need to refer to any other opinion, it is not surprising that the Statutes were not offered for debate by a representative assembly of the feudal estates.

For Hungarians, the most sensitive issue was the role of the palatine, and during the lengthy formulation process the authors of the Statutes were able to approach this question from a number of angles. Finally, and not surprisingly, the following was decided upon: the sovereign, if still under age, should be put into the care of a regent appointed by members of the dynasty. By appointing a regent rather than the palatine to substitute the king, a regent moreover whose hands were tied by the provisions of the family Statutes, Hungarian common law was completely disregarded. The Statutes assumed the unity of the Habsburg empire, and such unity left no room for Hungarian common law. Hungary and Transylvania were viewed merely as provinces, as a consequence of which the palatine, who had no legal influence over the dynasty, was deemed to be a negligible representative of the emperor.

The same idea underpinned Maria Theresa's recommendation that her successors should elect the palatine of the Hungarians, should they have one, from among the Habsburg archdukes. This was meant to ensure that the palatine would at all times remain under the control of the family Statutes—a principle laid down definitively by 1839—and, in case of a conflict of loyalty, the palatine would be faced with expulsion if he chose to take seriously his role of substituting the Hungarian king in defiance of the dynasty.

It should be added that, according to the Statutes, the sovereign (or regent) ruling at any given time was also the head of the dynasty, without whose consent family members could not even travel abroad. This demonstrates that, in the event of any conflict between Hungarian common law and the Statutes, the palatine could easily be prevented from appearing before his Hungarian subjects.

Needless to say, Francis Joseph was unlikely to have acquired any in-depth knowledge of Hungarian common law, as his curriculum did not include detailed consideration of this topic before 1848. Neither could he make more than formal preparations for his inauguration ceremony, as he learned only a few days prior to the event that he would be required to deliver an address. On the other hand, he would have been all too familiar with the Statutes of the dynasty, even if not in every detail for the fundamentals—the absolutist nature of the dynasty and the unity of the empire—were hammered into him throughout his education. Consequently, he felt somewhat bewildered by the great enthusiasm which he seemed to generate; one having to do with the values and rules of his family's Statutes seemed to render that enthusiasm almost superfluous.

There was another reason why Francis Joseph reacted so coolly to the scene at the County Hall, his calculating personality and the nature of his education. His public appearance even if it was merely an instrument in the hands of policy makers, could have been interpreted as a great personal success, which might have flattered his vanity. However, the religio-ethical nature of Francis Joseph's education and his own strong personal principles prevented him from overestimate his own importance. Already at the age of thirteen he referred to vanity as a "hideous sin" in a school paper, and expressed the conviction that one had a duty to rise above the temptations of this sin by means of rigorous self-examination and hard work. Even if, secretly, he may not have been entirely free of this vice, he did not regard the audience of the county assembly—and the subjects of the monarchy in general—as factors to be given serious consideration. Popularity is valuable only when something depends on it. Francis Joseph had been taught that he and his family had been granted their status by the grace of God, not by their subjects, whose acclaim or disapproval was therefore of little account. One knew when one had it, but no connection should be made between acquiring popularity and being a ruler. Had he been more politically experienced, of course, he would have taken a more prag-matic approach to popularity, which does have its uses, but his funda-mental views on the subject would have remained the same. His world view, education, and habits simply did not allow him to regard his sub-jects as citizens from whom the legitimacy of his power derived, even partially. On the contrary, Metternich and his history tutor, Abbot Rauscher, drummed it into Francis Joseph that to take such a stance was to invite conflict. Both Francis Joseph and his family dwelt in a sphere different from their subjects: it was their task to crush anyone whose actions encouraged discord.

It may seem that we have dwelt too long on Francis Joseph's first public appearance in Hungary, but it is important to have at least some understanding of the background of an absurd situation, the features of which resurfaced every so often in the relationship between the Hungarian people and Francis Joseph, as well as in the people's views of their ruler's personality; The public naturally needed to identify something which might enable them to interpret the words and actions of the archduke in accordance with their own, often changing, motiva-tions. With some political cunning—for the time being provided by others in ready-to-use form— it was not too difficult for Francis Joseph to give the public what they wanted. However, personality and values in this case constitute no more than the appearance that a person chooses to project, or what others instruct that person to project, to the outside world. Therefore the relationship between the public figure Francis Joseph and most of his audience was quite superficial, and even then was interpreted differently by the two sides. The absurdity of the situation resided in the fact that, while Francis Joseph and his audience really had nothing to do with each other, it nevertheless seemed as if the two existed in the closest synergy. Accordingly, Francis Joseph's first public appearance created a good impression. He was increasingly seen as the undisputed heir to the throne, and the image of a fine-looking young man of upright posture delivering a patriotic speech in a flawless Hungarian accent was transmitted even to those who had not been present in the County Hall.

The archduke visited Hungary once again in 1847, for the fifth time, but made no public appearance. He was in Pozsony (Pressburg), at the opening of the last session of the feudal estates. He listened to the speech made by Ferdinand V, delivered in Hungarian, and he saw the enthusiasm with which Ferdinand was greeted. In a letter in which he mentioned this event, Francis Joseph remarked that he too had experienced something of the sort, and that the explanation of such enthusiasm was very simple: Ferdinand was the first sovereign to address his Hungarian subjects in their own language in three hundred years. The tone of the letter, reflecting to the writer's general attitude, is not very emphatic: in places where the writer does not identify with his subject, it is not descriptive but rather objectively explanatory, signaling that the writer is fully cognizant of the causes of the things he is talking about. Or at least that he believes that he is.

Chapter Three

AN AMATEUR ACTOR AMIDST THE TURMOIL OF 1848

At the outset of 1848 the archduke Francis Joseph was looking forward to two pleasant events with some certainty: his studies were drawing to an end and he sensed that he was about to embark on an important mission. A growing number of voices around him were suggesting that he might soon attain a very high office. The prerequisite of this, of course, was his coming of age on his eighteenth birthday, 18 August 1848. Although under the Statutes of the dynasty the heir to the throne could come of age at the age of sixteen, Francis Joseph was not the direct heir—in line with the order of succession, Ferdinand was to be followed on the throne by Francis Joseph's father, Francis Charles. Coming of age was a good thing in itself, however, as it meant that one would be established on an independent footing, with one's own allowance. As far as the political atmosphere was concerned, however, 1848 was fraught with uncertainty.

For the time being, this uncertainty did not touch the young archduke's world. In January, Francis Joseph appeared before the royal family and the court in a comic play, *Prankish Pageboys*, staged for his father's nameday. August Kotzebue was the playwright. In February, he went on stage again. This time the play was called *Turmoil*, a particularly apt title in February 1848. Tidings of the revolution in France came in early March. In the evening of 13 March, Metternich, the renowned authority on the art of government, postponed his student's tutorials indefinitely. He did not have time to announce his decision, however, being forced to flee from the revolution in Vienna. Francis Joseph appears to have felt sincere regret at the loss of his professor; at least that is what his mother, Sophia, told the chancellor in hiding in a letter written on 23 March It may be difficult to understand how anyone could have felt sorry for Metternich, given that the inflexible nature of his regime had been largely responsible for the outbreak of the revolution. However, this is not how Francis Joseph viewed matters. In his eyes, the liberal reformers were malevolent figures, seeking to undermine the rule of the Habsburg dynasty. According to this logic Metternich deserved sympathy as someone who, as one manifestation of the Good, had been overcome by evil powers. Opinions did of course differ about what strengthened and what undermined the rule of the dynasty.

Even if Metternich himself lectured on the subject on Sundays, it is worth turning our attention to another "professor," aged forty-six at the time, who probably taught the archduke, then aged seventeen, many new things. This professor's approach was quite different from that of the chancellor. Apart from anything else, he provided guidance to Francis Joseph the private individual in those crisis-stricken times. The archduke could not listen to the professor's words himself, as they were delivered on 3 March in the Lower House of the Hungarian Diet in Pozsony. But news of them and their importance reached Vienna, and were even read in the Austrian Landtag; they were also circulated among courtiers.

What did this "new professor," whose name, incidentally, was Lajos Kossuth, have to say? Among other things, he stated that

> we think the time...has now come to grant people political rights...to develop our constitutional system into one of parliamentary representation in the truest sense of the word, to cultivate our spiritual values based on freedom, to fundamentally transform our national defense to suit the character of the Hungarian nation, and to reconcile the interests of the various classes making up the Hungarian state.

Speaking about the ways in which this could be achieved, Kossuth said:

Our laws which aim to extend constitutionalism and to bring spiritual richness and prosperity to our nation can only be brought to life...if their enforcement is put in the hands of a national government which is free from all external pressure and is accountable to the majority, which is a principle of our constitution....Bureaus and bayonets are a wretched bond...only the free can be loyal with all their hearts.

Dealing with the rest of the empire, Kossuth argued that

the gap between our own interests and those of our confederates in the empire may be addressed without injury to our independence, freedom, and prosperity only if we share the same constitution and sentiments...and I prophesy that there will be a second founder of the Habsburg dynasty, one who can take the empire's system of government in the constitutional direction by way of reform, and establish the throne of his royal dynasty upon the rock-solid foundations of the freedom of his faithful peoples.

Kossuth went on to mention Francis Joseph:

Let me now voice my strong belief that the real cause of the demise of the empire's tranquility and of all resulting erroneous conclusions lies in the Viennese system of government, and I am concerned that its persistence in conducting such anomalous policies, which go directly against the interests of its peoples and the justified need for a reasonable amount of freedom, will, in the final analysis, harm the future of the dynasty. Sometimes depraved political formations can last for a long time, because it is a long road from patience to despair, but...the moment arrives when it becomes dangerous to let them continue any longer, when they have lived long enough and are ripe for death. And while death can be shared, it cannot be avoided. I know that it is difficult for a derelict system, as it is for a decrepit old man, to relinquish the idea of a long life. I know that it hurts to see what was built up by the labors of a long life fall to pieces. But when the foundations are unsound nothing can save the walls from falling down, and we, to whom providence has entrusted the destiny of a whole nation, must turn our gaze away from the frailty of mere mortals. The nation lives forever, and we wish to see our homeland and the radiance of this dynasty—which we recognize as our rulers—last forever. Mortals from the past descend into their graves within a day or two, and I doubt that the Archduke Francis Joseph, offspring of the high hopes of the Habsburg dynasty, who acquired the love of this nation as soon as he made his first public appearance, and who is looking forward to the heritage of a radiant throne, will be able to maintain it in its ancient glory by means of the unfortunate machinations of Viennese politics: he will be empowered to do so only by the affection of his peoples, which in its turn derives its strength from their freedom.

The dynasty had to make a choice between its long-term interests and maintaining a political system that was in a state of decay. In this way, Kossuth's words went directly against what Francis Joseph had been taught by Metternich. Kossuth, an influential opinion maker, also made clear how the dynasty could take advantage of the success of Francis Joseph's public appearance in 1847, and what the Hungarian people wanted in return for their loyalty. Although Kossuth did not address his words directly to Francis Joseph, the message was meant for him too. Kossuth as well as the majority of the lawfully elected Hungarian Diet were of the opinion that both Austria and Hungary had to have a constitutional order based on liberal principles, such as a government accountable to majority rule, and popular representation. Hungary must be free from external pressure within the empire and have a constitutional order of its own. These were the conditions of consolidating the dynasty's rule, ensuring Hungary's loyalty, and avoiding crisis and chaos.

Kossuth's speech had another feature of special interest. He openly alluded to the fact that the days of the reigning powerholders were numbered. By jumping ahead slightly in the legitimate order of succession, he also painted the picture of a new, constitutional monarchy and linked that vision to Francis Joseph, referring to him as a sovereign who "derives his powers from freedom." There were a number of ways in which this part of Kossuth's speech could be interpreted; otherwise, he left no doubt concerning his repeatedly expressed opinion that liberal-national constitutionalism was at the heart of everything. One possible interpretation of his words was that the majority of the Lower House of the Hungarian Diet wanted to see a new Austrian emperor and a new Hungarian king—in other words, they wanted a new ruler for the empire as a whole. The idea of having a "'younger" or "young" king was akin to the spirit of Hungarian common law. The reigning king with the consent of the feudal estates, could appoint a "joint regent." (Emperor Francis I had had Ferdinand crowned during his lifetime—in 1830—only to have the latter be crowned again once his father died.) But those with a more lively imagination might even go so far as to conclude that Kossuth was calling for a new and constitutionally governing king for Hungary alone, an interpretation supported by the venue at which he gave his speech, and by the fact that he focused solely on Hungary's internal affairs. This interpretation would, of course, have been a little too far-fetched, as Hungary would have still remained under the Habsburg scepter, the only difference being that the Austrian emperor would have been different from the Hungarian king. Such a scenario would have ensured loyalty, constitutional order, and independence, but for the time being it lacked legal foundations, as the Pragmatic Sanction of 1723 did not envision such a possibility.

Kossuth's speech could therefore be interpreted in three different ways, depending on the scope of one's imagination. But it is a fact that this was the first time that the wish to see Francis Joseph on the throne had been publicly expressed in the Hungarian Diet, something which lent that wish a certain urgency. One might wonder how much of all this was grasped by the young Habsburg who was the subject of so many high hopes. One suspects, very little. He may have heard about Kossuth's speech, as everyone in Vienna was talking about it after 3 March. He may even have heard of the passage that directly concerned him. But he little understood what that message meant. As we have already seen, Francis Joseph had paid relatively little attention to politics until that point; he preferred to live in his own secure world. But tidings of revolution and subsequent events were putting increasing pressure on him to step out of his politics-free existence, at least to some extent, and to enter another one, characterized by the often obscure and confused course of events. In this latter world, much of what happened went directly against everything he had ever been taught or had come to believe.

The conference rooms at the Viennese court became loud with the clamor of demands and grievances; decisions made would be over-turned within a matter of hours or days; while at the same time the crowd would on occasion loudly cheer the archduke and the Habsburg family. How very far this was from everything that he had learned from Metternich, for whom he felt so much respect. Francis Joseph's father constantly wavered between acceptance and rejection of the laws demanded by Hungary. No one knew any longer what was right and what was wrong. Perhaps it was with Kossuth's speech in mind that the king and queen took Francis Joseph along to Pozsony for the announcement of the laws which had at last been sanctioned, enshrin-ing Hungarian reforms, at the last session of the Hungarian feudal Diet before it was dissolved.

Francis Joseph stood in the gallery of the Primate's Palace, listen-ing to the new Hungarian laws being announced. What must he have been thinking? He knew very well that his parents were opposed to these laws, and that his father had given his assent to them only because he had been put under political pressure to do so. He also knew that the sovereign was a weak man who, with a little effort, could be made to sign anything. He saw the enthusiasm and solemnity of the Hungarians, but deep in his soul he was probably irritated by the notion that his destiny in some way depended on their devotion rather than on the will of his family. He must have felt that "the time was out joint." And he was right. The question, at least from the point of view of the Habsburg court, was rather "who had been born to put it right?" The general opinion at court was that, for the time being, the person in question was not Francis Joseph.

Count Franz Bombelles, still Francis Joseph's active tutor, believed that it was advisable for the archduke to maintain a low profile during such revolutionary times. The archduke himself was tired of all the dis-order and the pitiful squirming of a dynasty which had once been so proud. How could they bow to popular demands? What is more, they could not even keep a promise! He hated to see them so humiliated, and he impatiently demanded to be sent to Radetzky's camp to fight the rebels in Italy. Count Joseph Radetzky was among the most loyal supporters of the dynasty. Francis Joseph obtained the sovereign's approval for this trip on 20 April, and on 29 April he reported to Radetzky in Verona.

Let us pause here for a moment. The empire and the Habsburg dynasty were in crisis. Nothing was as it should have been. How could a young man just turned eighteen cope? What if he felt compelled to reconsider everything that he had ever been taught? Might he not sink into a personal crisis, one which would make him susceptible to accepting the role offered by Kossuth? These were questions which would only be answered by future events. Historical events have a tendency to be used later on as evidence for or against a decision. At the same time, they provide little insight into the dilemmas of the individual, although it would be a mistake to assume that the actions of historical figures lack spiritual motives. Therefore, the question arises concerning Francis Joseph, whether, like the empire, he was at a crossroads at this point? On the one hand, the crisis of the Habsburg dynasty, even if he was not conscious of it, made it obvious that this young man would be unable to find in his immediate surroundings a role model to show him how to be a sovereign. The head of the Habsburg family, the emperor, was not exactly a manly character, and his feeble-mindedness, which in peacetime could be patiently tolerated, was, at a time of crisis, nothing but a source of humiliation for his relations, repositories of the grace of God as they supposedly were. The memory of Francis Joseph's beloved grandfather, Emperor Francis I, could not serve as an example either, as he had died when his grandson was only five years old. Francis Joseph's father was a jovial type, lacking in fortitude, who—as his reaction to the political upheavals demonstrated—failed to live up to the principle that Metternich so consistently insisted upon: he had no authority—all he could do was drift with the tide. His younger brothers were no help to Francis Joseph either, and of little consequence.

The only remotely "masculine" character close to him was his mother, Sophia. Understandably, she was the greatest influence over her son. Her willpower, resolve, and dutifulness exemplified the character traits of a sovereign, yet she was not eligible for the crown. All she could do was to exert her influence, but she could not provide an example which could be directly copied.

Who was left? There had to be someone to follow; after all, Francis Joseph had been brought up to be a sovereign and a man. Where could he look for a role model with whom he could identify, if not absolutely, then at least partially? He felt respect for Metternich, and was truly and sincerely saddened by the prince's absence. But Metternich was an old man whose time was over. Influenced by his mother's personality and his own education, Francis Joseph—as we have already seen—was ready to embrace the military spirit, particularly now, when most traditional values seemed to have lost their relevance, and the army alone was willing to stand against the current. Our young hero wanted certainty and a role model, but he could not find either. His own previous experience and objective circumstances both conditioned him to find what he was looking for in the army. And if he was lucky, in a campaigning army he might even meet someone whose personality could satisfy his quest for a role model. This was the reason why he kept demanding with such impatience that he be allowed to fight, to go to the front like a man. In this sense, Francis Joseph's Italian mission did much to promote his spiritual development. The stakes were high: if the army turned out to be a disappointment too, our young hero might have lost his last (and only) chance to find a model which could reconnect him to the world view and values conferred upon him by his mother, his family, and his education.

In the spring of 1848, therefore, Francis Joseph was going through a crisis, and he needed to find peace of mind. This crisis was of the sort to force him to reconsider his views about the world. However, it would have struck with full force only if his search for a sense of identity had failed. Such failure would have caused Francis Joseph to lose sight of his values, while success would provide him with a sense of absolute self-assurance.

Radetzky probably had little interest in the refinements of human psychology, and had not fully slept off his fatigue when, at 4 A.M. on 29 April, Francis Joseph reported to him for duty. An aged but revered military commander, Radetzky was not pleased by the news. The thought of having another archduke in his army was an irritation (he already had a number of them), because if any harm came to him it would have grave consequences.

Francis Joseph wanted to fight at all costs. He did not have to wait very long: on 6 May he smelled gunpowder for the first time, and was even slightly injured. Francis Joseph remained with Radetzky until early June. The Italian adventure was a decisive experience for him. He could see and feel for himself what it was really like to be in a campaigning army; what it was like to be victorious and to be defeated, to a greater or lesser extent. In Radetzky, whom he got to know very well, he found someone who was everything that Francis Joseph had been taught to be as a soldier. Besides, Radetzky's soldiers were fighting for a cause with which Francis Joseph could fully identify. Francis Joseph also became aware that the army was a force in which the national differences so frequently talked about in Vienna did not matter. At the Battle of Santa Lucia Francis Joseph headed the 52nd Infantry Regiment of Pécs, which was named after his father. Francis Joseph addressed his soldiers in Hungarian, who marched into battle for him and for the Habsburg dynasty. It was an object lesson in obedience and the willingness of his subjects to sacrifice themselves. During the same battle, a cannon ball tore off the right arm of a colonel of the Pécs regiment. The elderly officer, aged fifty-eight, rode to his commander in chief to report that he had lost an arm, and asked leave to retire from the battle. His request was, of course, granted; what is more, Francis Joseph made sure that he retired with the rank of general. The case of András Pottornyay—the colonel in question—served to underline that one's duty and discipline came first, even when it was no longer possible to meet the requirements of either. Nothing illustrates better than a difficult situation such as this that loyalty and respect for orders lend one dignity and masculine integrity, even in defeat. This was the kind of integrity that Francis Joseph had seen little of in Vienna. During the month that he spent in the army in Italy, Francis Joseph also learned the importance of obedience, and that the ideal of a unified monarchy was manifested in the army. In other words, he finally encountered a living confirmation of his own values.

Even more important, however, was his quest for a role model with whom he could identify. The army served him well on this point, too. Finally—although he had already had intimations to that effect—he realized how to be masculine in a manner befitting a sovereign. He was not yet eighteen, but already knew instinctively how to command and direct others—and how to treat others in the spirit in which he had been taught. He had had a taste of a particular model of power, and he had finally found the peace of mind that he had been looking for.

But his subjects had to pay a heavy price before they could teach him a different model of behavior. In early June 1848, Francis Joseph traveled to Innsbruck (to which the court had fled from Vienna). He was going there to receive the mandate for his new assignment, although it was one he never managed to complete. Francis Joseph was supposed to be sent to Bohemia to become viceroy. These plans were thwarted by the Prague uprising, although the military governor Prince Alfred Windischgrätz's soldiers quickly gained the upper hand over the rebels. For Francis Joseph, this was another example of success obtained by means of military intervention rather than wretched political maneuvering!

Otherwise, Francis Joseph's life was fairly uneventful. At least he had ceased to suffer from anxiety, and no longer wished to be active at all costs. Bombelles retired, and Count Karl Grünne became Francis Joseph's lord chamberlain. Grünne was a staunch supporter of absolutism—he was unlikely ever to give his ruler cause for concern. Francis Joseph resumed his studies, albeit irregularly—he studied when it suited him. Among other things, he tried to learn the violin, without much success. Instead of embarking on formal studies, he would haphazardly join his younger brothers' classes. He did not take much interest in politics. Sometimes, he would engage in conversation with Prince Pál Esterházy, the Hungarian government minister responsible for the king's person. In addition, Francis Joseph would hunt for chamois and go target shooting.

In August 1848, the Habsburg family returned to Vienna. Francis Joseph's eighteenth birthday was drawing ever closer. Rumor had it that he would become emperor. But nothing was actually happening, although a Hungarian master felt coat maker from Vác sent him a fine, long, sleeveless frieze cape as a present, with the Hungarian crown embroidered on it. Such an act of generosity could not, of course, crown Francis Joseph, but in early August the honorable master crafts-man was not alone in thinking that Francis Joseph would become king of Hungary. Kossuth himself pointed to this possibility on several occasions. (It should be remembered that, to begin with, Palatine Stephan was also mentioned as a possibility.) If we recall the speech delivered in the Diet on 3 March, this should not come as a surprise. However, by August, circumstances had begun to change. Hungarians were seeking a legitimate way to avoid the escalation into military conflict of the increasing tension between the Austrian court and Hungary. They reasoned that if Hungary had a Habsburg king, a Habsburg emperor would not take up arms against him. In this way, Hungary could retain the achievements of spring 1848: constitutional order and national self-determination. The laws of 1848, ratified by Ferdinand V, furnished the legal foundation that was still missing in March for the legitimate election of a Habsburg king for Hungary who was not the same person as the emperor of Austria: in 1686, the Hungarian estates had passed a bill granting the Hungarian royal throne to the male line of the Habsburg dynasty indefinitely. In 1723, this rule was extended to include the female line of the Habsburg dynasty as well, and the Pragmatic Sanction ruled that the two main parts of the empire, Austria and Hungary, were "indivisibiliter and inseparabiliter." In 1790, a bill was passed demanding recognition of Hungary as an independent state and that it should be ruled accord-ingly.

These laws, taken together, could clearly be interpreted in a num-ber of different ways, in terms of how distant or close the relationship between Hungary and the empire should be: should they constitute a real union, characterized by common policies and affairs, or merely a personal union, united by the person of the sovereign alone. One thing was certain: the sovereign would be one and the same person for both Hungary and Austria. Whichever of the two interpretations one pre-ferred, the existence of such a union could not be called into question without challenging its legal foundations. When, in early March, Kossuth referred to Francis Joseph as a potential constitutional monarch, nei-ther the constitutional order for which he called nor the possibility of making a distinction between the Austrian emperor and the Hungarian

king existed in a legal sense. The legal foundations, however indirectly, were created only in the course of 1848. The spirit and, somewhat
ambiguously, even the letter of the 1848 laws reflected the vision of a
personal union, and in a sense went one step further. Given the intentions of the legislators, it was probably not by accident that they left a
"legal loophole" in the text. The Press Act incorporated a half-sen-
tence, interpreting the Pragmatic Sanction, which stated that Hungary
and Austria were linked by virtue of being ruled by the same dynasty.
Note that the basis of their union was defined as the dynasty and not
the sovereign! If this was the case, and given that the Act had been ratified, Hungarian politicians had every right to consider electing a
Habsburg as Hungarian king who did not also wear the emperor's
crown. They were acting lawfully because, according to the principles
of Roman law, whenever the Pragmatic Sanction was in conflict with
the provisions of the law of 1848, the latter took precedence. The intention of the Hungarians was both lawful and politically justified. But it
had one great weakness: it had no chance of becoming reality, at least
as far as those who would have been affected by it were concerned.

Palatine Stephan fled, while Lieutenant General Count Josip Jelačić,
ban or governor of Croatia, launched an assault on Hungary in the
king's name and with his consent. In early October, the king officially
announced his decision to dissolve the Hungarian parliament, put
Hungary under martial law (declaring all laws passed by the
Hungarians invalid), and send in the army to crush the "rebellion." The
royal Letter-Patent was issued without the relevant minister's coun-
tersignature, however, and so it had no legal force. While the
Hungarian leaders sought a legal escape route from the increasing tension, and one that would also suit their own interests, the Viennese
court opted for unlawful schism. Vienna and Pest came into open conflict, and any possibility of Francis Joseph becoming a crowned and
constitutional king in 1848 with the consent of the Hungarians was
lost. Vienna did not realize that it had let a historical moment slip
away, nor was Francis Joseph likely to have regretted his failure to
become constitutional Hungarian monarch. He was one of those who
supported a full-scale military assault, prompted partly by his own
experience, and partly by the fact that he was not yet in a position to

assert his own political standpoint: he was not yet involved in decision-making.

In any case, Vienna did not have much time to contemplate whether this had been a historical moment or not. The Viennese revolution which took place in October—the outbreak of which was to a great extent caused by the court's anti-Hungarian actions—once again forced the royal family to flee. After a bumpy, eight-day journey by carriage and on horseback the Habsburg family arrived in Olmütz (Olomouc), Bohemia. Here, the event which insiders had been talking about for so long finally took place: Ferdinand abdicated, and Francis Charles renounced the throne. Consequently, Francis Joseph was to become the new sovereign. This decision, which had been in the cards for some time, was dictated by political necessity. The court finally made up its mind—to some extent under the influence of the events of early October 1848—in order to break Hungary and to crush its lawful order which was considered to be nothing more than a rebellion. Vienna preferred to introduce a new regime as soon it had achieved victory, and so a ruler was needed who was eligible under the rules of succession set out by the Pragmatic Sanction, the principal law in their eyes, had the appropriate personal qualities, and was not bound either by former promises (this ruled out his father) or by any law associated with his name or passed with his direct involvement.

Francis Joseph had already demonstrated his deep commitment to the ideals of a unified empire and the unrestrained power of the sovereign on a number of occasions. He was an energetic young man, who had never exposed himself politically, not even during the chaos of 1848. As already mentioned, he had never actually taken up his appointment as viceroy of Bohemia, and his only active military involvement in Italy had been in connection with the armed suppression of the revolution.

Francis Joseph was being presented with a mission that fully matched his character and personal beliefs. At the same time, everything which he was required to do was diametrically opposed to the wishes of the supporters of Hungarian constitutionalism. Full-scale confrontation between nation and individual was therefore unavoidable. On the other hand, the reasoning of the archduke and of the court was quite different. Francis Joseph believed that the clash was taking place between God's law and the dark forces of rebellion; by standing on the side of righteousness he would be acting in the interests of, rather than against, the Hungarian nation. His mission was to bring a flock which had gone astray back into the camp of the loyal, by force of arms if need be. On 20 November 1848 he welcomed the 37th Infantry Regiment of Nagyvárad (Oradea) as it passed through Olmütz. The unit fought on the emperor's side and against their own compatriots. Francis Joseph saw confirmed once again what he had experienced on the Italian campaign—that the army had a supranational loyalty to the dynasty. In a speech—delivered in Hungarian—Francis Joseph talked about loyalty and the uplifting effect of taking the military oath. His words were enthusiastically greeted with an ovation. In autumn 1848, however, the significance of loyalty and of oath-taking became ambiguous, since it was unclear to what they should apply: the law-breaking Habsburg dynasty or the law-abiding Hungarian government which was willing to take up the fight provoked by the dynasty? The overwhelming majority of Hungarian regiments were clearly in support of the latter. At the same time, Francis Joseph had no doubt that the 37th regiment—one of the exceptions—were right to do what they did. Already in September, Francis Joseph had spoken elatedly of Jelačić's pamphlet which communicated to the Hungarian people the author's determination to restore the king's violated rights, authority, and order.

There was no reason for Francis Joseph to have changed his mind by November 1848. His life had changed little in the meantime: he had continued the studies which he had begun back in Innsbruck. However, things were now slightly different: he was being kept informed concerning political affairs by the ministers Count Felix Schwarzenberg (who later became prime minister) and Count Franz Stadion. In the meantime, preparations started for a coup, which was scheduled for 2 December. It was not decided right up to the last minute what name Francis Joseph would assume as sovereign: Francis II or Francis Joseph? Finally, Schwarzenberg decided that all documents should feature the name Francis Joseph I.

Chapter Four

THE YOUNG HERO OF THE BATTLEFIELD AND A BIRTHDAY PRESENT

On 2 December, Francis Joseph became the sovereign, but strangely enough, from a Hungarian point of view, not the Hungarian king, regardless of the fact that both Ferdinand and Francis Charles had left the Hungarian royal crown to Francis Joseph in a declaration of abdication written in Hungarian. Francis Joseph, on the other hand, emphasized that his accession to the imperial throne should also entail his taking control of Hungary and Transylvania. (Note that this treatment of Transylvania as a separate country signified the new sovereign's determination to revert to the state of affairs which prevailed before the adoption of the laws of 1848, which he did not recognize.)

This change in the throne's occupant was never officially communicated to a Hungarian parliament which was considered to be rebellious, and so the Hungarian nation never officially consented to it. Besides, none of the physical requirements had been satisfied: the crown itself, for instance, was still in the possession of the "rebellious" Hungarian government. It would be pointless to go through all the things that were lacking, as those who organized the coronation on 2 December well knew; indeed, their aim was to ensure that the enthronement of the new sovereign would be unlawful from a Hungarian point of view. If they had accepted the validity of either the centuries-old laws or the new laws of 1848, that would have amounted to recognition of the very Hungary which they were trying to crush, to which end changing the sovereign was merely a means.

The new sovereign promised his peoples who lived in a united Austria freedom, and an elected parliament. At the same time, he reverted to a phrase which had appeared to fall into desuetude in early September 1848: Francis Joseph started to say that he ruled "by the grace of God." His choice of this expression gave every reason to cast doubt on the sincerity of the new sovereign's intention to share power with elected representatives. This doubt was reinforced by the fact that, at the same time, Francis Joseph's army was busy suppressing the Hungarian "rebellion" one which had already made freedom a reality. At the time of his accession to the throne, the adulatory voices which welcomed the new emperor were mixed with the opinion, emphatically expressed by Schwarzenberg, among others, that by raising a "rebellion" the Hungarians had abandoned their constitution and that therefore there was no need to crown Francis Joseph as Hungarian king.

What could the Hungarians do? Effectively, their fate had been decided. Recognizing the legitimacy of the events of 2 December would have amounted to a denial of their own laws and of their very existence as a nation. Therefore, they were compelled to reject what had happened. Whether one took a more or a less radical stance, the essence remained the same. Samu Jósika and Count Antal Szécsen, frequent visitors at Olmütz, were among those who opposed the 1848 reforms, yet they too reacted angrily to such total negligence of Hungary's historically established rights, even those acquired before 1848, on the part of the new sovereign. The city of Pozsony petitioned Francis Joseph, asking him to regain the love of his Hungarian subjects by letting himself be crowned in a constitutional manner. Newspapers in Hungary, then at war with Austria, expressed the same wish, but with a little more frankness. They wrote that, while Ferdinand had every right to put Francis Joseph in charge of his own flock, Hungarians were no sheep and Hungary was no sheep fold. Saint Stephen's crown was no mere nightcap that could be taken off one head and put on another without having to ask the owner's consent. The crown belonged to the nation and so the nation's consent had to be sought before it could be transferred to a new sovereign.

The official reaction was absolutely clear: on 7 December, Parliament ceremonially declared that no one was authorized to dispose of the Hungarian royal throne unilaterally, without Parliament's support, knowledge, and consent. Anyone obeying an unlawful ruler was guilty of treason. The Parliament's resolution clearly refused to recognize the change on the throne, although at an earlier session some members of Parliament had supported granting that recognition. They had done so not so much due to a lack of principles but rather because they believed that in that way it might become possible to restore peace and obtain recognition for Hungary's rights. However, the majority did not share their naiveté, and acted in a manner dictated under the given circumstances by law, political self-defense, and morality.

Both politically and morally it was characteristic that the resolution of parliament did not oppose Francis Joseph personally. It merely rejected the unlawful manner in which the throne had been passed from one incumbent to another. The resolution left open the possibility that the court might one day decide to act lawfully, in which case relations should not be impeded by the memory of irresponsible ad hominem remarks, however well founded. The Hungarian Parliament maintained the position it had held consistently since spring 1848: if Francis Joseph recognized the laws of Hungary, there would be no reason why he could not become Hungary's lawful king. The resolution therefore carefully avoided making any personal reference. Nevertheless, the new sovereign's image, as it had been formed back in 1847, had been tarnished. Even more importantly, on 2 December a split occurred between Francis Joseph and Hungary, and henceforth they were to stand on opposite sides. This still did not amount to a personal criticism of Francis Joseph, but it did present the prospect of an intensifying conflict between him and the Hungarian people. Events were to validate this analysis. Windischgrätz's imperial army was drawing closer to Pest, and he demanded unconditional surrender, as he informed the delegates of the Hungarian Parliament. He also had Count Lajos Batthyány, Hungary's first prime minister, who had been appointed in the spring and later resigned, arrested.

The country was at war and Windischgrätz's soldiers fought for Francis Joseph's empire, to the new sovereign's great delight. In 1848, Francis Joseph's Christmas present from his parents included three portraits of persons the initial letters of whose surnames made up

"WIR," the infamous "slogan" of the counterrevolution: Windischgrätz, Jelačić, and Radetzky. Jelačić firmly believed that the Hungarians, this "Mongol population [,]...must be exterminated utterly." (Clearly, Jelačić's rabid anti-Hungarian sentiments were motivated partly by personal failure: his military campaign waged against Hungary is not counted among the shining successes of Habsburg military history.) Radetzky had excelled in the crushing of the Italian revolution, and it was in his military camp that Francis Joseph had gained the impressions that would last him a lifetime and give him inner strength. Finally, Windischgrätz crushed the Viennese and Prague revolutions, and was to occupy Pest in the early days of the new year.

Everyone in Vienna was looking forward to a happy new year, as the commander in chief of the imperial army assaulting Hungary reported that the resistance he encountered was pitiful and victory was near. Francis Joseph believed Windischgrätz: on receiving Windischgrätz's infamous telegram after the Battle of Kápolna, which read: "I have smashed these rebellious cattle," Francis Joseph thought that the time had come to translate into action the motto that he had chosen for himself as sovereign back in February 1849: Viribus unitis—"by united efforts," which in practical terms meant "for a united Austria." It seemed that he might just be able to achieve what many of his Habsburg predecessors had dreamt of in vain: a united empire.

From a distance, Metternich warned him against this chimerical notion, but he went unheeded. The idea was that as soon as Hungary had been crushed by the imperial army and the flames of Italian resistance had been extinguished, nothing would stand in the way of the consolidation of power. On 4 March 1849, Francis Joseph issued the Olmütz Constitution, which had been under preparation since January. The "perfect time" for promulgation of this document arrived when Francis Joseph dissolved the Austrian constitutional convention assembled at Kremsier, which would have granted Austria's many nationalities far-reaching autonomy, and when Vienna believed that they had crushed all resistance in Hungary.

On the face of it, the Olmütz Constitution was a liberal one, but the rights enshrined in it were guaranteed by nothing more than the sovereign's sense of responsibility to God. This complete absence of guarantees of any sort must have made the supporters of liberalism uneasy. Further cause for concern lay in the fact that Francis Joseph had used armed force to disperse his own Parliament, and had promised to reintroduce rights only after "order" had been restored.

The Olmütz Constitution, at least as far as issues of freedom are concerned, gave rise to doubts from the beginning. Liberal concerns apart, this constitution was totally unacceptable from the point of view of the Hungarian national cause. The emperor invalidated Hungarian laws on his own whim; to be more precise, the only ones he allowed to remain in force were those that did not clash with the empire's own constitution.

His general approach was not fundamentally new. What was new, however, was the termination of Hungarian nationhood by carving it up into five provinces, with Vienna as capital of a united empire. This is how the Olmütz Constitution "solved" the uncertainty that existed in December. Francis Joseph openly declared that he did not want the Hungarian crown. To be more precise, he did not need what the crown signified. He wanted five provinces, but no Hungarian kingdom. And if there was no so-called "Hungarian Constitution," there could be no Hungarian nation. The laws of the empire would be the only new laws, and as soon as "order" was restored among his subjects, everyone would be subject to these laws as citizens of a greater united Austria.

Francis Joseph could not have done much more to distance himself from his Hungarian subjects. He believed that he was doing the right thing, however, and that Hungarian resistance would be crushed in only a matter of days, perhaps weeks. But he was wrong. Windischgrätz failed to accomplish his mission, and he was recalled. On 13 April, Field Marshal Ludwig Welden was appointed to replace him. In the winter, small Russian units came to the aid of the imperial troops in Transylvania, but the long-awaited victory could not be attained. A new, more decisive force was needed.

Nicholas I, "Tsar and Autocrat of All the Russias" and the new hope of reactionary Europe, seemed willing to solve the problems faced by Austria. First Schwarzenberg, then Francis Joseph invited Tsar Nicholas to send an army to Hungary. The tsar acceded to their request and sent General Ivan Fedorovich Paskevich with 200,000

Russian troops to fight in a country that did not even exist in the eyes of the rulers of the Austrian Empire. The Hungarian response to the Olmütz Constitution had not yet reached the Habsburg court when the latter requested Russian intervention. When news of the April Declaration of Independence reached him, Francis Joseph is reported to have said: "So much the better." The Declaration furnished him with an excuse to proceed.

The opinions of the Hungarian politicians then in session in the town of Debrecen differed. They all more or less agreed that, after what had happened, they could not talk to the new emperor. However, some thought that the solution would be to bring back Ferdinand V from Prague and to restore him to the throne. Of course, this was no more than a theoretical possibility, given that Ferdinand had already abdicated. In any case, where was the political force which could bring back an abdicated king from Prague to Hungary? The majority agreed with Kossuth: if it was the case that Francis Joseph did not want to be the king of Hungary, and if Hungary did not exist as far as he was concerned, then Hungary should refuse to recognize him. On 14 April, Kossuth submitted a motion (with detailed argumentation) to the House of Representatives, then sitting in Debrecen's High Church. Two paragraphs of this motion were a direct response to the Olmütz Constitution:

It should be declared in the name of the nation by way of a resolution: first, that Hungary, lawfully united Transylvania, and all countries, partiums, and provinces thereof, should be declared a free, sovereign, and independent European state, and that the entire state and its territorial integrity should be declared indivisible and its territory inviolate; secondly, given the betrayal, treachery, and taking up of arms by the Habsburg-Lotharingian dynasty against the Hungarian nation, its desire to compromise the country's territorial integrity, and tear Transylvania and Croatia away from Hungary, and the fact that it was not ashamed to attempt to eradicate the country's independence by the use of armed force, and to involve a foreign army to murder a nation, it destroyed the Pragmatic Sanction by its own hands, just as it generally destroyed all relations between Hungary and its provinces and itself. In the name of the nation, this treacherous Habsburg-Lotharingian dynasty is hereby declared forever excluded from ruling Hungary, lawfully united Transylvania, and all countries, partiums, and provinces thereof. It is expelled from the country and excluded from the enjoyment of all civil rights. Similarly, it is hereby declared dethroned, excluded, and expelled in the name of the nation....

The Declaration of Independence, which was drafted by a number of people on the basis of Kossuth's motion, was adopted by Parliament on 19 April 1849. This legislative act, which did not omit to mention Francis Joseph's personal responsibility, stated:

Had the Hungarian nation's consent to the change in occupancy of the throne on 2 December been sought in a lawful manner, and had the young prince offered to take an oath to the Hungarian constitution before he soaked his hands in civilian blood, the Hungarian nation would have accepted him as its king without delay by a diplomatic bond and crowned him with the crown of Saint Stephen,

but Francis Joseph,

having forsaken everything that is holy before God and humanity, not only failed to offer that, but proceeded to cast off the innocence of a youthful bosom, and, with his first words, hurried to cry out that he would take Hungary, which he, the rebel, dared to call rebellious, by force of arms, and that he would make it his life's mission to strip that country of its thousand-year-old independence and to merge it into the Austrian Empire. And he has tried everything he could to make his words become awful reality.

Therefore "that treacherous dynasty shall be expelled from the Hungarian royal throne and be given up to God's judgment, and the abhorrence of public opinion, morality, and honor."

The Declaration of Independence, together with its argumentation, clearly demonstrated the gulf which had opened up between the

Hungarian people and Francis Joseph. For the first time, he was made personally responsible. The question of responsibility would henceforth arise quite often. To begin with, Francis Joseph came to power with little knowledge of Hungarian law. As we have seen, this was to have formed part of his studies in 1848, but events made regular study impossible. Although he became a soldier he did not learn how to be a general, and as a future Hungarian king he had no idea what his rights and responsibilities were. He could, of course, have gained some practical experience: just as his military experiences in Italy taught him how to be a soldier, his visit to the 1848 parliamentary session in Pozsony (Pressburg) could have been equally instructive in the political field. But Francis Joseph's natural inclination towards military matters in equal measure hindered any inclination he might have had, or might have acquired, towards parliamentary politics.

Needless to say, as sovereign (and being of age) he had an obligation to make himself familiar with the basic institutions of the countries over which his rule extended and his own rights and duties under the law. However, just as he had had no practical experience in politics prior to his accession to the throne, only seldom had he come anywhere near the actual process of decision-making. It could also be cited in his defense that he was still very young, and so was still reliant upon those who had promoted his rise to power. Yet he was no mere puppet when he came to the throne. Only three days after his accession he was already chairing the Council of Ministers. At the end of the first session, which lasted five hours, he summarized what had been said, performing his task with precision and in accordance with established procedure. His comments indicated that he had listened attentively the whole time and followed the discussion closely.

He continued to chair Council of Ministers meetings later on, and not just formally. In addition, he drew attention to himself through his "hands-on" approach to administration, even in insignificant matters: for example, Francis Joseph used his influence with Parliament to make them vote an exceptionally high allowance for the widow and seven orphans of a certain Lamberg who had been murdered in Pest.

Undoubtedly, Schwarzenberg was the greatest influence on Francis Joseph. One could say that Schwarzenberg was the paramount figure of a new era. Having said that, Francis Joseph did nothing that he personally did not agree with. In such a case, Schwarzenberg would have had to give way. As far as we know, however, they never disagreed, not even slightly on anything important. On the contrary, whenever the interests of the dynasty and royal pride demanded it, Schwarzenberg broke, in the politest way possible, even with those to whom he owed a great deal. It was in the prime minister's own interests to have Windischgrätz dismissed, but his recall would not have been quite as rapid if the commander in chief of the imperial army had not forgotten to send a particular report to his young sovereign.

To be sure, at this point Francis Joseph did not yet possess the authority of an experienced sovereign. A few years later, Windischgrätz would not have dared to lash out angrily at Francis Joseph upon being dismissed for neglecting his duty towards the emperor's domain. ("Your Majesty would have no such duties to worry about, had it not been for me." There was a great deal of truth in this, as Windischgrätz had suppressed a number of revolutions.) Francis Joseph was trying hard to acquire authority, however, listening to the advice of some, while dismissing the advice of others without giving them a second thought. For example, the advice of anyone arguing for more concessions to Hungary rather than calling in the Russians was bound to fall upon deaf ears. On the other hand, anyone who took the view that there was no need for political reconciliation was deemed to be giving "wise advice." Those who said that Windischgrätz had been too lenient for having pardoned two Hungarians sentenced to hang (one as young as Francis Joseph himself, and the other a father of three), were bound to meet with approval. Those who, like Schwarzenberg, argued that there was no need to be sensitive towards Hungarian national sentiments in the occupied territories, were welcomed. Formally, however, responsibility rested with the sovereign, as atrocities were committed with his approval and in his name. In this sense, the Hungarian Parliament was definitely justified in holding Francis Joseph personally responsible.

If we look at the actions of Francis Joseph during these months, not just as sovereign but also as a person, then we realize that this was the time when he was beginning to face up to the moral and political consequences of his deeds. Even more importantly, he was more than happy with the unfolding of events. Nevertheless, it would be inaccurate to say that he alone was responsible for what happened. Many others shared the blame. At the same time, Francis Joseph was doing everything in his power to exercise as much influence as possible over events. He had acquired a taste for his new role and was trying to create his own "image." He was prepared to engross himself for hours on end in reading reports: he wanted to be better informed than anyone. Sometimes, he tried to acquire first-hand experience of the real situation. He—and members of the Council of Ministers—even thought of assuming personal leadership of the imperial army in its campaign against Hungary.

General Artúr Görgey's success in April prevented Francis Joseph from doing this, but it could not prevent him from trying to obtain personal knowledge of the military situation. On 10 May, the sovereign, who had been excluded from the country by act of parliament (then sitting in Debrecen), stepped onto Hungarian soil for a three-day trip around the western borders. At the Vág River, he was very close to the Hungarian border guards, while at Óvár, Pöltenberg's hussars were preparing to give chase to the emperor, but he managed to avoid meeting them.

Another trip—which he again made in connection with his Hungarian subjects—led to a slight setback in respect of Francis Joseph's image-building and his stature as an independent sovereign. On 21 May (the same day on which Görgey occupied Buda), he arrived in Warsaw. Francis Joseph was to meet the tsar, whose assistance was making Francis Joseph's victory over Hungary a certainty, in order to thank him. The Russian host did everything he could not to overawe his young guest. The tsar had Francis Joseph stay in his own quarters, and passed before him with sword held down, saluting Francis Joseph as an inferior would his superior. Yet it could not be clearer who was indebted to whom. On the balcony of the Lazienki Palace, Francis Joseph kissed the hand of the Tsar of All the Russias. He was clearly grateful, and with good reason. In the feudal world order under which Francis Joseph had been brought up, a kiss on the hand signified much more than a mere courtesy. It was the middle of the supposedly enlightened nineteenth century, yet both Francis Joseph and Tsar Nicholas I embodied the spirit of a bygone age. This is the explanation of the apparent selflessness of the ruler of the Russian Empire; in the same spirit, a kiss on the hand signified subordination to the other's superior might.

After reigning for only four-and-half months, Francis Joseph had to accept that his rule was unstable without the goodwill of his mighty neighbor. This represented a real failure, but who was to blame? Needless to say, the emperor of Austria was unlikely to find himself or Schwarzenberg's policies at fault. Instead, he put the blame on the rebels. The Austrian Empire identified the rebels as the Hungarians, while the Russian Empire identified them with the implacable Poles. The two mighty rulers understood each other well, and their sense of justice was reinforced by the fact that a number of Poles fought on the side of the Hungarians. Now the tsar's armies were marching against the latter, too. In any case, Francis Joseph's visit to Warsaw constituted a humiliating slap in the face, for which the Hungarians were responsible, at least according to his own logic. Needless to say, the Hungarians would have to be taught a lesson.

Upon his return in Austria, Francis Joseph dismissed Welden and appointed Julius Haynau to lead the military campaign against Hungary. The emperor must have read General Haynau's personal file prior to making the appointment, as was his custom. There was little need from a military point of view to appoint a new commander in chief, as the Russian intervention alone was enough to decide the outcome of the war: Welden would have done as well as anyone else. Radetzky, the general so admired by the young emperor, recommended Haynau's military capabilities in the strongest terms. Haynau had served under Radetzky and had great respect for him as the commander in chief of the Italian army. But what would Haynau's personal file have told Francis Joseph about him as a person? In anticipation of certain victory, the emperor needed someone who could not only pursue military operations successfully, but also direct the occupying forces.

Haynau's personal file included an assessment by Lieutenant General Pittl, Haynau's commander at Temesvár (Timişoara). In 1847:

> Haynau is sixty-one-years old, but he looks seventy, and has a sickly disposition. He has a thorough understanding of the nature of military service, but has a tendency to twist the rules in order

to achieve glory and to make accusations against persons against whom he has cultivated a dislike. Such people he abuses with calculated hatred. He is very knowledgeable in military affairs, but he is also characterized by a meanness not entirely in keeping with military dignity. Given his moral character, everyone would like to see him recalled, because no one likes to serve with him. Perhaps the best thing would be to retire him.

These character traits may have seemed exactly what was required in late May 1849. Rebellious Hungary could not expect to receive from Haynau, the certain victor, even the little mercy it had been shown by the now recalled Windischgrätz. In all likelihood this was why Haynau was selected for the task.

Haynau invited Francis Joseph to Hungary, and the sovereign accepted his invitation. He was heading for battle, so providing him with the perfect opportunity to demonstrate that he was ready and able personally to defeat the hydra of rebellion. He knew that his tarnished authority as sovereign could be repaired by demonstrating personal courage. Francis Joseph also had pleasant memories of his army days in Italy. Besides, he wanted to boost the troops' morale: the army had suffered too much in the teeth of a Hungarian resistance which Windischgrätz had prematurely dubbed "pitiful." The soldiers also had to live with the thought that, although they had fought for months, the victory laurels would not be theirs alone.

Francis Joseph may also have felt that he had to lend some kind of personal weight to the pamphlet in which he had addressed the people of Hungary before his trip to Warsaw. In this, he had announced his alliance with the Russians in order to "'liberate" Hungary

from the heavy yoke imposed by villains both within and outside the country [a reference to the Poles who had come to the aid of Hungary]...Under the false pretext of protecting their nation and their family from danger [these subversive elements] are willing to shed the blood of their brothers and their kindred, to destroy the wealth of peaceful citizens and the well-being of their thriving homeland, and to call them to arms against their own king, who grants all his peoples a free constitution, even those that never previously had one, and grants equal rights to all the nations and citizens in his vast empire.

The Hungarian people took slogans announcing their forthcoming "liberation" with a grain of salt, to say the least: they knew full well what was likely to be in store for them. Francis Joseph's desire to demonstrate his benevolence was therefore addressed not so much to them, but to the other nations of the empire, which had as yet seen little of the "blessings" of the Olmütz Constitution.

The desire to make a fight of it was mounting. Ten days after the Russians had crossed the Hungarian border, Francis Joseph took part in the battle for the reoccupation of Győr. His involvement is interesting, as it demonstrates his desire to show himself as independent ruler at all costs. During the siege, Francis Joseph expressed a wish to head the first battalion (a small, but not insoluble psychological riddle!), but General Schlick humbly invited him to accompany his own third battalion into the town. Francis Joseph assented, but, the moment the one-eyed Schlick's back was turned, the emperor climbed over to the opposite bank of the Rába River along the beam of a burned-out bridge, and headed towards the main square, accompanied by adjutant Grünne, as well as his ministers Schwarzenberg and Gyulay. By the time Francis Joseph got to the square, it had been occupied by the Imperial Army. The wholly pointless exercise of climbing across a beam may be attributed to a nineteen-year-old young man's desire for adventure. Knowing Francis Joseph's strong sense of discipline, however, it seems more likely that he wanted to underline his freedom to do as he pleased even in the face of rational argument.

Francis Joseph was celebrated as a hero for his action at Győr, which did a great deal to enhance the image which, according to both him and his inner circle, corresponded to the greatness of a sovereign. (Tsar Nicholas I, who begged Francis Joseph not to put his life at risk for the sake of his subjects, sent his fellow sovereign the Cross of the Order of Saint George.) The almighty Schwarzenberg was also concerned by the emperor's adventurousness, and upon his return to Vienna submitted a request to His Majesty that he return to the Austrian capital in order to safeguard his life.

Francis Joseph continued to argue that he could do as he wished. On 2 July, he participated in another battle, this time near Komárom— he was involved in the fighting in the forest of Ács. Strictly speaking, there was nothing to justify the emperor's personal presence on the battlefield, although his courage did serve to boost the soldiers' morale. (His mere presence alone would have had the same result). Apart from anything else, Francis Joseph's direct involvement also served to demonstrate to Schwarzenberg and the Council of Ministers that he would take whatever action he saw fit. No one was to assume that the emperor would listen to them: however influential they were, they would be powerless if the emperor decided otherwise, with the result that people tended to restrict their advice to what they thought the emperor wanted to hear.

In any case, Francis Joseph was not needed for the final act, and on 4 July he returned to Vienna with heightened self-confidence. On 18 August, his family spent the day together at his summer residence at Ischl, celebrating the emperor's nineteenth birthday. Around a sumptuous table sat the emperor's parents and his brothers and sisters. The emperor's aide entered the room with a cheerful face, holding a telegram, which he passed to the young ruler at his bidding. The message was short and referred to an event which had happened five days earlier: Görgey, the commander in chief of the Hungarian army, had surrendered to the Russians at Világos. On hearing the news, Francis Joseph's family rejoiced, raising their glasses for a second time. A welcome birthday present, indeed!

Chapter Five
THE ANOINTED MURDERER

The late summer of 1849 was the beginning of the "dark years" for Hungary, continuing through the 1850s and lasting until the mid-1860s, with only a brief respite. The last four months of 1849 and the first half of 1850 showed that, unlikely as it might seem, Francis Joseph was capable of increasing the distance which now separated him from the Hungarian people, as great as it already was as a result of the Olmütz Constitution, the Declaration of Independence, and the ensuing armed struggle. At this stage all fighting had come to an end, to be replaced by repression.

Needless to say, any conqueror is unlikely to be loved by those whom he has defeated. He can expect only hatred for having crushed the cause for which a nation rose up in arms in the first place. However, the intensity and duration of this hatred depends upon the victor's attitude towards the defeated. But how should the defeated be dealt with? Some called for nothing less than the death penalty. Even a number of conservative Hungarians who were loyal to the dynasty took this view, including Samu Jósika and Emil Dessewffy. Other loyal Hungarian aristocrats, however, including Count Johann Coronini, a former tutor of Francis Joseph, argued that mercy befitted the victor. In the circumstances, therefore, the wisest action would be to forgive and forget. Significantly, however, Coronini added: "as far as possible." The pro-Russian Hungarian Count Ferenc Zichy would also have been satisfied by fewer deaths and called for mercy.

The Russian position, similarly, was not unanimous. Count Karl Nesselrode, the tsar's minister of foreign affairs, proposed a full amnesty without the need for an investigation. The tsar and his military commander, General Paskevich, advocated a combination of just severity and mercy. This general—and rather ambiguous—advice had been tilted in the direction of mercy by the fact that the Russians had asked that Görgey be pardoned, a request which was granted. In moral or legal terms, it would be difficult to justify bringing to trial the subordinates of an army commander who had been pardoned when they had only been obeying his orders. The tsar did not ask for an unconditional pardon, but the inner logic of his advice did support mercy overall. There were also clear signs that the international community would welcome a policy of forgiveness. Lord Henry Palmerston, the British foreign secretary, spoke in this spirit. His French counterpart at the time was Alexis de Tocqueville, whose famous book on democracy in America had been available in Hungarian translation since 1841: his writings had instructed many of those who were now awaiting punishment. Faithful to his ideals, the French minister talked of the heroes of a noble and courageous Hungarian nation, and suggested that the victors should not to treat them as traitors.

It seems clear that there was widespread support for the principle of forgiveness or at least for emphasizing amnesty rather than punishment. The same principle was reinforced by the fact that the Hungarians had not ill-treated any of the officers of the Austrian Imperial Army whom they had captured; on the contrary, some of these officers were allowed to go free upon their word of honor that they would never again take up arms against the Hungarian people. One of these officers was Heinrich Hentzi, commander of the Buda Castle, who, having broken his word, fought against the Hungarian national army in its attempt to recapture Buda, and was repaid by being fatally wounded.

The Austrian Council of Ministers had not yet been informed of the Hungarian capitulation at Világos when, on 16 August, they took a resolution to allow Haynau to negotiate with the Hungarians and to permit those Hungarian officers and political leaders who wished to do so to go abroad, as long as they did so within a given deadline, and to subject anyone who decided to stay to a "lenient" investigation. Francis Joseph was not present at this meeting: he was visiting his family at Ischl. Former Hungarian officers of the Austrian Imperial Army who had fought on the Hungarian side in the uprising would be readmitted to the army with rank undiminished or could apply for retirement, while soldiers from the lower ranks could return to their families; only politicians would be called upon to account for their actions during the revolution.

Görgey had surrendered to the Russians, not to the Austrians, and so refused to talk to Haynau. When news of the surrender of the main Hungarian army arrived, the Austrian Council of Ministers adopted a new resolution, this time in the presence of the emperor, whereby they declared that any promises made hitherto were not binding. This decision, taken on 20 August, marked a fundamental change compared to the decision made on 16 August. The order was now given to capture every political and military leader of the Hungarian uprising; to try all pro-Hungarian former Imperial Army officers; and to recruit all able-bodied lower ranks into the Imperial Army. At the same time, Haynau was instructed to submit any death sentences to the emperor before carrying them out. In the space of only four days everything had changed as a result of only one new development: units of the Hungarian army had begun to lay down their arms one after another. Now the punishments meted out depended only upon the whim of the conqueror. As soon as all Hungarian resistance had ceased, repression was unleashed at full strength. Now the principle of revenge began to come to the fore.

The use of terror had an ideological foundation adhered to by the two persons whose influence on the ruler of the Austrian Empire was decisive. Despite all the advice coming from both inside Austria and abroad, both Sophia and Schwarzenberg agreed that rebellion was the paramount danger. Given that the spirit of rebellion tends to live on in hearts and minds long after it has been physically crushed, it was the task of absolutism to demoralize rebellious souls and to "sever the head" of the insurgent leadership. "Mercy is a good thing, but we must do a little hanging first," the prime minister is said to have remarked. "We should not be afraid of instigating a blood bath," he professed in the autumn of 1849.

In keeping with this way of thinking, he issued an order to Haynau on 29 August to report only death sentences which had already been carried out. In this way, the sovereign gave Haynau a free hand, a man who, despite his military prowess, was morally corrupt and whom, given his thirst for revenge, should have been recalled in such circumstances. After Világos, the Austrian warlord had no more fighting to do in Hungary; his only task was repression, something which suited his character perfectly. A prostrate Hungary now helplessly awaited the meting out of death sentences and terms of imprisonment.

We do not possess detailed information concerning the ensuing terror. We can barely say with certainty how many lost their lives fighting for the rights of their nation in 1848–49. Generally speaking, only the victors draw up statistics. According to Austrian calculations, some fifty-five thousand Hungarians fell in the fighting. The period of repression, which lasted through the autumn and winter of 1849, saw 120 judicial executions: the number of those executed without due process, "shot while escaping," as the grim saying goes, remains unknown. Around forty to fifty thousand were forcibly recruited into the army or deported, while 1,200 were imprisoned. Thousands emigrated. The lack of adequate statistics speaks for itself. Similarly expressive was the manner in which the resolution of 20 August was enforced. Haynau had wanted to stage large-scale executions as early as 24 August, but the Russians and the Habsburg court had restrained him.

The Russians tried to stop him principally because they did not want to witness the consequences of their intervention. The Habsburg court had intervened because not all Hungarian resistance had been eradicated: some Hungarian corps were still capitulating, partly to Austrian troops, and the castle of Komárom was still holding firm. An agreement was reached only in late September allowing Captain György Klapka and his Komárom defenders, who numbered in the tens of thousands, to leave the encircled fortress under an amnesty. At this stage, forgiveness was motivated not so much by moral principles as by fear of losing the political power-game. However, as soon as the last nest of Hungarian resistance had been smoked out, the heavy fist was ready to strike. On the first anniversary of the revolution in Vienna, twelve generals and a colonel of the Hungarian national army were executed in Arad, and Count Lajos Batthyány, the lawfully appointed prime minister of the first responsible Hungarian government, was executed in Pest. Those who passed these sentences created, against their will, the first national symbols of the myth of 1848–49.

The executions provoked condemnation on an international scale. Palmerston expressed his personal opinion that the Austrians were the "worst beasts" ever to make the claim that they were a cultured people: "Their cruel atrocities committed in Galicia, Italy, Hungary, and Transylvania are comparable only to the behavior of African and Haitian tribesmen." The Austrian authorities were made to feel distinctly uncomfortable by the protests of other countries. Besides, they were also alarmed that many of their own army officers were against treating a defeated foe in this manner.

Needless to say, Haynau was not moved in the slightest by the argument that one of the thirteen officers executed in Arad, Ernő Pöltenberg, had treated his Austrian captives very decently, and that many of his Austrian counterparts still remembered the meaning of military honor and *ius armorum*. Of course, an armed foe has to be defeated, and, in the course of any struggle, death is always a possibility: in principle, the possession of arms granted both sides an equal chance of winning. But killing an already defenseless foe was against military honor: this was not the outcome of a fair fight, but cold-blooded murder.

Under pressure from protests and general discontent, but primarily because most of the "ringleaders" who could be caught had already been punished, on 26 October the Council of Ministers and Francis Joseph decided to call a halt to the executions. They continued to dole out prison sentences and forced labor, however. They wanted to stop only the most public forms of repression, those which gave rise to the greatest consternation. But Haynau remained unconcerned: he continued to issue and to carry out death sentences against the emperor's orders. Despite the embarrassment this caused, for the time being the emperor did not react to Haynau's brazen insubordination. It seems that he did not lack "patience," "human understanding," and the "spirit of forgiveness" after all (what is more, Francis Joseph even decided to pardon some, albeit low-ranking, offenders).

According to news emanating from Hungary, the public mood was such that its new absolutist government could not hope to win its affection even with the passage of time. The general hatred had reached boiling point not only in relation to the new government, but also in relation to the powers-that-be who had acted in breach of the law from the outset. The Hungarian people were now further apart from their de facto rulers than ever. In hindsight, while Francis Joseph's responsibility can be shared out among others, it cannot in any way be diminished. Naturally, both Schwarzenberg, the prime mover of events, and Haynau, who had acted under orders, were complicit. But Francis Joseph could have withdrawn his consent at any time. As we have seen, he had demonstrated on a number of occasions his readiness and ability to act as he saw fit when he felt the need to demonstrate his free will and sense of responsibility as a sovereign. He had every opportunity to make up his own mind about the policy of repression, if he had thought differently from his advisors. Furthermore, this would have been a wise course, given that a willingness to be merciful was part of the image of a sovereign, and that there were some who actively urged him in that direction. Had he exercised mercy, his rule over Hungary would not have been undermined. However, showing mercy was not a matter of principle for him, but rather one of tactics.

This was also the reasoning of those to whom Francis Joseph owed his ascension to the throne in 1848. Francis Joseph believed that the spirit of rebellion had to be stamped out, by hanging, shooting, or imprisonment, if need be. His education, personality and life experience, which underpinned his values, all conditioned him to think this way. He was still a young man, just turned nineteen. Had he been more experienced, he would probably have considered more carefully the political pros and cons of the repression suggested by Schwarzenberg. At the same time, his youth prevented Francis Joseph only from considering his actions wisely, not from having strong beliefs, which under the circumstances constituted the most powerful driving force.

In the autumn of 1849 he had every reason to feel that, at last, there was a real opportunity to create a unified empire and a truly all-powerful emperor. In order to realize that goal, however, he needed to institute a lasting deterrent: to have shown mercy would have been a sign of weakness, a lack of determination. Francis Joseph's principles, his notion of how a man should behave, his character and political inexperience, his opportunity to take revenge, and his exposure to influential advice all combined in the making of this decision. This is why he did not call a halt to the repression, and why his personal responsibility cannot be diminished. At the time, he thought that he was doing the right thing and he was willing to do whatever was necessary. He did not care—nor would he ever—whether his subjects liked him or hated him. He did not want to govern them, but to rule over them. Events had proven to him that terror was just another form of rule, not the most attractive perhaps, but not to be frowned upon should the need arise. Terror serves a purpose: to make people obey. And what could be more important than obedience? On 31 December 1849, Pest City Council passed a resolution making honorary citizens of Baron Julius von Haynau, Count Josip Jelačić, and Prince Ivan Fedorovich Paskevich. In this way, the magistrates of the rebellious city conferred, voluntarily, the highest honor upon the very persons whom they had deemed their enemies just a few months previously. This was a sure sign that terror was an efficient way of making people change their attitudes. This act signaled to Francis Joseph that Hungary was slowly coming to accept that it had been led astray—when it finally embraced that idea, it would become worthy of a milder form of rule.

Granting honorary citizenship was indeed a symbolic act. But the official position and the public mood did not coincide. On the contrary, they were worlds apart. It is difficult to assess the public mood by objective means. This was a time when the country lacked freedom of the press and people lived in fear, not daring to speak their mind other than in secret, and even then fleetingly and in words which could subsequently be taken back. But there were some who wrote their thoughts down, despite the risk that, if they were found out, they would be thrown into prison. Gyula Sárosi, a government commissioner in 1849, as well as a member of parliament, editor, and poet, was mostly a fugitive and a prisoner after 1849. His poems written in 1850 talk of those who had been executed with deep sorrow, and engage in word-play with some of their names. One of his poems gives a faithful reflection of the general mood and of attitudes towards Francis Joseph: "Where is God Now?"

> These people have become servants and fugitives in their homeland, burying their sorrow and bitterness in their bosoms. They cry

when they cannot be seen by anyone. How can you, my God, watch this in peace?

How can you watch what this King does, what he perpetrates in your holy name? Why do you let the tyrant, go unpunished, when he claims to be your representative on Earth!

But what is God to me?!?...Am I not talking to someone who is the creation of mere fancy?! And fancy, since it has created you can also destroy your lofty throne in the skies.

And here below, he who claims to be your representative, is but an anointed murderer of millions. But he shall be crucified one day by the people and shall be crowned!

Sárosi clearly laid the responsibility for tyranny at the sovereign's door. Similar sentiments were expressed by quite a few Hungarian intellectuals more prominent than Sárosi himself, if not so explicitly. In late 1849 and 1850 the poetry of Mihály Tompa, János Arany, and Mihály Vörösmarty gave expression to almost exactly the same ideas. Tompa writes in his well-known poem "To the Stork:"

Don't walk in the meadows, they are a burial grounds;
don't walk into the lake, it is flooded with blood;
When looking around from the top of a tower, expect to step on
smoldering ash rather than find a place of quiet.

János Arany wrote in one poem, entitled "The Lute Player," about the destiny of the poet:

What used to delight him was now a barren wasteland!
Nature and the surrounding world have changed.
The blood has frozen in peoples' veins, and the brook has become
silent; wild beasts roar in groves where nightingales used to sing!

He looks for his home only to find it in ruins:
below the rubble are buried the smashed deities of the house!
He looks at it in horror and flees from fear,
and walks where there is no road.

He is chased by a mortal enemy:
a horrific ghost called Reality.
The tinkling birds of a fairy's vision
have all abandoned him and do not dare to fly to him.

Vörösmarty's poem *Prologue* portrays terror as something almost superhuman; the poet describes it as the anger of "hostile gods":

Tempest is nigh. Its blood-curdling hand
throws human heads up into the skies like a ball-game,
while its feet trample on human hearts.
Life has shriveled from its breath,
The spiritual world has gone,
and lighting has made a mark
of the anger of hostile gods
on the faces of a darkened sky.
And the tempest keeps on roaring
like a monster maddened with anger.
Wherever he walks, his steps are followed
by the curse of nations torn apart rising up like a sigh
from among bone heaps;
and destitution lays its poor head
on towns burned to ash.
Now it is winter and stillness and snow and death.

These poems are fundamentally similar, despite the fact that the poets lived at some distance from one another, and were probably not aware of what their fellow poets were writing. Each of them felt that the country was defenseless, and all refused to accept "reality." They might not name those responsible, but nevertheless make it absolutely clear to the reader to whom they are alluding. The essential thing is the emotional denial of reality. Their powerful response to events, which became deeply ingrained in the minds of Hungarians, continued to resonate for many decades, although with varying intensity.

Francis Joseph in all likelihood never considered that his whole life, and his "afterlife," would be dogged by the shadows of those who had been unjustifiably executed and persecuted. He managed to make retaliation as unforgettable for his people as the actions that it was supposed to punish. The emotional, moral, and political rejection of terror drove even those who had frequently voiced their concern at the course of events to embrace the memory of 1848–49. In this sense, Francis Joseph's assignment for Haynau was completed "successfully." Haynau managed to create circumstances in which the country could be ruled without the loyalty of its subjects. In 1850, even the most conservative Hungarian aristocrats, those most loyal to the Habsburg court, including Count György Apponyi, Baron Samu Jósika, and Count Emil Dessewffy, expressed in a memoir their "disapproval of the latest changes." Although these aristocrats hated everything that 1848–49 symbolized, and had been prepared to serve the ruler of a downtrodden country, Francis Joseph little cared about these once loyal Hungarian aristocrats and even less about the general public mood, not to mention mere poets. Schwarzenberg boasted that "thank God" his sovereign was not the sentimental sort. With his experience as an amateur actor, Francis Joseph had a fascination for actors and actresses, but the young emperor did not open himself up to poetry or to the emotional and intellectual message of drama. For example, he considered Johann Wolfgang Goethe's *Torquato Tasso* "mere empty declamation." In the theater, he much preferred Austrian patriotic themes or somewhat simplistic comedy (his favorites were comic actors). The only thing he liked in William Shakespeare's *A Midsummer Night's Dream* was the actor who played Bottom, mainly because of his ass's head. Otherwise, Francis Joseph thought that the play was an exceptionally boring and stupid fairy tale.

When Francis Joseph sent Haynau into Hungary in July 1850 he was not hoping to win the sympathy of a subjugated people. But the general, who was later made a baron, overstepped the bounds of his mandate and increasingly acted as he saw fit instead of showing unconditional obedience. Recalling Haynau would have pacified those in Western Europe who were protesting against his terror. Soon afterwards, Francis Joseph required Haynau's assistance once more. After Brescia, the general was to teach his emperor's unbridled Italians another unforgettable lesson, and was prevented from doing so only by his sudden death.

Chapter Six
THE TYRANT

Retirement of the tyrant Haynau was suggested by Alexander Bach, minister of the interior. The 1850s in Hungary, a period generally known as the "Bach regime," was a time of fear coupled with dour bureaucracy. From Bach, Francis Joseph learnt that the bureaucratic machine was almost as important as the army. The minister of the police, Baron Johann Kempen, went further, proving that a network of informants and a well-established gendarmerie could be used effectively to intimidate civilians. We can be certain that by this time the emperor had established his independence as a fully empowered and grown-up sovereign. In April of 1852 Schwarzenberg died, but advisors old and new quickly surfaced to take his place. Some held high office, some did not. Interestingly, Metternich, the emperor's former tutor and chancellor, whom he continued to hold in great esteem, exerted his influence only from behind the scenes. Metternich's position was strengthened, however, by the fact that Baron Karl Kübeck, head of the Reichsrat (Imperial Council), established in 1851, also respected his opinion. The Reichsrat had two Hungarian members, whose loyalty to the emperor had been proven on a number of occasions: Counts Ferenc Zichy and László Szőgyény. In 1852, Archduke Albrecht, the emperor's nephew on his father's side, became the governor of the Hungarian province, its official military and administrative head.

This list of official and informal advisors could be continued, but the main point is that Francis Joseph increasingly wanted to rule the empire himself. In late 1851, he declared the Olmütz Constitution void in a proclamation (so vindicating the concerns expressed by skeptical liberals), and introduced absolutism, all power now resting with the emperor. Francis Joseph's new philosophy of government had been foreshadowed in the speeches he made in August: he declared that the government was accountable to the emperor alone, that the ministerial right to ratify legislative acts was merely a formality, and that the Reichsrat was only a consultative body, whose advice it was the emperor's majestic right to seek and listen to only as he saw fit. The December Imperial Patent declared that the countries of the Crown making up the empire were dependent administrative units. All public officials (including town and village dignitaries) could be appointed and confirmed in office only by a government accountable directly to the emperor. Although Francis Joseph had promised to introduce the liberal Austrian civil and penal codes, the judiciary did almost all its work behind closed doors. After Schwarzenberg's death, the sovereign went as far as to eliminate the Council of Ministers, replacing it with a so-called "ministerial meeting." In effect, the emperor made it clear that he was not going to appoint a prime minister and would take all matters of government under his own direct control. He considered ministers to be officials responsible to their emperor alone—the "emperor's ministers"—not an independent body within the state, but bureaucrats individually dependent on their sovereign's will.

By the age of twenty-two, Francis Joseph had done everything he could to establish himself as an absolutist imperial ruler. By late 1852, his dream of a unified empire under absolutist rule was finally realized. The underlying idea was very simple. As one scholar of the period has aptly put it: "The emperor ruled, the government legislated, the administration, supported by the military, enforced, and the people obeyed." In this scheme of things there was no room for civic participation, and for the same reason the power holders gave a much greater role to bureaucracy and administration than ever before, making it almost the cornerstone of their rule. Perhaps this was one of the reasons why the period was named after the minister of the interior rather than after Francis Joseph, despite the fact that it really bore his mark, something which contemporaries were fully aware of. His political regime was a reflection of his own world view, will, and personality, and a confirmation of all his past actions. It was preferred, at least from a Hungarian point of view, to name the period after Francis Joseph's powerful minister rather than Francis Joseph himself because anti-absolutist public opinion believed that officials enforcing the decisions of an absolutist power could be more easily removed. Only a revolution could remove Francis Joseph, whereas a simple political crisis was believed sufficient to overturn a minister and end the official terror.

The regime was, of course, governed by an ideology. This embodied the view that absolutism and its officials—even the sovereign who stood at the top of the hierarchy—were dedicated servants willing to work hard to bring happiness to their people, for which they should be thanked. The emperor, as a benevolent father figure, took care of his children. Anyone who refused to recognize that this political regime was the only correct one must be punished—this was the father's duty, after all! In relation to Hungary, the same philosophy was expanded by adding a postulate formulated in late 1848 in accordance with which Hungary had "forfeited" its former rights by rising against its lawful king. The idea was far from original, formally it went back to the seventeenth century, but in the 1850s it was decided to revive it: absolutism, planning for the long term, obstinately referred to it again and again.

From this it logically followed that the absolutist regime should do all it could to make sure that Hungary ceased to exist. Consequently, the territory of the Hungarian state was carved up: Croatia, Slavonia, Serbian Voivodina created from the Délvidék (Southern Region), and the Temes Banat became separate entities. Transylvania was also separated, and a military and civil governor was appointed. (Eduard Bach, younger brother of the Austrian minister of the interior, became the civil commissioner of Transylvania.) The remainder of Hungary was divided into five military and civil districts, their boundaries drawn up so as to leave the Hungarian population at a disadvantage. This territorial segmentation also interfered with people's daily lives—this was perhaps the most characteristic feature of absolutism.

This policy was made easier because martial law was maintained officially until 1854, allowing the army to intervene directly in domestic affairs. This continued even after the state of emergency was lifted, but thereafter, at least formally, the army was required to seek the consent of the civil authorities before they took action. The highest civil and military authority was in fact vested in one person, the governor, Archduke Albrecht.

There was a plentiful supply of soldiers to be called into action, should the need arise. Naturally, every effort was made to recruit the majority of soldiers stationed in Hungary from other nations in the empire. An even greater cause of daily inconvenience and fear for the civilian population than the presence of a largely foreign army was the presence of a state police, a gendarmerie, and countless official informers. Order was enforced by the police in towns and by the gendarmerie in the villages. A contemporary wrote in his memoirs: "Gendarmes were seen frequently, and an encounter with one was not a happy event. To begin with, people feared them; later on, they were only worried by them; then, they got used to having them around; and finally they came to despise them." Gendarmes were empowered to enter houses at any time and to carry out a search. Naturally, they preferred to go about their business at night: in this way, they were able to make people feel even more vulnerable. Throughout the country, the image of gendarmes beating on the door with their fists at night was synonymous with fear. Regulations did not require gendarmes to present proof; a gendarme's testimony, given under oath, was accepted as sufficient in itself. Gendarmes were encouraged to take such oaths because the pay of these dedicated defenders of public order was related to the severity of the punishment meted out to those brought to trial.

The work of the police and the gendarmerie was assisted by a network of informers, who were protected by the authorities. Among the things to be reported to the authorities was anyone seeking accommodation, since these were potential fugitives. There was an almost paranoid persecution of anything that might be interpreted as a manifestation of national feeling, at least in the early stages of repression, it was considered a crime to wear Hungarian national dress, as was the sporting of a Kossuth-style full beard. The diligence of those charged with maintaining public order was sometimes comically extreme. In one instance, a suit cut by a tailor named Császár ("emperor") and already paid for was not finished on time; this provoked the customer to express his indignation, loudly abusing the "emperor." Not for long, however, because he was soon locked up: use of the word "emperor" in a negative context was interpreted as sedition.

The administrative apparatus was made up largely of bureaucrats. All official matters were processed by them; all documents and applicants had to go through them. The sovereign was proud of his officials: he thought that with their assistance he could create a uniform and professional administrative system for his empire. However, the use of the apparatus for political purposes considerably reduced the value of his initiative. As with the police, the intention was to root out national feeling and constitutional procedure. Needless to say, neither its general role nor its daily activities endeared the all-powerful "Bureau" to Hungarians. Its officials, the so-called "Bach Hussars," were typical characters of the regime that employed them. They derived their name from the uniform they were required to wear, this satisfied the sovereign's aesthetic sensibilities, since these uniform-wearing bureaucrats must have created the impression of a "civilian army." They were instantly recognizable, and lent an air of homogeneity to state rule in the eyes of the often poorly dressed petitioners, members of the general public who came to the Bureau on various matters of business. Hungarian officials were required to wear a so-called "attila" suit with hussar-knots instead of buttons, complete with a cock-feathered "kun" hat and a scimitar with a mother-of-pearl hilt. On ceremonial occasions—the emperor's birthday for example—these officials were required to wear the Hungarian parade dress—but with the double-headed eagle on their rosettes and their sword hilts. As already mentioned, it was forbidden to wear a full beard; on the other hand it was strongly recommended to grow side-whiskers, as a sign of loyalty, especially since the sovereign himself started to grow them. After a while, this newly created "national dress" was also made mandatory for prison officers, at which point the whole thing began to take on an air of self-parody.

It was very costly to run a regime based on fear and oppression. Nearly half of the whole government budget was devoured by the army and public administration. (In contemporary Europe, the Habsburg empire spent more on the latter than any other country.) Given the extra duties of an occupying force, maintaining this army cost seven times as much, even in peacetime, as the development of industry, agriculture, and trade taken together. We have no exact figures about what it cost in the 1850s to finance the police or the network of informers, but we do know that even in the years directly preceding the Compromise, when a much milder form of absolutism held sway, per capita expenditure on the police force was forty percent higher than in Prussia, ninety percent higher than in Russia, and three hundred percent higher than in Great Britain. As is usually the case absolutism was financed by those who were being oppressed by it. Before 1848, Hungary's direct tax burden was the Austrian equivalent of twenty-one million forints. By 1857, this had increased to fifty-four million, and by 1864 to seventy-five million forints. More than one-third of all tax revenues was exported from Hungary directly to enrich other parts of the empire. An already extraordinarily high tax burden was further aggravated by a number of additional taxes. In 1854, a so-called "national loan facility" was launched amidst propaganda issued by the authorities which asked the population to contribute to the scheme, "voluntarily" for the sake of "building a better future." Contributions were allocated to towns and villages, and the bureaucracy was instructed to administer the money. Naturally, people gladly came to their much loved sovereign's assistance.

Francis Joseph was becoming increasingly in need of such help. The expensive absolutist regime caused the empire to run up a government deficit in the period 1848–63 which was two-and-a-half times what it had been previously. The following Hungarian folk song concerns exploitation by the state and subsequent reprisals:

> There are as many finance officers,
> As pleats on a skirt,
> And our chains resound as loudly
> As clapping in an applause-dance.

What were the feelings of the Hungarian people about all this? While the full spectrum of possible reactions was represented, the general mood was clearly one of opposition, although, as we have seen, it could not be openly expressed. There was no freedom of the press. In

1852 censorship was institutionalized—one hour prior to publication newspapers had to be presented to the censor, and if he disapproved of anything, the whole run was confiscated. Afraid of incurring heavy losses, publishers carried out a kind of preliminary self-censorship, and likewise required their contributors to exercise "self-restraint."

What were the self-appointed guardians of the press seeking to prevent? Among other things, "incitement to overturn the existing order by force," for which the punishment might be up to twenty years' imprisonment, and "holding the public administration in contempt," which carried a penalty of up to five years' imprisonment. Those who published an opinion which "posed a threat to law and order" (note the vagueness of the wording) could get up to six months in prison. In the event, the combination of a stringent press regime and the personal incompetence of the censors did not leave untouched even those newspapers which exercised strict self-control. For instance, the politically harmless *Hölgyfutár* (Lady's Courier) was banned for three months for publishing a short story. The hero of the story, clearly written in a spirit of loyalty, is a young Hungarian man who meets a young Austrian woman from the Tyrol. The young man becomes infatuated, and when the time of parting comes, he says goodbye to the lady of his heart with the words: "God be with you, daughter of the strange mountains!" The ban was preceded by an investigation in the course of which the Governor's Office of Buda found that there were no "strange mountains" in the Tyrol; the Tyrol was part of a single empire, and the reference was deemed to amount to nothing less than an attack on its unity.

Given the press situation, no dissident voices were allowed publicity, only political supporters of the regime. Pro-regime Hungarians generally justified their position by arguing that the overriding concern should be economic development rather than national or constitutional issues. The popularity of such views is confirmed by the fact that many took up civil service jobs or became informers. In Hungary, no one could stay underground for long; sooner or later, the fugitives would be reported. But even those who chose to serve the regime, for financial reasons, due to a lack of strong moral principles, did so without a particular emotional attachment. Such people fulfilled an important function but could not be relied upon either politically or in times of crisis. Not even those conservatives who were normally noted for their staunch loyalty as officeholders, for instance, were fully committed.

The majority suffered in silence, choosing to remain passive. The model for this stance was provided by Ferenc Deák, who was personally unaffected by the wave of terror. (This despite the fact that he had been involved in the events of 1848 for exactly the same length of time as Batthyány, and had been both minister and Member of Parliament. While Batthyány was executed, Deák got away scot-free.) In April 1850, Minister of Justice Anton Schmerling convened a meeting on Hungarian private law in Vienna. Deák was among those invited. However, he politely turned down the kind invitation. "After the sad events of the recent past, and under the circumstances which continue to prevail, I cannot actively participate in public functions." Up until 1860, Deák practically withdrew from direct political involvement. He could remain passive because the authorities, as already mentioned, did not take a stand on social participation. (For instance, after the above incident Deák simply received no more invitations.) All that Deák and similarly minded people could do was to remain passive, which could be accomplished successfully as long as they did not have to take up public office for financial reasons. This stance was not provocative, but it did signal that the regime was merely endured rather than accepted. Of course, there could be a number of reasons for "remaining aloof," but it was commonly understood what it meant in relation to absolutism: a refusal to accept what was unlawful and an insistence upon the rule of law. On this view, the last laws considered legal were the April Laws of 1848: in the opinion of many, these laws cradled the ideals of independent statehood and an even greater expansion of rights, the heritage of 1849. There were differences of opinion on some issues.

More drastic forms of resistance included short-lived conspiracies and armed coups. Károly Jubál, József Makk, Gáspár Noszlopy. The list of those involved could be continued. Suicide, flight, execution, imprisonment became their lot. They were the ones who, often in conjunction with emigrants, kept alive the spirit of active resistance, and even if they could not boast of notable successes, their actions indicated that absolutism had been rejected, not only as a political regime, but also on emotional ground. Women also played their part: Blanka Teleki was imprisoned because she educated her students in a revolutionary spirit.

Emotional rejection was reinforced by intellectual resistance. Vörösmarty's lines written in 1854 came to symbolize hope: "There will be another day of celebration in this world!" The Hungarian emigration, in common with similar movements, was characterized by divisions and disunity, and it was often too weak to assume the leadership of the resistance movement. (Kossuth, for instance, was interned in Kütahya in Anatolia until the early 1850s.) Nevertheless, the emigrants did everything they could to organize Hungarian public opinion, and to develop schemes which might lay the foundations of a future Hungary—a democratic state living in peace with its national minorities and independent of the Habsburg empire.

Kossuth, who had become a national symbol, was, of course, the most famous emigrant, although while still in Hungary he had received the honorary title, the "Hungarian Moses." The peasantry saw Kossuth as its savior, and not without reason, since he had done most to lift the yoke of serfdom. A miniscule but significant sign of resistance and hope for the future was the fact that large numbers of people continued to hide 1848 money, so-called "Kossuth notes," whose destruction had been ordered, and possession of which was illegal. What would the young emperor have thought if he had known about this? Francis Joseph was aware of how ambivalent Hungarians were in terms of their feelings towards him and his reign, and, slowly but surely, it became clear to him how little he and the notion of a unified empire associated with him was welcomed.

In his determination to observe his empire with his own eyes he visited each country in turn. His visit to Hungary took place in 1852. This was his seventh major expedition, after visits to Moravia, Bohemia, the Italian provinces, Galicia, and Silesia. The sequence in which he made his visits may be taken to indicate their order of importance. It seems that he was in no hurry to visit Hungary.

His Hungarian tour lasted from early June to mid-August, covering fifteen thousand kilometers. In those days, railway lines were few and far between, and so the emperor had to travel across the country by steam boat and carriage, and on horseback. He visited nearly all the major towns, from Pozsony to Buda, and from Orsova to Lőcse. Everywhere he was welcomed by triumphal arches, speeches which simply oozed loyalty, bouquets, and young women dressed all in white. He paid visits to government offices, attended popular festivities and the theater, went hunting, watched military parades, held audiences, and addressed matters of state. He also sailed along the Danube and on Lake Balaton, of which he had such pleasant childhood memories—he also floated on a log raft along the Tisza and Vág Rivers. He was young and the journey did not tire him. He was pleased by the homage paid him by Archbishop János Scitovszky and his twenty-two bishops. He saw the triumphal arch erected for him in Transylvania and adorned with black-and-yellow flags. He was already becoming accustomed to being greeted by placards reading: "Absolute homage to the founder of a great united Austria, Francis Joseph I." Songs and poems of praise were performed for him. In the course of the journey he also issued a number of pardons: in Arad, 135 political prisoners and 386 common criminals were given their freedom (note the disproportion!).

Foreign newspapers suggested that this was an excellent opportunity to forgive and forget, but Francis Joseph had other ideas. He visited all the major battlefields, and at every opportunity awarded medals to soldiers who had served him. The archbishop himself encouraged Francis Joseph in the belief that he was doing the right thing: after all, it was his victorious army which had saved Hungary from ultimate destruction. Francis Joseph laid the foundation stones of some memorials and unveiled others. In Buda, he unveiled a statue dedicated to Hentzi, the Austrian commander killed defending Buda, and Allnoch—who had wanted to blow up the Chain Bridge but had accidentally blown himself up instead—and his 418 soldiers, who were also killed. He made Hentzi's son a baron, and treated those defenders who were still living to a feast.

Francis Joseph also received and honored insurgents from the national minorities who had fought against the Hungarians. It had been planned that Francis Joseph would spend a night with Avram Jancu, a leader of the Romanian uprising, but in the end organizational problems meant that he had to make do with Uniate Andrei Şaguna, the Romanian Uniate bishop who had been the first to invite Russian troops to Transylvania to fight the Hungarians.

In the meantime, the newspapers continued to announce the latest sentences meted out in political trials. At first sight it may have seemed to Francis Joseph that everything in the garden was rosy. He was being publicly celebrated and the imperial colors were everywhere, with no sign of the Hungarian tricolor. At the same time, those who spoke to Francis Joseph in Hungarian he addressed in Hungarian; he even drank from the mythical Hungarian chieftain Lehel's Horn—and the empire did not collapse around him. To the more acute observer, however, it was clear that most of those who came to greet Francis Joseph were officials. How different from the atmosphere at the County Assembly of Pest in 1847 or the Pozsony session of the Diet on 11 April 1848. These earlier encounters with Francis Joseph were also official functions, but the chorus of acclamation had clearly come from the heart. Where were the Hungarians, those who ought to have been grateful to Francis Joseph for having "saved the country from ultimate destruction?" Newspapers described Francis Joseph walking bareheaded in the Thanksgiving Day's Procession in the following terms: "the bond between the prince and his devoted people has been sanctified by the heavenly powers of religion." On the other hand, the same procession had also included those who were highly unlikely to attend an official celebration.

It may be, however, that Francis Joseph was all too aware of how much his minister of the interior had had to do to ensure that His Majesty would be greeted everywhere by crowds of people. In any case, only eight months later he would have been left in no doubt that the archbishop had been exaggerating when he talked of the unanimous gratitude of the Hungarian people. On 18 February 1853, in Vienna the emperor took his usual walk after lunch. He had just reached the castle's bastion when his adjutant looked down into the moat. Just at that moment, someone sprang out from behind the emperor and tried to stab him in the neck. The tip of the knife was turned by the high collar of Francis Joseph's uniform, and so he was only slightly injured. The assassin was captured by the adjutant and two passersby.

János Libényi was an unmarried Catholic tailor, twenty-one years of age, and was born in Csákvár in Fejér County. When asked to account for his actions, he replied:

> I have been arrested for stabbing the emperor with a knife this afternoon.
>
> The treatment which my country is now receiving under the reign of this emperor has shaken me to the uttermost depths of my soul. I love my country more than anything else, even more than my life, but I have had to endure seeing my fellow countrymen executed, even noblemen of the highest rank hanged or shot in the head, or sentenced to imprisonment by the dozen. I have also had to witness the loss of all our freedoms.
>
> I could not stand this any longer, and because I realized that under the current strict surveillance implemented by the army, the gendarmerie, and the police, there was no hope for improvement in my country's situation, I made up my mind in 1850 to liberate my country from its current servitude by some other means, namely, by assassinating the emperor...The verdicts which I continued to read in the newspapers...only fuelled my determination.

The assassin declared in his confession that he had acted alone, and that he had had the idea "free from any external influence or instruction, motivated purely by love of country, and with the intention of freeing it from its current state of servitude." The assassin had never talked about his plan to anyone. Libényi was hanged just over a week later, on 26 February. His testimony that he had acted alone was not accepted, however, and seventeen of his fellow workers were sentenced with various degrees of severity. In the weeks after the assassination, 379 individuals were arrested in Pest for supporting Libényi's act. Students were flogged and imprisoned in Pozsony on the same grounds. According to an official communiqué, many tried to outdo each other in "uttering the most hostile speeches and scornful remarks," while in Pest "workers dissatisfied with the new order of things whispered in factory workshops, inns, and hiding places that the emperor had to die." Francis Joseph was kept constantly informed by his minister of the police, the "thousand-eared" Kempen. He signed the death sentences, and a glance at the list would have told him that one-third of those executed between 1852 and 1854 were peasants. Not only Hungarian noblemen, but also workers and peasants dared to raise their hand in defiance of their king and emperor.

The assassination attempt served to confirm the reports of the minister of the police. In this way, Francis Joseph discovered beyond any doubt that behind the veil of official adulation and the politics of passive resistance both his person and his regime were hated. In vain did a delegation of more than one hundred Hungarians come to see their "father" after the assassination attempt to express the joy of the Hungarian people over his deliverance from danger; in vain did Hungarian noblemen make donations for the construction of a votive church (consecrated in 1879) on the site of the assassination attempt. The despair which had motivated the act could no longer be hidden (it was also rumored, although no evidence has ever been produced, that Libényi had been partly motivated by personal revenge, the emperor allegedly having seduced his sister). Libényi's own words and the reports of the secret police indicated the general mood prevailing in much of the country.

Francis Joseph gradually discovered from such reports, as well as from personal experience, what the Hungarian people thought of him. For the time being, he had no thought of making any concessions, however, and he continued to refuse to be crowned king of Hungary, despite the fact that the royal Holy Crown had been discovered in September near Orsova, where it had been buried by Prime Minister Bertalan Szemere. Valuable information about the crown's location had been supplied by an informant called Wargha, acting as a "mole" inside the leadership of the Hungarian resistance movement. For Hungarian public opinion, the Hungarian crown was not merely a museum piece, but a living symbol of Hungarian statehood. It is believed to have belonged originally to Stephen (later Saint Stephen), the country's first Christian king. The priceless national treasure and symbol was now taken to Vienna by Archduke Albrecht and Archbishop Scitovszky to be presented to Francis Joseph. The emperor said it was a fine looking crown, at which the archbishop asked,

"Would it not look even finer on Your Majesty's head," to which the emperor is reported to have said: "That will also happen in due time."

After this conversation, Francis Joseph decided to return the crown to Hungary, keeping it under guard in Buda. Francis Joseph liked to talk of his "imperial benevolence" towards Hungary, and advocates of loyalty interpreted the emperor's gesture as a sign of his trust in the Hungarian people and his determination to become king. It is more likely that Francis Joseph attached so little importance to the Hungarian crown that he was quite happy to let it go.

Francis Joseph had no need of what the crown symbolized—a separate Hungarian kingdom—he believed only in the ideal of a unified empire of all his subjects (the "common homeland"), and wished to speak to all thirty-eight million citizens of a united Austria and empire as a single body. The Austrian poet Seidl wrote a new text for *Gott erhalte*, and in March 1854 Joseph Haydn's beautiful music was filled with new content and became the imperial hymn. It is a very long poem, and its first and last two stanza run as follows:

> God save and protect our
> Emperor and the common homeland!
> Make us find strength in holy faith,
> Let him give wise commands!
> . . . .
>
> Let us all stick together! Strength lies
> in being joined by consent;
> If we can unite, our strength
> can easily conquer any obstacle.
>
> We should remain together like brothers
> with a common patriotic goal!
> Long live the emperor and the homeland!
> Austria shall live forever!

The hymn also repeats the message of the imperial motto: "*viribus unitis*" or "with united strength." Even more importantly, the hymn talks only of Austria, not of Hungary. Francis Joseph would not compromise on the position which he had adopted at the beginning of his reign. He was aware that the "patriotic goal" alluded to in *Gott erhalte* was not palatable to the vast majority of Hungarians, but for the time being he did not care. And the singing of *Gott erhalte* in Hungarian schools became compulsory.

The new national anthem made its first appearance in connection with a notable family event. On 24 April 1854 the emperor, then aged twenty-four, married his cousin, Elizabeth Wittelsbach, then seventeen years of age, a member of the Bavarian royal family. Getting married was another step towards greater independence. Francis Joseph's mother had originally chosen Elizabeth's sister, Helena, but Francis Joseph decided otherwise. Sophia would have preferred Helena, who would have acknowledged her mother-in-law and cousin as her superior; Elizabeth, on the other hand, was known to be somewhat self-willed. Nevertheless, Sophia was determined to make her future daughter-in-law embrace her own and her son's values, under duress if necessary. Of course, Francis Joseph's choice was not motivated solely by a desire to demonstrate his independence. Elizabeth was a beautiful young woman, and the young emperor had always had a weakness for female beauty. The list of the emperor's former lovers includes countesses, dancers (one of whom was rumored to be Margit Libényi), and actresses. Apart from his personal preferences, however, his choice had to be governed by the strict rules of the Pragmatic Sanction. In Elizabeth, everything came together: beauty, charm, and a good family. It did not matter that the Wittelsbachs were not rich, since Francis Joseph was more than wealthy enough himself.

The wedding was to take place in the Augustinian Church in Vienna. The ceremony was celebrated by Joseph Rauscher, Francis Joseph's former tutor, by that time prince bishop of the Austrian capital. All twelve of Hungary's highest ranking churchmen and many Hungarian aristocrats were also present as part of a delegation of one hundred and seventy-nine, come to pay its respects to the new empress in the name of the Hungarian provinces. The delegation was accompanied by Archduke Albrecht.

Members of the delegation could only confirm the news: Elizabeth was indeed very attractive. The Hungarian press was full of news about Elizabeth and the wedding. In this connection, the press was subject to no restrictions. A particular point was made of the fact that Elizabeth was distantly descended from the Árpád dynasty, the oldest dynasty of Hungarian kings. She was a granddaughter in the fifteenth degree of Saint Elizabeth (who died in 1321), the daughter of Andrew II. This fact was emphasized in the hope that it would endear the sovereign's wife to the Hungarian public, but for the time being it was not moved. There was no sign of the Elizabeth-cult that came into being only a few years later.

Elizabeth's descent from the Árpád dynasty was taken to be of little consequence, since Francis Joseph himself, as diligent researchers have verified, could count nine women from the Árpád dynasty among his ancestors. Indeed, all Europe's royal dynasties were in some way related, comprising as they did only around three-hundred families. As far as Elizabeth's looks were concerned, although beauty was definitely not a disadvantage, it was not sufficient to melt Hungarian hearts straightaway. Francis Joseph's mother had passed for a beauty when she was young. The Bavarian King Louis I, Sophia's younger brother, once created a so-called "Hall of Beauty," comprising paintings of attractive women, and Sophia had been included. Although the emperor's mother was little known in Hungary—and few remained alive who had seen her when she was young—she was not popular. The poet Gyula Sárosi even condemned her in the newspaper, *Arany Trombita*, published around the time of the War of Liberation of 1848–49. Many believed that the emperor's mother was the chief ideologist of the post-1849 repression. Some went as far as to spread the rumor that Lajos Batthyány, the Hungarian prime minister, had been executed because Sophia had felt herself romantically slighted by him. However that may be, she certainly resented the fact that Batthyány had made her leave the room whenever he was talking to Ferdinand V in an official capacity.

Like Sophia, Elizabeth was a Wittelsbach, but at least she had presence, something which encouraged hope of positive change. This hope was reinforced by the fact that, shortly before his wedding, Francis Joseph had declared a wide-ranging amnesty: five hundred and eighty-six political prisoners were freed and treason trials ceased. Elizabeth's entry onto the stage of Hungarian history seemed to have brought relief to many.

Francis Joseph sought to educate his wife, who, after all, was still an adolescent, in conformity with his own world view. At the reception after the wedding she was introduced to Windischgrätz, Jelačić, and Radetzky, officially among the greatest figures of the empire. If she had known her husband better, she would have been in no doubt what he, with his strong sense of duty towards his family and the empire, expected of her. Over the next four years, Elizabeth gave birth to three children. (Fourteen years after the first child, in 1869, she gave birth to yet another, Maria Valeria.) However, she had to continue until she had given birth to a son: after Sophia in 1855 and Gisella in 1856, in 1858 she finally gave birth to Rudolf.

Gisella's arrival signaled more concessions to the Hungarian people. A short time before her birth the emperor declared a general amnesty for those who had been imprisoned for their participation in the Freedom Fight. Former prisoners even had their property restored. The political system did not change, however, and the amnesty did not include those who had been imprisoned for anti-absolutist subversion. But at least those who had been sitting in prison since 1849 or 1850 were now released. It was characteristic that, although the amnesty had been granted by the emperor, most Hungarians nevertheless took it as a sign of Elizabeth's good influence; many did not believe that Francis Joseph was capable of such an act by his own volition. They were wrong, however. It is true that Francis Joseph had not declared an amnesty because he had given up his dream of a united empire or absolute imperial power, but he did believe that to issue pardons every now and then was proper to a sovereign, particularly on joyful family occasions. Within the framework of the feudal world view, the strongest unwritten law demanded that the sovereign share his personal happiness with his subjects in this way. Marriage or the birth of children were not private occasions for emperors.

It is not by accident that the royal pardon now came to be extended primarily to political prisoners rather than to common criminals, as had usually been the case in earlier times. With his partial political amnesty, Francis Joseph was relieving people from punishments meted out for actions committed seven or eight years before. For the first time, Francis Joseph had taken a small step towards accepting a

Hungarian reality which was different from his own. These seven or eight years had made it clear to him that all was not necessarily as he would wish it to be in Hungary. Furthermore, he could no longer ignore the fact that maintaining "order" in accordance with his wishes was becoming ever more costly, necessitating increased borrowing and higher taxes. By 1856, no one could seriously claim that the policy of oppression could be continued. At the same time, while something clearly had to change it had to be carried out with as little actual reform as possible. This stimulated Francis Joseph to begin thinking with a politician's head. Declaring an amnesty seemed the wisest course.

Why the choice of beneficiaries fell on political prisoners can be explained in terms of Elizabeth. During the years since the 1848 revolution Hungarians had been given no cause to believe that absolutism was weakening its grip: for example, the Citadel fortress had been erected on Gellért Hill overlooking Pest. Most of the fortress's cannon were directed towards the city center, where the revolution had started. This massive structure towering over the city reminded both residents and visitors to Pest of the strength and determination of the ruling power. Hence the Citadel came to be commonly known as the "Hungarian Bastille."

But intimidation cannot usually be maintained forever. In October 1855, the soldiers guarding the Citadel would have witnessed far below them the gathering of a large crowd dressed in black, taking the opportunity presented by the poet Vörösmarty's funeral to protest against the regime. This was the first large-scale demonstration after six years of absolutism. The regime hoped that the granting of pardons would relieve the tension, and would ultimately reassure the Hungarian people that their lot was not too burdensome after all.

Chapter Seven

EDWARD AND THE WELSH

On 4 May 1857, the imperial couple and their children arrived in Hungary. At the reception held at the Assembly Hall in the royal palace Francis Joseph said: "I have come to find out for myself about the state the country is in and to fulfill its wishes insofar as that is possible." His words echoed the poem which had been published the previous day in *Vasárnapi Újság* in order to glorify him and Elizabeth, written by Kálmán Lisznyai. It was addressed to Francis Joseph as king of Hungary and expressed the hope that "the homeland [would] rise to glory once again." This poem (paraphrased below) clearly illustrated the prevailing official position and the ceremonial atmosphere of the royal visit:

King of the Hungarians!
Songs are sung all over the Hungarian land, emanating from the hearts of the people.
Wherever YOU and our beautiful queen
walk let your journey be a glorious triumph!
And let there be a celebration across the hills, valleys,
and meadows of this land.

YOU are our powerful lord here on earth,
which was conquered by Árpád,
and then held by heroes and saints of shining virtue,
sitting on the throne which is now yours.
They were at the center of a victorious nation
descended from heroes, the conquerors of the homeland.

Even today you have an army of strong,
young heroes, whose loyalty to their emperor
is solid and unshakeable,
like the cliffs of a mountain.
They are the pillars of your throne amidst tempest and danger,
while YOU are the Father of this fine and cherished homeland.

Here they are now, the faithful, standing near you
to welcome your Majesty
and your beloved Royal Lady
whom you brought to this holy land.
And the sweet smile on your lips
brings new serenity to our beautiful homeland.

Your gracious smiles shall be the precious pledge
that this homeland will rise in glory once again,
and its pious people will shed tears
of joy along your path.
And they will say prayers of blessing for you in their happiness.
Let your crowns shine for a long time to come!

The sovereign's promises and the purchased message of loyalty may have awakened hope in some. Those most favorably disposed towards the Habsburg dynasty in Hungary produced a "Declaration of Devotion," asking the primate to deliver the document, with one hundred and twenty-five signatures, into His Majesty's hands. The conservatives, who were the initiators of this act, had repeatedly demonstrated their unconditional loyalty, even in "hard times." They hoped that their requests would be treated favorably, as they were not asking for anything in the spirit of 1848–49, but seeking merely to end disharmony within Hungary. They believed Francis Joseph when he said that he had come to grant the country's wishes. These conservatives were convinced that, as the poem said, all the Hungarian people needed was a gracious smile, and that all they wanted was to shed tears of joy. These conservatives asked only to have the country's integrity reestablished, the Hungarian language recognized, and pre-1848 institutions restored. Francis Joseph would not even receive their "Declaration of

Devotion." He would listen only to individual requests: a petition was tantamount to a political demonstration. In this way, he signaled that he would never allow the concept of a united empire to be called into question, however tentatively.

But if this was the case, why had he gone to Hungary? To enjoy the celebrations? They were not much different from those he had attended in 1852, with triumphal arches, double-headed eagles, black-and-yellow draperies everywhere, theater plays, welcoming speeches in both Hungarian and German, receptions, and, once again, Lehel's Horn. László Szőgyény-Marich, a member of the Reichsrat and a loyal Hungarian conservative, wrote that the celebrations

> seemed glorious to the outside observer, as if the country had become enveloped by a sense of complete satisfaction and well-being, but they had very little substance, since we all knew very well that all the glitter had been created by means of the orders and threats of the bureaucrats, and financed by voluntary levies so as to further the private interests of particular individuals.

As already mentioned, Francis Joseph had come to observe personally how his regime was working and to that end held discussions with citizens of various ranks. In Szőgyény-Marich's opinion, however:

> It is difficult to imagine what benefit the emperor's visit could have provided because His Majesty saw nothing in its real or natural state; everything was artificial; problems were hidden from him; people and things were dressed in a festive cloak; the emperor discussed matters of public concern only with bureaucrats, who presented everything in the best possible light for their own advantage. With the independently-minded, the emperor discussed only neutral topics; and with ordinary folk he had no contact at all.

All in all, a rather ineffective way of gathering experience. Furthermore, the author of this account, as someone loyal to the regime, is likely to have softened its edges somewhat: for example, the "independently minded" to whom he refers were considered reliable enough by the powers-that-be to be invited to the welcoming receptions: the really independent men stayed away, in the knowledge that they could have little to discuss with an all-powerful emperor. As far as the "ordinary folk" are concerned, the following anecdote illustrates the general mood of the time. Francis Joseph was given a ride in the renowned five-horse carriage in Debrecen, driven by the famous Pista Kallós. The ride across the Hortobágy plain started at a slow pace, and the emperor's entourage trotted alongside. However, the emperor threatened to have Kallós thrown off the carriage if he did not drive faster. Kallós, who had little experience in the ways of etiquette, replied offended: "I have driven greater men than you!" His royal passenger, slightly surprised, asked him who he meant. "His Majesty Lajos Kossuth, of course!," came the reply, no doubt to the emperor's consternation. In any case, Kallós loosened his reins, and the five horses broke into a gallop, leaving the entourage far behind. When he had overcome his initial surprise, the slightly embarrassed passenger asked, "And where is my entourage?" The driver replied, in a matter-of-fact way: "the Germans have been left behind!"

The sovereign's visit gave rise to countless anecdotes, all of which were conceived in a spirit of protest and "non-acceptance." The protagonists are always people who took part in the official celebrations, their function usually having been to demonstrate their loyalty. These anecdotes were formulated with the kind of frankness characteristic of a split consciousness: in other words, the official standpoint and reality are juxtaposed in an absurd way. The protagonists themselves tend to occupy an ambiguous position, not unusual for Hungarians at the time. To illustrate how these anecdotes break down all social barriers, let us give two further examples. Both stories have an almost folkloric aspect in that they are told about both the 1852 and the 1857 visit; lacking a real time element, they demonstrate the collective consciousness of the period.

The first story, from the collection of Béla Tóth, involves a dignitary. When visiting a town in the Hungarian Plain the young emperor asked the town magistrate why there were so few gendarmes among the officials paying their respects to him. "There were more, your Majesty," the judge replied, "but we have beaten the others to death."

The hero of another incident is an aristocrat, Baron József Eötvös. When the Council of Magistrates asked him for advice on how they could hold a reception which would both surprise His Majesty and please the crowd, while not costing too much, Eötvös thought for a while and then asked the magistrates whether His Majesty would ride across the Chain Bridge. Having been answered in the affirmative, Eötvös went on to say that, in that case, the vice magistrate should have his chief of police hanged on one of the two pillars which stood at the head of the bridge and himself on the other. This would certainly be cheap, give His Majesty a surprise, and please the crowd.

We could go on telling anecdotes of this kind, but they all have the same, very simple message. A more interesting question is whether this message ever reached Francis Joseph: if it had, perhaps his journey could be said to have had some purpose after all. But intimations of the populace's negative opinion of his person and regime could not have reached him directly. The journey had been arranged in such a manner that the truth would never be revealed. Francis Joseph would never have been given the opportunity to learn what János Arany had written about him, unless it had been a hymn of praise; in any case, neither the emperor nor anyone else in his inner circle could have seen the full text of Arany's ballad *The Bards of Wales*, since it was not completed until 1861 and was published for the first time in 1863. By writing a single hymn of praise Arany could have made as much money as from writing ten ballads. Yet he refused to follow Lisznyai, who had agreed to write to order because he was in financial trouble.

Arany wrote *The Bards of Wales* for nothing. In the poem, King Edward, visiting the province of Wales, is "greeted" by the court poets, who were supposed to confine themselves to telling legends about the great king, with the words:

> "Grim death rattles, the brave battles
>   And blood bestains the sun,
> Your deeds reek high, up to the sky:
>   You are the guilty one!
>
> "Our dead are plenty as the corn
>   When harvest is begun,

And as we reap and glean, we weep:
  You did this, guilty one!"

"Off to the stake!" The king commands,
  "This was churlishly hard.
Sing us, you there, a softer air,
  You, young and courtly bard!"

"A breeze, so soft, does sweetly waft
  Where Milford Haven lies,
With wailing woes of doomes widows
  And mournful maidens' cries.

Maiden, don't bear a slave! Mother,
  Your babe must not be nursed!..."
A royal nod. He reached the stake
  Together with the first.

But boldly and without a call
  A third one takes the floor;
Without salute he strikes the lute,
  His song begins to soar:

"The brave were killed, just as you willed,
  Or languish in your gaols:
To hail your name or sing your fame
  You'll find no bard in Wales.

"*He* may be gone, but his songs live on —
  The toast is: King beware!
You bear the curse and even worse
  Of Welsh bards everywhere."

The scene, as Arany describes it, could be taken from the 1850s, even if Francis Joseph had already retired Haynau and declared an amnesty. The emperor's visit to Hungary in 1857 was a new occasion for issuing amnesties. Now people who had been forced into emigration were allowed to return to Hungary: they could even get back their property. In return, they were required to take an oath of loyalty. More political prisoners were freed. But Arany and many others felt that the image of the "anointed murderer" had not yet faded. Although amnesties were being issued, the regime did not change. Unchanged absolutism was perceived as being still more than capable of disregarding people's rights in any way it saw fit. This explains why the image of Francis Joseph had remained unchanged since the first wave of repression. Arany's poem also reflected the contemporary situation in that there was one "Welsh bard" who was willing to glorify the king, albeit for money rather than as a matter of principle. Such people certainly existed, willing to serve a hated regime and its ruler.

Arany was not the only famous Hungarian writer who had criticized Francis Joseph, unbeknownst to him. Count István Széchenyi, the "greatest Hungarians," and at that time resident of the Döbling mental institution, accused him of the moral destruction of a people forced into submission. Széchenyi's writing was entitled the *Great Hungarian Satire* and was published by Árpád Károlyi in 1921. It was not meant for publication by its author, and in it Count Széchenyi expressed his innermost feelings and ideas in the form of an imaginary dialogue between Francis Joseph and Minister of the Interior Alexander Bach. Széchenyi, who was otherwise well disposed towards the Habsburg dynasty, passionately condemns Francis Joseph and his policies. His essay is worth quoting at some length because few unrestrained confessions are available from the period. At one point, Bach says:

> Please believe me, Your Majesty, no one loves you other than your immediate family, your mother, myself, and Count Karl von Grünne; therefore—according to Machiavelli's axiom—Your Majesty cannot govern your people on the grounds that they love you; as I have already pointed out, you must continue to rule as before, that is, by terror, if you don't want to be overthrown. Your Majesty, I hope that you are not deluding yourself that it is possible to combine the two systems, that is, to have a system whereby a ruler who is intent on torture and who reeks of human blood can also be loved. Only dogs can feel that way, if at all, since they can sometimes love even the cruelest master, at least to the extent that a dog can love. A nation, however, can at best pretend to have

such feelings, but it will never really nurture love in its bosom, with the possible exception of a few human oddities, who would make perfect dogs. Or does Your Majesty really believe that your subjects, in particular the Hungarians, love their emperor? No, my emperor's positive character cannot contemplate such illusions. It would be so ridiculous! I hope that Your Majesty has more wit than that! I cannot tell you how much the long-whiskered fool, the general and executioner Haynau, that excellent ass, made me laugh and how much fun it was to see that he, in good faith, allowed himself the sweet delusion that the Hungarian people loved him....

Dear Sir, it is a crime to deceive others, but to deceive yourself is stupidity; and in politics, a crime is of much less significance than stupidity. As Talleyrand said of the murder of the Duke d'Enghien by Napoleon: "It's worse than a crime, it's a mistake," by which he meant roughly that, while a sin can be forgiven, a mistake is inexcusable, and sooner or later it is bound to give rise to revenge.

Your Majesty has probably heard the little joke with which Hungarians like to confuse their children, who do not yet possess the power of judgment, asking them to distinguish love from love: "Tell me, my dear." they say, "How do you love me? Like a dove likes grain, or like a goat loves the knife?" and many innocent little children do not know how to reply straightaway, because their soft little heads cannot yet make the essential distinction between these two kinds of love.

But Your Majesty's head has long since hardened, I hope, because, as I have said, self-delusion is the height of absurdity. So, in all the demonstrations of love which we recently made the Hungarian people act out before Your Majesty, or rather to seduce European opinion, Your Majesty should not see any other kind of love than that which the goat feels towards the knife, and this is all we need as far as the creation of the Neuösterreich is concerned; because to be honest we prefer to treat Hungarians as a goat—which abhors the emperor's knife and of being knifed—rather than as a gluttonous dove, which would prefer *imperinenter* to pick grain-by-grain from the emperor's hand, etc., etc., etc.

Or does Your Majesty really believe that at some point in time you might gain the love of your Hungarian subjects, when the older generations die out and the new generations can be merged into a common empire by ties of interest, custom, time, finding the secret trigger, religion, royal pomp, etc., etc., etc? I do not think so, because, although the Hungarian people are perhaps the least vindictive of all human beings in the world, there are grievances which no nation will ever forget, unless all feeling is extinguished from their hearts.

This nation could perhaps forgive Your Majesty for having mercilessly executed and thrown into unspeakable misery hundreds of thousands, if not millions, of people when you acted as a usurper, because it can at least revere as martyrs those of its sons who shed their blood and died in misery, whose deceased souls will keep coming back to purify, empower, and make more godly the souls of the living; and the nation could even forgive Your Majesty for having injured the entire nation with most despicable death, because just as the most perfect order will be tainted by a single moral stench, so even the most deplorable of punishments will shed its stench with the passage of time, if it is conferred upon an individual of pure virtue. It will not be long before no gallows will any longer be able to impress the reviled stigma upon anyone, because so many innocent Hungarian patriots were punished by hanging for the disloyalty of their hearts alongside the guilty. Your Majesty excluded all Hungarians from your council and were unwilling to grant an audience even to the nation's best sons or would listen to them with adverse feelings or even hatred, acting instead like an immature schoolboy or passion-addled woman, and listening only to those who flatter your haughtiness. Your Majesty seems to be unaware that if there is anyone in the world who must not fall into the sin of *primae informationis*, it is the leader of nations, whose most holy duty is to remember the following law of justice by all possible means: "*audiatur et eltera pars*": the Hungarian nation could forgive Your Majesty even for forgetting that. The Hungarian people can forgive Your Majesty for all that, and what it cannot forgive, it can forget. But there is one sting that nothing can ever remove from the bosom of the Hungarian people, namely the sting with which Your Majesty hurt the heart, soul, and dignity of the Hungarian nation: when, after all the unspeakable indignities you forced them to enact a travesty of

gratitude...before the whole world and to their own total humiliation, when you last visited Hungary to show the lady empress the
fine views of Hungary. However admirable the saint may be who,
when slapped on one cheek, offers his other cheek, and when he
receives a slap on that side, proceeds to kiss the slapping hand
with much gratitude, such saintliness exercised by a whole nation
is a more deplorable stigma than being marked on the forehead for
hanging: because the mark of the latter will be erased at the end of
a short human life, but a nation which has to live with the stigma
of an unspeakable disgrace, will long for something lost and will
suffer, short of falling into despair, for centuries.

In another passage, Széchenyi refers again to the emperor as "reek-
ing human blood" and "a usurper of the apostles." The author's criticism also targets the existing political regime, and more explicitly than
most protestors, blaming absolutism for the nation's moral decay and
split political and human consciousness. Both Arany and Széchenyi
spoke about things which Francis Joseph may already have learnt from
the reports of his informers, but could not have come face to face with
during his journey in 1857. Therefore, it would be a mistake to conclude that Francis Joseph's Hungarian visit was meant to acquaint him
with his critics. It should not be forgotten that he even refused to
accept the conservatives' "Declaration of Devotion." Still less can it be
asserted that Francis Joseph came to Hungary because he wanted to
change anything. On the contrary, his journey was meant to demonstrate his determination not to deviate from his former beliefs and policies—despite all hopes to the contrary and the discontent of the
Hungarian people.

In March 1857, Francis Joseph convened a Crown Council meeting with a Hungarian agenda before setting off on his journey. The
minutes defined the agenda as follows:

His Majesty included several Hungarian matters on the agenda.
In this country (said His Majesty) various intrigues have resulted
in active agitation in two directions: on the one hand, agitation to
destroy the positive impression which His Majesty was aiming to
create by his planned journey; and on the other hand, to obtain

redress for particular grievances which had been rejected in the past. This circumstance, and the difficulties arising from it, will make His Majesty's Hungarian visit an epoch-making event both for this crown province and for the whole state. His Majesty is determined to continue to adhere to the basic principles which have hitherto governed his reign over the imperial state, in contrast to attempts which he expects to encounter in Hungary to alter his will. We should be careful not to fuel false hopes in this country, which His Majesty has no intention of fulfilling, and it is essential already at this stage to make sure that the highest government authorities use every opportunity to speak in this spirit, leaving no doubt that His Majesty is determined not to deviate one iota from the aforementioned basic principles.

At the end of his journey, on 9 September, in Laxenburg, the emperor addressed a letter to Archduke Albrecht, Governor of Hungary:

On the occasion of my journey, which took in a large part of my Hungarian kingdom, and which I have just completed, I was met everywhere and by all the peoples inhabiting this country with the most vivid expressions of faithful devotion and by often shining and always well-intended signs of sincere and loyal reverence. I was glad to see the tremendous progress which this country seems to have made in every respect, compared to my journey here five years ago, and I concluded that the measures taken as a result of my royal decree of 31 December 1851, in view of Hungary's particular conditions, have clearly done much to facilitate the country's development. I trust that, with the continuing growth of industry, trade, and transport, and due to measures already in hand to address proprietary rights, not to mention the constant improvement of the administration, these positive influences will exhibit their effects on an even larger scale next year. I am determined to adhere firmly to the basic principles which have governed my reign so far, and I would like this resolution to be made known to the widest possible public. Furthermore, I expect all my government officials to conscientiously bear these basic principles in mind at all times. I shall take care that the peculiarities of the various peoples and national minorities are safeguarded and that they shall be able to use and cultivate their mother tongues in the appropriate measure. Let me warmly thank you for the devotion and care with which you have administered my kingdom, and I ask you to communicate my special esteem to all the authorities, which are functioning amidst a great variety of difficulties but with diligence and devotion. I expect them to continue to enforce my good will for the benefit of the country and so its citizens.

Conservative Hungarians fishing for compliments, however small, from their emperor would be disappointed. For this reason, emotional and political rejection continued to be the predominant notes, and it was becoming increasingly difficult to maintain appearances. The emperor's trip of 1857 and its intended purpose betray a great deal about the emperor's personality. His obstinacy and inflexibility were striking, but fully in line with his character. It is more interesting to discover that—as the minister of the police wrote in his diaries— Francis Joseph had told him that he had found the general mood in Hungary to be at its lowest ebb since the 1848 Revolution. Nevertheless, he acted as if nothing needed to be done. It seems never to have occurred to Francis Joseph that he should attempt to draw some political lessons from his clear understanding of the state of public feeling. At the same time, he remained entirely self-consistent in his belief that there was no need for his Hungarian subjects' approval. All he was aiming for was acceptance. He cared nothing for devotion: he simply did not recognize any intrinsic value in such attachment. The "will of the people" was of absolutely no significance to an emperor reigning by God's grace.

He did, however, recognize the need to give God and the Church what was due to them: in 1855 Francis Joseph signed a treaty with the pope, promising generous privileges, and he also donated money for the construction of Esztergom Cathedral. National and liberal initiatives met with a good deal less favor, however. Francis Joseph believed in the need to repress them not only because he saw in them a threat to the imaginary unity of his empire, but also because his power as he saw it, did not depend on them. The inflexibility and haughtiness with which Francis Joseph rejected all grievances was extremely narrow-minded. His unpopularity continued to increase and in response he became even more hostile to those who refused to accept him. This political-psychological vicious circle could not be broken.

The emperor's trip had scarcely got under way when it was interrupted by a tragic event: Sophia, the imperial couple's baby daughter, died in Buda. Official manifestations of sympathy were plentiful. However, real sympathy was directed only towards Elizabeth, then aged nineteen. Although in the mid-nineteenth century deaths in infancy were still relatively common, it was no less shocking than it is today. Whenever a child died, the mother tended to receive the most sympathy, but in this case the compassion had its own special psychological mechanism, and contributed significantly to the creation of the cult of Elizabeth which later flourished in Hungary. After the execution of the thirteen revolutionary generals in Arad in 1849, a strange yet perfectly understandable belief was born in the public consciousness that Francis Joseph had thirteen sacrifices to make in order to redeem the blood of thirteen innocent people. It was popularly believed that Francis Joseph and his despicable regime would receive "divine punishment." This "punishment" was to be severe, demanding the lives of thirteen family members. However inhumane this popular belief might have been, the crime which had provoked it was fully its equal in that respect. Sophia's death, however terrible it may seem, was interpreted by many as the first sign of God's wrath. What is more, the innocent girl was named after Francis Joseph's mother, and so her death represented the symbolic death of the archduchess who was reputed to harbor anti-Hungarian sentiments.

But what did all this have to do with the young and fragile Elizabeth, who had not even known her husband-to-be when the hangings were taking place in Arad? In recognition of this fact, people naturally extended their sympathy and understanding to Elizabeth, whose share in the "punishment" was due to no fault of her own. This tragic event directed public attention to her for the first time: until now, she had been only her husband's "tag-along accessory." Before the emperor's visit, the organizers had wanted to produce an Elizabeth Album, but they encountered the same resistance as when they tried to commission a poem glorifying the emperor. (In the end, the Saint Stephen

Society offered a Hungarian illustrated edition of *The Legend of Saint Elizabeth* for this purpose.)

Francis Joseph's visit to Hungary in 1857 did nothing to change his relationship with the Hungarian people. The emperor continued to refuse to be crowned, and the nation refused to accept an uncrowned king as its ruler. No amount of protest was enough to make Francis Joseph change his mind and agree to concessions. Other ways had to be sought. And the time was near.

Chapter Eight

THE COMPROMISE OF AN AUTOCRAT

Viscount Palmerston the British foreign secretary, wrote in 1849:

Austria's governors (one cannot call them statesmen) have let things come to such a pass that in a number of areas their emperor's rule reaches only as far as the three neighboring powers will allow; he can extend his rule in Italy only as far as France will allow it. In Hungary and Poland he can extend his rule only as far as Russia will allow it. His possession of the German provinces turns on ideals and feelings which Austria's ministers can hardly connect together and find it hard to defend themselves against.

The events of 1849 proved the English statesman right, at least in relation to Hungary, and in relation to Italy he was vindicated by the events of 1859. In 1858, Piedmontese Prime Minister Count Camille Cavour entered into an alliance with French Emperor Napoleon III for the liberation of northern Italy. A passage of arms with the Habsburg empire was unavoidable for the Italian reunification movement, given that Lombardy and Venetia were still held by the Austrian monarchy. Napoleon III asked for Nice and Savoy in return for his assistance. Members of the Hungarian emigration initially hoped to achieve Hungary's independence and the restoration of its constitutional order by armed struggle, and their hopes seemed well founded. Kossuth entered into alliance with Cavour and with Napoleon III, but he also made an agreement with the Romanian Prince Alexandru Cuza to the effect that the liberating army would be permitted to use the Romanian principalities as a military base.

War broke out, and the Austrian army, with Francis Joseph as commander in chief in its later stages, suffered a decisive defeat in June 1859 at Magenta, and later at Solferino. Defeats were soon followed by armistice and a peace agreement. Austria lost Lombardy but was allowed to keep Venetia. It became obvious to both the Viennese court and the emperor that something had to be done. The empire had not had to face a major international challenge since 1849. It had stayed out of the Crimean War, abandoning Russia in its fight against Britain and France. Russian assistance of the kind which had defeated the Hungarian revolution was thus called into question in the event of another internal crisis. Austria was now facing a major challenge and it immediately became clear that Francis Joseph's Austria could not handle it. Palmerston's conclusion, made ten years earlier, now became acute reality: if the empire wanted to survive, it could not afford in times of crisis to have its army and resources tied up domestically in expectation of nationalist discontent which might explode at any minute. Continued insistence on the status quo might prompt the Hungarian emigration to lead the country into revolution under the aegis of the continuing conflict between Italy and Austria over Venetia. The empire might be forced to wage a war on two fronts, perhaps with no hope of Russian intervention.

This basic necessity motivated change in accordance with the usual political "script": the replacement of personnel, followed by limited concessions, and finally a compromise proposal. The ministers of the interior and of the police were dismissed, and, by a strange twist of fate, two influential figures died almost at the same time: Jelačić and Metternich, Francis Joseph's former "professor." The grip of absolutism was finally being eased. The public increasingly found the courage to demonstrate publicly. Any occasion was seized for this purpose. There were demonstrations both at Kazinczy's grave and at the premiere of Ferenc Erkel's opera *László Hunyadi*. Soon, virtually any occasion involving a large audience would turn into a demonstration for the national cause. In 1860, demonstrators even dared to go out on the streets on 15 March, the anniversary of the revolution. The police intervened, however, and a student, Géza Forinyák, was fatally wounded. His funeral was yet another occasion for a demonstration, and, at the end of April, a crowd of no less than eighty thousand gathered at a church in Pest for Széchenyi's requiem mass: it was generally considered that his persecution by the regime had led to his suicide. There were also protests against the proposed imperial decree limiting the rights of Protestants, and on such a scale that even its announcement proved difficult. The emperor was forced to revoke it. Absolutism was in retreat.

The emperor was also now beginning to discover for himself that what he had heard about Kossuth was true—that his words, even from a great distance, could ignite Hungary at any time. Francis Joseph probably knew that Kossuth was forging an alliance with the supporters of the Hungarian national cause to create an independent and democratic Hungary. The emperor must also have heard that Kossuth had addressed the Hungarian soldiers of the Imperial Army, telling them:

> You owe no loyalty to Francis Joseph! Francis Joseph is no king of Hungary. According to our laws, Hungarians owe loyalty only to their lawfully crowned king. Francis Joseph obtained his power by foreign force and so it has been sanctioned neither by coronation nor by election....You owe loyalty to the nation and to no one else!

Kossuth's speech did not cause the army to disband, but his message was intended not so much for the soldiers as for the nation as a whole. And the nation did not fail to respond, as the wave of demonstrations indicates. It was in these circumstances that the emperor finally made up his mind to grant the "great concession," the so-called "October Diploma." In this document the emperor declared that rights could be granted or withdrawn upon his sole discretion, and that now he was minded to grant them, motivated by a feeling of "paternal care." The October Diploma was valid for the empire as a whole, but it was the Hungarian people who really understood its special significance. The Diploma decreed that the united empire would be maintained, as would a large part of absolutist rights (for example, in the areas of national defense and foreign affairs). It also decreed, however, that the Hungarian Parliament would have its former powers restored, the only stipulation being that it would send representatives to the Reichsrat (the resolutions of this body would still not be binding on the emperor, however). The emperor also promised to convene the coronation assembly of the Hungarian Parliament in accordance with the terms laid out in a document attached to the Diploma. (The coronation assembly was a forum whose competence was limited to specific issues, such as domestic affairs, religion, general education, and justice.) The Diploma also promised to restore pre-1847 institutions, including the Council of Magistrates and the Hungarian and Transylvanian Court Chancellery. It made Hungarian the official language of administration, the judiciary, and—at least in part—education.

What more could one want? A great deal, as it happens. Being governed under the sufferance of the emperor was unacceptable to Hungarian public opinion. Although Francis Joseph was now willing to have himself crowned as king of Hungary, he would still be only a "semi-constitutional" king, since the Hungarian parliament would have only very limited powers. There would be no accountable government, and the Hungarian kingdom would be only a subordinate member of the empire. Of the Laws of 1848, the October Diploma kept only those which could no longer be reversed, such as general taxation, liberation of the serfs, and the termination of church tithes. In terms of political rights, however, the Diploma did not recognize the achievements of 1848 and the most recently sanctified Hungarian laws. So did Francis Joseph really want to be the legitimate king of Hungary? A demonstration against the October Diploma was held in Pest as early as 23 October; what is more, opposition was nationwide. Imperial double-headed eagles were smashed, and it became fashionable to wear Hungarian costume as a sign of protest. On 2 December, the anniversary of Francis Joseph's enthronement, demonstrations were held all over the country, signaling that Hungary did not want him.

The emperor now took the view that he had to make a personal contribution to promoting the October Diploma. For the first time in his life he took time—as long as thirty minutes!—to exchange views with two former Hungarian ministers who were committed to the ideals of 1848. In late December, he invited József Eötvös and Ferenc Deák to visit him. News of this meeting spread rapidly and created an atmosphere of hope. In a letter addressed to his brother-in-law, Deák described the general mood and prospects as follows:

> It seems that it is an exclusive property of human nature to enjoy deluding itself with sweet dreams, and to unfold the colorful wings of its imagination and apply the tiniest circumstance and every insignificant event to enhance the illusion. This would all be very nice and very pleasing if the subsequent disillusionment were not so unpleasant and sometimes even full of danger. Such daydreaming can cause much harm, particularly when it is applied to the fundamentals of life, which tend to depend on cool and abstract calculation, whereas these are days of change and commotion, and our hopes are all excited
>
> ...and God knows what colorful dreams you have conjured up for yourselves, imagining that everything is all right and that we have everything that we need.
>
> I am sorry, but I have to disturb your dreams with a faithful reflection on cold reality; daydreaming is not a matter for politics, and especially not for older men: they must remain awake at all times....
>
> People like us regard the laws of 1848 without restrictions and limitations as the basis for everything. His Majesty's new Diploma has in many ways come closer to embracing them, but in some respects seeks to have them amended....
>
> Otherwise, I am convinced that Hungary's situation has never been so uncertain as it is at present, even if we assume all sides to be as well intentioned as can be and forget about the absolutistic goals above and the overheated revolutionary hopes below....
>
> Many believe that the twelve years of absolutism are over and have been replaced by constitutional rule, and so that henceforth, everything is going to be fine. But listen, my friend: these twelve years of absolutism have corrupted all the instruments of the state's operation, and spent the revenues of two, three, or possibly even more generations, usurped all vitality, and dragged industry and

trade down to their knees. Not even constitutional rule can now make good the painful consequences or restore wasted power. A serious illness has been conquered, but will a weakened organism be able to overcome any remaining pathological germs?

You ask me what the future holds. God alone knows the answer to that, and probably no man can tell with any certainty. It can easily, very easily be that the future holds the decay and crumbling of Hungary and the empire.

Those citizens determined to look beyond what is negative even in this difficult situation, and who will not be satisfied with pointing their finger at one law or another, but are instead resolved to actively do something to save the homeland, must confess that they have no clear idea themselves about the "how." And how can someone influence others and point the way to them, when he cannot clearly see the way out of this multitude of troubles himself?

My head is dizzy and my chest is tight when I try to look in the face of the chaos of possibilities which lies before us, knowing that one wrong step can toss our homeland into ultimate destruction. Retreating for the sake of finding leverage can be just as pernicious as letting things reach the breaking point by rigidly sticking to our demands.

I think this will suffice to make you understand, if not the nature of the whole situation, at least this much: we are sitting daydreaming on top of a volcano, deluding ourselves with rosy imaginings.

Deák's assessment of the situation well illustrates the prevailing atmosphere and the vulnerability of a particular section of society unwilling to surrender its achievements. At the same time, this way of thinking was open to compromise, if not on the basis of the October Diploma and its ideal of a united empire. When they finally met, Deák reminded Francis Joseph of the Laws of 11 April 1848, their only "encounter" up until that point. Deák and Francis Joseph were both in Pozsony for the occasion, but although they saw each other they did not talk. It took twelve years for Francis Joseph to find so much as half-an-hour for the most influential Hungarian political figure. The emperor hoped that this meeting would make Deák and his supporters more open to compromise, that is, willing to adopt the October Diploma.

In late December, Francis Joseph had a meeting of a different kind. This time the visitor came neither for politeness' sake nor as a matter of principle. Nor had any invitation been issued. The visitor was in fact taken to see the emperor as a prisoner. Count László Teleki had been captured by Saxonian police and extradited to Austria. Teleki's arrest was a great coup: he was one of the three leading figures of the Hungarian emigration. He was to be tried by an Austrian court, but refused to cooperate and declared that he would answer questions only before a lawfully appointed Hungarian court. Hence the unexpected development: on the last day of the year, Teleki was escorted to see the emperor. Francis Joseph told Teleki that he knew about everything he had done against the Habsburg dynasty during the past eleven years. Nevertheless, he was willing to forgive him. Francis Joseph cautioned Teleki to keep away from politics for the time being. What is strange about this story is not so much the act of forgiveness, but that this meeting took place at all. It signals that under the prevailing political circumstances Teleki could not be imprisoned, still less executed, as this would have provoked yet another wave of mass protests, and so might have severed the already slender thread by which stabilization of the internal political situation hung. Even so, there was no need for the emperor to meet Teleki just for the sake of pardoning him. There must be another explanation for his extraordinary conduct: the emperor was seeking Teleki's silence. Since Teleki's entire political career was characterized by a refusal to recognize Francis Joseph as sovereign, his silence could never have been obtained, even in principle. Furthermore, less than one week after this meeting Francis Joseph was to declare a general amnesty for those who had actively opposed his regime. As a result, Teleki was in no way bound by anything the emperor might say. This makes it even more difficult to understand what Francis Joseph sought to achieve by this meeting.

The Hungarian Parliament now reselected a number of people for office despite the fact that they were still unable to take up their posts. This was bound to antagonize Francis Joseph, signaling as it did a refusal to embrace the ideal of a unified empire. The list included Kossuth, Klapka, and even Giuseppe Garibaldi, the famous Italian republican adversary of the Habsburg throne. The emperor always vetoed such measures, but that only served to fuel the opposition: more and more counties protested against the violation of their rights and some declared in a resolution that Francis Joseph was not a lawful king of Hungary. Francis Joseph's royal prestige was deteriorating. Those with political experience said that there was little chance of Francis Joseph's being elected king of Hungary on the basis of the concessions granted by the October Diploma.

However, the pessimism—or optimism, depending on one's point of view— of those weighing the chances of his coronation did not matter to the emperor. He was now determined to become king, and he had no intention of giving much ground to Hungarian grievances. To demonstrate his determination, Francis Joseph issued a new patent in February 1861 which stipulated the exact number of representatives that the Hungarian Crown had to delegate to the Reichsrat. He wanted the Hungarian government to be accountable only to him and not to the Hungarian Parliament, and wanted to remove certain important areas of decision-making (foreign affairs, military affairs and army command) from the control of imperial deputies. These were the prerequisites that the Hungarian Parliament had to agree to before Francis Joseph was willing to have himself crowned.

But the February Patent turned out to be another bitter experience and disappointment for Francis Joseph. The "deceitful" Teleki not only refused to renounce his views, despite the emperor's generous forgiveness, but also became leader of a new political party. And Teleki was a radical speaker: compared to him, even Deák was a reliable supplicant, whom Francis Joseph described after their meeting as someone who "thinks that much is possible, even if it requires conquering almost insurmountable difficulties."

Teleki gave his parliamentary election speech on 26 March in Abony. Francis Joseph convened Parliament to have the Diploma and the Patent adopted in Hungary, and to have himself crowned. Teleki's position was radically different and in the temporarily more relaxed environment, his speech even received press coverage. Those who chose to support Teleki knew exactly what he stood for. His speech started on a note which was not calculated to please Francis Joseph:

It is now thirteen years since I last had the honor of meeting my fellow countrymen. It was a beautiful day, when the ideals of national independence, equal rights, and national unification became reality. How rosy the future then looked! But what we took for roses was rather ivy covered in blood. Bloody battles and so much glory, followed later on by so much mourning and twelve years of oppression and suffering.

And so we meet again for the first time since those days, which now seem to belong to a different time, as if they had happened before the biblical flood. Shall we tell one another what we have suffered? On the one hand, there are those who stayed at home and disobediently kept a vigil over the fate of their cherished homeland despite the most bloodthirsty absolutism, martial law, courtmartials, foreign laws, aggressive Germanization, and the burden of unfair taxation, monopolies, additional burdens imposed by tyranny, and threats to increase these burdens even further...[such people] stayed behind to care for, heal, and revive others. On the other hand, there are those who ate the bitter bread of exile in foreign countries in order to tell our story and to promote the national cause abroad, and to promulgate its teachings and glory, and to prove its oneness with the European ideals of civil society and freedom....

All this was in the past. But did Teleki define the present in terms of continuity or as a new beginning? He continued his address as follows:

After many years during which every right and law in this country were trampled upon, we are now reassured: "Have faith and accept this Diploma and Patent, which will restore your constitutional rights."

Suppose that the Hungarian constitution is restored, and all other Hungarian laws are recognized as effective without prejudice, including those of 1848? Even if this came to pass, how could we forget what has happened since 1848; how could we forget our glorious heroes whom we mourn, our martyrs, and so much bloodshed, and the horrific oppression of so many years?

But in any case, there is no talk of "restitution" here. What we are supposed to found our trust upon is nothing but [coercion], a new Diploma ignoring our most holy and most fundamental rights; instead of being a two-way attachment, it is but a charitable gift from absolutism, and one which could be taken back by absolutism at any time. And they are asking us to trust them? It is no more than a gift that they are offering, and what sort of gift? It is but a painted constitution, without any of the things which would serve as important pledges of our national constitutional independence, such as finance, defense, and the right of disposal over levies of either money or blood.

It is without any accountability, without independent ministries, and without so many other things! And they are asking us for our trust?...Alongside so many other things, now the press and the police have been taken out of our hands! Can we trust them under such circumstances?

Teleki continued his speech by describing the direction of development as he envisaged it, laying out a program which ran directly counter to the emperor's wishes:

We must not bargain, we must firmly insist upon all our rights, and in this respect we must not make any distinction between rights and rights, and between laws and laws, because any waived rights could lead to further waivers, and thus lead us into a vortex. It is a sad kind of wisdom which teaches that it is better to have a bird in the hand than two in the bush!

But under the current circumstances, if we agreed to rest content with the one bird we have in our hand, the two in the bush are likely to remain forever beyond our reach. Therefore we must give ourselves up entirely to the thought that we must not step back from the laws of 1848, not even a little, and that it would not be a tragedy if parliament was dispersed without achieving anything, [since] it would be a catastrophe indeed if we were to relinquish any of the pillars of our constitutionalism. I would go even further: we must not rest content with restoring the status quo of 1848. It is only a basis which must be developed, both constitutionally and in terms of the equality of democratic rights. We need

more guarantees than may be found in the status quo of 1848,
guarantees which will make the restoration of absolutism impossible once and for all. We have been taught that lesson by everything that has happened since 1848. I insist upon the laws of 1848
together with all their consequences.

The message was clear. Teleki challenged the legitimacy of
Francis Joseph's rule, not only on moral grounds, but also in terms of
a political course within the framework of which there was no room
for Francis Joseph. The frequently emphasized willingness to "face all
the consequences" was no less than a revival of the spirit of the
Declaration of Independence. And in any case, what was a sovereign
insisting upon his absolutist rights doing in a democratic country?
Teleki was not the only one who thought in this way, and this was the
greatest problem for absolutism: the atmosphere of parliamentary
elections and the position of the newly reestablished legislatures signaled that most of the Hungarian population embraced Teleki's speech
and wanted to follow him.

Francis Joseph had been right in 1857: the general mood had
become worse than it had been in 1847, before the outbreak of the revolution. So what did the emperor hope for? Mostly that the Hungarian
upper classes would not persist in their views, since sooner or later that
would lead to another major conflict. Moreover, the Hungarian upper
classes were very much divided: Deák and his supporters also
embraced the laws of 1848, but not their consequences, and they were
ready to accept the joint Austro-Hungarian responsibilities arising
from the Pragmatic Sanction of 1723. At the same time, while they
rejected the idea of a unified empire they were more open to the idea
of "joint affairs" or joint ministries. As Deák and his circle were under
pressure from Teleki and his supporters, however, the former were
likely to become more radical.

The convened Parliament was a disappointment to both camps,
for no one got what they wanted. Teleki was on the verge of being
abandoned by some of his party, something which did take place some
time later, contributing much to Count Teleki's suicide. Deák and his
supporters concluded that they had been flexible enough in the past

and refused to accept the October Diploma and the February Patent, but on the other hand signaled their willingness to review the laws of 1848 when they were restored and to accept the idea of joint ministries with Austria. But even the more moderate of the two political camps was to be disappointed: the emperor had no intention of satisfying even Deák's wishes, as that would have meant relinquishing the ideal of the unified empire and surrendering a number of his cherished absolutist rights. And just as Teleki had emphasized the importance of the "trust" of the Hungarian people, it must also have been a cause for concern to Francis Joseph. Why should he trust the Hungarians? Even if the laws of 1848 were restored, what was the guarantee that the Hungarian people would be willing to do what Francis Joseph asked for in return? The public response to the absolutism of 1848–49 and afterwards had only fuelled his suspicions: these Hungarians must be rebels deep in their hearts, and therefore they must also be hypocrites. While Francis Joseph was to all intents and purposes acknowledged as sovereign by Deák and his circle, who addressed their parliamentary speeches to the king, Teleki and his circle were drafting a resolution to declare their rejection of Francis Joseph as their legitimate king, and made every effort to prove that Francis Joseph's uncle had abdicated in violation of the country's laws and therefore that Francis Joseph's coronation would also be illegal. How could such behavior be explained other than as a manifestation of low cunning? What could be behind it all? In any case, why were the Hungarians rejoicing over the emperor's concessions? Francis Joseph asked Deák when they met what the Hungarians had against a unified empire. The stockily-built Deák answered by making reference to various laws which meant precious little to Francis Joseph, who could only feel that his suspicions were confirmed.

Teleki was disappointed because a certain section of his party did not want to follow him. Deák was disappointed because the emperor was not open to accepting Deák's legalistic stance, despite the fact that it was oriented towards compromise. Finally, Francis Joseph did not get what he wanted from this parliamentary session, which was the support of the Hungarian people for what he thought of as nothing less than a political compromise. On the contrary. Deák's attitude contin-

ued to harden as the session progressed, and his second draft address
to the sovereign included elements which were reminiscent of Teleki.
Deák said:

> The approach reflected in the highest royal patent—that is, when
> it claims absolute power over our laws and rights, and wishes to
> make the Diploma of 20 October and the Patent of 26 February
> the basis for the Hungarian constitution, although it may well be
> an attempt to introduce a coerced constitution—will not lead to
> the restoration of the Hungarian constitution. But we shall never
> relinquish the country's constitutional rights, in terms of which
> legislative power must be jointly exercised by the head of state
> and the nation; and therefore we cannot recognize any unilateral
> and absolutist legislation as constitutional or as binding upon our
> country. Power and authority would then once again suspend our
> constitutional rights, impose its wishes by coercion, and make
> decrees. We declare any such suspension, decree, and coercion
> anti-constitutional, and just another way of keeping an absolutist
> regime alive after twelve years. Therefore, we must refuse to give
> our consent...because by doing so we would thereby be unfaithful
> to our laws, our homeland, and our conscience.

Deák ended his speech by alluding to the possible consequences
of the current state of affairs, and formulated the ethics of remaining
unshakably faithful to one's principles.

> Difficult times may come upon this country once again, but we
> must not buy our way out of them at the cost of failing in our duty
> as citizens. The country's constitutional freedom is not ours to
> dispose of as we please; the nation has entrusted it to us for its
> faithful safeguarding, and we have a responsibility to the home-
> land and to our consciences. If suffer it must, then must the nation
> suffer for the sake of saving for posterity that constitutional free-
> dom which it has inherited from its ancestors. And it will suffer
> without dismay, as its ancestors suffered and endured their suf-
> fering while continuing to defend the nation's rights, because that
> which is taken away by...force, can one day be restored, with good
> fortune; but that which a nation relinquishes from fear of suffer-

ing is relinquished of its own accord and it is always more difficult to get it back, and the outcome is always uncertain. This nation will suffer with forbearance, hoping for a better future and trusting in the justice of its cause. We, who otherwise remain your humblest servants, in deep respect for Your Imperial and Royal Highness, the representatives of the convened Hungarian Parliament.

Compare this with the corresponding entry in the minutes of the House of Representatives: "his words were accompanied by deafening expressions of approval and thunderous applause—a unanimous and stormy ovation which, it seemed, would never come to an end."

The emperor decided to dissolve the Hungarian Parliament. In November 1861 Francis Joseph announced his intention to introduce a new system of government in Hungary. Under the provisional government, as it was called, the legislature was disbanded, a state of martial law was introduced, and the powers of the Council of the Governor General were restricted. The new Governor General was Count Móric Pálffy. He was a cavalry general who at one time had been Haynau's adjutant. Absolutism stayed, but in a much milder form. The 1850s were not yet consigned to the history books, but absolutism was no longer all-powerful, although it did make a conscious effort to remind its subjects that it was still in charge. Court-martials were still in use, and new anti-Habsburg plots were severely punished, although death sentences now tended to be commuted by the emperor to long terms of imprisonment. Less press censorship also meant more libel trials, and many were imprisoned for writing controversial newspaper articles.

The emperor found himself in a strange and difficult situation. In 1860–61, Francis Joseph had to placate his anxious mother repeatedly with the assertion that he had no intention of allowing real constitutionalism. And he probably meant it: both Francis Joseph and his mother hated the words "constitution" and "constitutionalism" so much that for several years it was forbidden even to utter them. The Diploma and the Patent, which Francis Joseph had advocated as compromise gestures, were in fact covert attempts to prolong absolutism, but the Hungarian people would not accept them. For the first time, Francis

Joseph had expressed his wish to be crowned king of Hungary, but those whose task it was to crown him refused to accept the emperor's conditions.

Although Francis Joseph had undoubtedly made some progress in the direction of accepting a kind of reality different from his own, he still had a long way to go. He had failed to consolidate his rule over Hungary and the restoration of absolutism was no longer an option. At the same time, he had come to realize that, although the Hungarian people were more or less united in their rejection of absolutism, concessions could be used to divide and rule. The situation was rather absurd because everyone knew that the state of affairs was not final and so decided to wait and see.

Francis Joseph demonstratively reverted to absolutism—the appointment of Haynau's former adjutant as governor general was intended partly as a warning—but oppression was weakening. The Hungarian Members of Parliament who applauded Deák so enthusiastically could once again feel themselves united, although many were clearly open to compromise, often going against the inclinations of those who elected them. Others uncompromisingly insisted on "facing all the consequences" of the transformation of 1848, and rejected Francis Joseph as king of Hungary. Their position was that a Hungary independent of Austria might not even be a monarchy, but even if it did remain one, it would not tolerate being ruled by the Austrian emperor. There were also disputes concerning the interpretation of the laws of 1848: was Hungary only willing to share a sovereign with Austria, or were the two countries supposed to be governed jointly in certain areas, beyond mere personal union? The situation was indeed provisional, and only time could determine under what terms Francis Joseph could become king of Hungary.

Chapter Nine

"THE EMPRESS IS LEARNING HUNGARIAN"

Elizabeth started to learn Hungarian. To begin with, she practiced with Rudolf's nanny, but from spring 1863 she employed Emma Mendelényi, the daughter of a court councilor, as a companion and began to study Hungarian in earnest. More and more people watched the efforts of the young empress with admiration: her interest in the Hungarian language was interpreted as a sign of her interest in the Hungarian people and culture. It was also "common knowledge," although in fact based purely on anecdote and rumor, that Elizabeth and her mother-in-law Sophia, not exactly a favorite with the Hungarian people, did not get on very well. Needless to say, this made Elizabeth even more popular among Hungarians. Furthermore, the empress was known not to like staying at the Viennese royal castle, the Burg, just as the Hungarian people did not like being part of an empire governed from the Burg. In terms of political psychology, this affection for Elizabeth was also enhanced by the fact that it provided public opinion with a vehicle in terms of which it could demonstrate its dislike for Francis Joseph while maintaining the appearance of loyalty to the dynasty. Showering the emperor's wife with tokens of love could be justified in terms of gallantry towards a lady, while the husband was afforded no more than the official respect dictated by protocol. Had Francis Joseph not been hated so much, Elizabeth would probably have received far less attention.

But now this fragile young woman was perceived as a secret supporter and ally of the Hungarian cause, who would be able to favorably influence her husband. Because of this she deserved her subjects' love.

It was very simple, but people ignored one thing: Francis Joseph was not the kind of person to allow his wife to interfere in politics too much, not to mention the fact that Elizabeth did nothing that might have suggested any "independent" political aspirations on her part. But this was a negligible detail compared to the power of political psychology. The essence of the matter was that for one reason or another, one could love Elizabeth in accordance with the requisite loyalty to the dynasty, while maintaining a mildly oppositional stance and hating her husband. It is important to recall what Francis Joseph's public appearance in 1847 had signified: at that time, the Habsburg dynasty of which he was a member was something with which those committed to the national cause chose to identify with. During the Age of Reform, Palatine Joseph had been the most suitable person to fill this role, after which national sentiment, which constantly needed a focus, turned to his son Stephen, who succeeded him as palatine. At the time of his first public appearance, Francis Joseph was the recipient of this affection and the object of expectations. However, subsequent events made it impossible to maintain the image of a "Hungarianized Habsburg" in relation to either Stephen, who fled in September 1848, or Francis Joseph when he became emperor.

On the other hand, it seemed that Elizabeth could reduce the tensions arising from the discrepancy between an existing need and the absence of the right person to satisfy it. The need harbored by many Hungarians to identify with a Habsburg who was willing to become assimilated to the nation remained so persistent for a good reason. It made it possible to combine a traditional loyalty to the monarchy going back several centuries with the need to belong to a modern nation and a civil society with a rich history. With a "Hungarian" palatine—essentially a regent representing the king—the two needs could be reconciled, thereby eliminating any conflict which might arise between the great Habsburg empire and Hungarian nationalism, which preferred an independent Hungarian state. This was only one step away from combining the liberal ideals of national revival with the image of the "Hungarian Habsburg": during the Age of Reform, for example, nation and liberalism had constituted an integral whole. At the same time, rationally justifiable politico-psychological attitudes went hand in hand with some clearly irrational aspirations, even illusions, as disillusionment with Stephen and then with Francis Joseph did not eliminate the need to find an object of national affection, an innate feature of Hungarian national character.

As long as the Hungarian state and nation were embedded in the Habsburg empire in one way or another, this need remained a reality which constantly reappeared. The Declaration of Independence marked a kind of political reckoning with this deep-seated but illusory need, but because the independent Hungarian state did not survive for long, it failed to bring about a decisive change in public consciousness. On the contrary, the crushing of the War of Liberation brought many to the view that there was a greater need for a "Hungarianized Habsburg" than ever before, as only such a powerful figure would be able to address the grievances of the Hungarian people. After 1849, Francis Joseph's every gesture signaled a rigid distancing of himself from any such expectations, and Archduke Albrecht, the new governor, adopted a similar approach. Consequently, Elizabeth was the only person within the Habsburg dynasty who could possibly play the role of "patron of the Hungarian people"—at least for those committed to the idea of combining loyalty to the Habsburgs with the pursuit of national interests. So a myth of Elizabeth was gradually created which gathered momentum in the first half of the 1860s.

Hungarians were seeking some sort of emotional link with the Habsburg dynasty. The desire for a compromise was slowly but surely taking shape. Some Hungarian politicians were motivated by the lessons of the Polish uprising of 1863. All the rest of Europe had done was to express its sympathy for the Poles. The Tsar of All the Russias, however, cruelly crushed the rebellion. The anti-unionist position of Hungary's national minorities and the unlawfully convened Transylvanian Parliament, which excluded Hungarian representatives, along with an appalling drought and a number of other factors led the majority of politicians in Deák's circle to seek a compromise with Austria. A number of conspiracies aimed at winning Hungary's independence all failed, one after the other. In 1863 a movement headed by András

Jámbor and József Somogyi was liquidated, and in 1864 a group headed by Pál Almássy met with the same fate, including a certain István Nedeczky, a close relative and friend of Deák. Political prisoners were no longer executed, but they faced long, hard years in prison. National minority movements also experienced something of a revival, from which many Hungarians concluded that it would be easier to make a compromise with the Habsburg court than with the national minorities. Most Hungarian politicians were alarmed by Kossuth's vision of a commonwealth of Danube nations replacing an obsolete Habsburg empire. In addition, Deák showed as early as 1861 that he was willing to accept a joint Austro-Hungarian government in some areas. Francis Joseph was also concerned about the future. Since Venetia was still part of the empire, he faced the prospect of new conflicts with Italy: it did not take much imagination to realize that an Italy gaining in strength would not simply abandon territory which lawfully belonged to it. Consequently, Austria was bound to be drawn into a new war sooner or later, and the fiasco of 1859 might be repeated if the empire remained disunited. On the other hand, the prospect of losing the highly developed Italian provinces lent greater economic and political importance to the retention of similar provinces elsewhere.

By the 1860s a new development overshadowed even the Italian question: the question of German unity, particularly the issue of the leadership under which a united Germany would be forged. The country which was able to assume this role would surely take the lead in continental Europe. There were two contestants: Austria and Prussia. As late as 1864 they were still able to combine to recover Schleswig, Holstein, and Lauenburg from Denmark, introducing a joint Austro-Prussian administration (thereby creating the possibility of future conflicts of interest). Austria needed a consolidated "home-base" if it wanted to enter into competition with Prussia. The "Hungarian question" had to be resolved to prevent Prussia from making the Hungarians their enthusiastic allies. Granting concessions would allow the emperor to concentrate all his resources on his principal foe. If Austria were to defeat Prussia, then Hungary might lose its significance for Austria— it might even become independent, as a united Germany would have no need of a multicultural hinterland. On the other hand—and this was a Hungarian concern—a monumental united German block under the Habsburgs could, if it wished, crush Hungary and create a situation even more hopeless than before. If Prussia were to prevail, Francis Joseph would in all likelihood seek to quell Hungary in an effort to hang on to whatever territories he had left.

The road to compromise was being paved by the conservatives, with the emperor's silent approval. Already in 1862 these conservatives suggested a so-called "equitable dualism," whereby the Austrian and Hungarian halves of the empire would jointly administer foreign affairs, defense, finance, and trade, which were important for the empire as a whole. In 1863, the emperor was still against the idea. It was not easy for Francis Joseph to accept that what he thought was both necessary and realistic had turned out to be simply beyond the bounds of possibility. The ideal of a unified empire turned out to be an illusion, and government without real constitutional rights was but a dream. What Francis Joseph had thought was the only way possible was now turning out to be unsustainable. In rational terms, his fundamental idea and nearly one-and-a-half decades of political practice lacked all foundation in reality. The conservatives also wanted to maintain the empire, but not in the same way as Francis Joseph had once imagined it. For Francis Joseph it was a very big personal step to renounce his notion of an "age of Francis Joseph" for a new and very different era. He had to accept rights, constitutionalism, and national interests, which were against everything that he had ever stood for and what he had been brought up to believe in. All of a sudden he had to recognize that God's grace alone was not enough for a ruler to stay in power. Francis Joseph's dilemma was clear: Would he take the rational course or remain a prisoner of his own personality and the past? The events of the mid-1860s demanded an answer.

Chapter Ten

FIVE MINUTES PAST MIDNIGHT

In 1865, *Pesti Napló* published Deák's famous "Easter Article," in which the leading Hungarian liberal announced for the first time that he would "be willing at any time to reconcile our own laws in a lawful manner with the security of the empire's sound continuity." In other words, Deák was willing to accept the existence of the empire as a primary interest to which Hungarian demands would have to be subordinated. Shortly afterwards, a series of so-called "May Letters" appeared in the Viennese conservative newspaper *Debatte*. The Letters were unsigned (as was the "Easter Article"), but everyone who read them knew that their author was Deák. Those who were able to read them, that is, because the last article in the series, which contained a script for the Hungarian Compromise, was never published in Hungarian, leaving most of the Hungarian public ignorant of what was being prepared behind the political scenes. Otherwise, the Letters expressed a clear view on every major aspect of the proposed "compromise." Besides accepting the Austrian emperor as the Hungarian king, the Letters also accepted joint government in foreign affairs, defense, and finance. The Letters also proposed entrusting the administration of so-called "joint affairs" and the accountability of ministers responsible for joint affairs to Delegations made up of parliamentary representatives—with equal rights—from Austria and Hungary. The scenario defined as a prerequisite of a legitimate compromise the restoration of the laws of 1848: in other words Parliament should be elected in accordance with the Elections Act of 1848, a responsible government should be appointed, and the sovereign should be crowned. This "new" king would then proceed to sanctify the laws underpinning the Compromise, already debated by the Hungarian Parliament.

Eighteen sixty-five was another year of concessions for Francis Joseph. Already at the beginning of the year he realized that convening the Hungarian Parliament would serve the imperial interest. After a long series of meetings, discussions behind closed doors, and new ministerial appointments, Francis Joseph decided to convene the Hungarian Parliament in September. He opened the first session of Parliament on 14 December 1865 after the elections which returned Deák's party with a majority. Francis Joseph greeted Members of Parliament in the Buda Castle, the first time he had ever done so: in 1861 he had not even attended the opening of Parliament. However, since the building of the House of Representatives was still not ready, many MPs thought that their invitation to the Buda Castle was simply for a reception, and so some did not even attend. Transylvanian representatives joined later on, after the Transylvanian Parliament declared the union. Others were offended by the black-and-yellow flag flying over the Castle in place of their preferred national tricolor.

The emperor had not yet fully embraced the plan of a Compromise: his speech from the throne still referred to the October Diploma and the February Patent. Clearly, the whole atmosphere was one of reconciliation and compromise, but when would it come into being? No one really knew. But work on persuading public opinion had already begun.

In the company of Pest citizens Deák awaited the sovereign at the Pest railway station. In return, Francis Joseph invited members of the Hungarian House of Representatives for lunch on 14 December, but only those whose surnames started with "A" or "B." Other invitees included Deák, Eötvös, Pál Somssich, Antal Csengery, and Menyhért Lónyay. Deák had another invitation, alone, for 16 December. Parliament sent a delegation to greet Elizabeth on her birthday. Empress Elizabeth received the delegation in Vienna in early January 1866. She was wearing a white dress adorned with emeralds and rubies (red, white, and green are the colors of the Hungarian flag). The empress, who was obviously well prepared addressed the delegation in fine Hungarian, making reference to a "tender and unbreakable bond" with Hungary.

She and her husband went to Pest in late January, and in early February the first court ball of the season was held in Buda. The queen was dressed in a white, Hungarian-style silk dress, and Francis Joseph, as was customary, paraded in a general's uniform. Speaking Hungarian— and dancing the "csárdás"—was acceptable according to court etiquette, and was very warmly welcomed by many Hungarian patriots wandering in a trance of loyalty. Elizabeth made so many polite gestures and was so charming that it came to be commonly believed that the pardoning of the conspirators in the Almássy case and the return of László Teleki's assets to his heirs had been her doing. Moreover, Elizabeth took care to return to her children with presents from Pest: Rudolf's present was fifty toy soldiers representing the Pest *banderium*, feudal mounted escort. and Gizella's was dolls in Hungarian-style dress. Rumor had it that the royal couple had come to like Hungarians so much that they had decided to spend the summer at Balatonfüred.

In fact, Elizabeth did spend the summer (or at least a large part of it) in Hungary—but not in Balatonfüred, and not entirely in the manner that she had planned. War had broken out.

The situation was lamentable for both Francis Joseph and those Hungarians seeking a compromise, jeopardizing all their efforts to persuade the Hungarian public. Despite being victorious on Italy's battlefields, the emperor lost Venetia, and what was even more painful for him, was left out of the North German Confederation after the Prussian victory. Austria had been defeated in the struggle to lead the German unification process. Italy, or at least part of it, had been under Habsburg rule since 1535. Now their reign was ended there once and for all. They had ruled in Germany since 1273, and that was now over, too. What is more, Austria had been defeated by two movements for national unification. These defeats signaled the obsolete nature of the dynastic-imperial principle, and the Hungarian people too entered upon a campaign for national interests. In the summer of 1866, however, the emperor was not yet ready to fully embrace the idea of a compromise—he envisaged continuing the administration of joint affairs in the spirit of the October Diploma and the February Patent—so that talks with Hungarian representatives reached a dead end.

When the war broke out, the emperor arbitrarily declared compulsory military service and ordered conscription for the second time that year, another signal of his disregard for Hungarian laws. This move was condemned even by Deák, who complained that Hungarian mothers gave birth only once a year. In general, Francis Joseph had the impression all along that the compromise-seeking Hungarians merely wanted to lure him into a trap, and refused to allow even the restoration of the laws of 1848. Furthermore, as befits a true autocratic despot, he was immeasurably irritated by the notion of responsible ministries. Francis Joseph's standpoint and his dislike for Deák is well illustrated by a letter which he wrote in February 1866. The intentions reflected in this letter and its spirit had to all intents and purposes shipwrecked the bargaining process by the summer of 1866. The letter was written at the very time the Hungarian "csárdás" had come to be accepted by court etiquette and Elizabeth had dressed in Hungarian style and spoken of her deep emotional ties to Hungary. Her husband's lines to his minister of state, Count Richard Belcredi, written from Pest, were in stark contrast:

> The situation here has become clearer in some respects since the Address of the Parliament [Parliament's official reaction to the speech from the throne—A. G.] was published....This address did not create the kind of positive response that its authors had hoped for. On the one hand...it was not warm and obliging enough, and on the other hand it reflected an emerging suspicion that Deák's principles of legality alone would not get them far....Yesterday, Esterházy and Mailáth had a discussion with Deák to see whether or not it would be possible to agree on a schedule for talks. He was very upset and wellnigh perfidious: from the position he took, in contrast to those other gentlemen, it became clear to me that there was nothing we could do with him right now, and the most we should use him for is to prevent a total interruption of talks with Parliament.
>
> I think that the government (I mean the imperial government) should not proceed as follows: immediately reject the desire for the restoration of the laws of 1848...and persevere in this position; ask Parliament to work out a proposal concerning joint affairs. As far as the question of the ministry is concerned, it seems to me that

the time has not yet come to issue a principle against the setting up
of the ministry, as people are not yet sensible enough [to under-
stand]....We should use our influence to make them [the
Hungarians] understand the necessity of having a common consultative body on joint affairs. Once this is proven to them, and
they have accepted it, then the idea of the ministry will automatically die.

Two days later, Francis Joseph wrote about himself: "I am making
great efforts to avoid everything which could give rise to unsatisfiable
hopes in the people here."

Based on the above it is understandable that the Hungarians seeking a compromise were losing patience. By June, when the emperor
decided to postpone the next session of Parliament—with reference to
the outbreak of war—Deák and his circle had already drafted a proposal for the Compromise. Postponement of Parliament also made it
clear that the emperor had no intention of accepting many of the fundamental demands of the Hungarians. Francis Joseph still regarded the
head of the majority party as an "instrument," and was still a long way
from accepting the idea of a Hungarian government that would not be
responsible to him alone. In other words, Francis Joseph had been
forced to retreat for political reasons, but he had no intention of surrendering either the idea of a unified empire or absolutism. By the
summer, however, when the empire was facing catastrophic international defeat, Francis Joseph was no longer in a position to implement
his will, not even in Hungary. In the seventeenth year of his reign,
Francis Joseph was faced with the total collapse of both his international and domestic policies.

The summer of 1866 showed that while he had no way of influ-
encing international events to his liking, he at least had a chance to
control domestic events, provided he gave up the absolutistic idea of a
unified empire. Pro-compromise Hungarians must also have been worried. Deák and his supporters had to face the reality that conservatives
considered their demands too farfetched, while at the same time those
who wanted a return to the 1848 status quo accused them of voluntarily forfeiting rights which had already been obtained. Francis Joseph

was clearly still against them rather than with them. Despite their July meeting, the positions of Deák and Francis Joseph were not getting any closer. This was immediately after the catastrophic Austrian defeat in the Battle of Königgrätz, yet Deák did not seek to exploit the situation by asking for anything further. Nevertheless, Francis Joseph was still unable to make up his mind to accept the constitutional rules, even when he realized that he would not be able to turn Count Gyula Andrássy—Deák's proposed choice for prime minister of Hungary— against Deák. (Talks with Andrássy lasted until September.) No material change took place in the meantime; what is more, even the idea of federalist reforms was raised, without however abandoning the ideal of a unified empire, despite the fact that by this time the Austrian Empire had proven itself a complete failure. It was already past the last hour, even if only by five minutes.

This moment, the summer of 1866, served as an excellent opportunity to irreversibly consolidate the affection felt by the Hungarian people for Elizabeth—as a means of alleviating an otherwise hopeless situation. Francis Joseph sought to turn this emotional capital gathered by the empress to his own advantage. He wanted volunteers to fight in a war which, as usual, was entirely unrelated to Hungary's national interests or emotional inclinations. To this end, he sent his wife to Pest, dressed all in black. The empress visited wounded soldiers at a makeshift hospital in Orczy Park. According to rumors spread across Pest, the emperor's wife granted an injured gypsy's request that she sit by his side while his leg was amputated. Shortly afterwards, Elizabeth returned to Pest, this time accompanied by her children, where they stayed until early September, interrupted only by short breaks. The nation was acting the role of the gallant gentleman, offering refuge and support to a mother and her children fleeing from the dangers of war. This woman just happened to be the emperor's wife, and one of her children just happened to be the heir to the throne. It was loyal gallantry indeed. But in contrast to her husband, Elizabeth was genuinely humane. Throughout her stay in Pest she was busy looking after her children, visiting the wounded, carriage riding in the City Park, participating in a pilgrimage, and learning about Hungarian culture. After her stay, she invited Miksa Falk, the learned lead columnist of newspaper *Pesti Napló* and Eötvös's former personal secretary, to teach her Hungarian literature and history. In other words, Elizabeth, whose personality was the complete opposite of that of her husband, found herself in a situation in which the Hungarian people vested all their faith in her rather than in her husband. They were looking for a "patron" once again as the situation looked bleak. When Elizabeth left Pest, she was showered with tokens of affection by the Hungarian people. Despite the fact that she was not politically minded, this trust placed in her did acquire political momentum.

Her husband was a powerful man, but his actions as sovereign prevented him from winning the affection of his people, not even those who supported political compromise. However, such a compromise had no future without some sort of emotional underpinning, particularly when so much national feeling was centered around the events of 1848–49, blame for the suppression of which was directly pinned by Francis Joseph, who was now about to be crowned king of Hungary. In any event, he demonstrated little willingness to make himself more popular, even as late as 1866. This is not surprising since his personality had changed little in the meantime, and he was motivated to temporize only by a belated yielding to external pressure rather than the force of his own principles.

Only Elizabeth, who returned the affection of the Hungarian people and demonstrated her liberal-mindedness and humanity by getting Falk to give her banned literature (for example, she started to read about the history of the Hungarian War of Liberation), but had no influence whatsoever on power politics, could serve as some sort of emotional conduit. The empress ignored the censors—their prohibitions only made her reading more interesting. Moreover, Falk is said to have deliberately started the rumor that Elizabeth and her husband had deeply regretted the terror of 1849, and would have loved to bring back to life those who had been executed. Perhaps Elizabeth really did feel that way. But her husband showed no sign of remorse...for the time being. His attitude was the result of a particular way of thinking as much as of his personality: a ruler who believes that his powers have been bestowed on him by God's benevolent will is unlikely to go in much for self-criticism. But there is a major difference between God and the recipient of his benevolence: while God could restore lives he had taken away, he who merely acted in his name did not have the same ability. If Francis Joseph could not restore what he had taken away, the least he could do was to show remorse, something rarely found in those claiming to rule by divine right. But all this is mere speculation: Francis Joseph had a long life ahead, one which would give him plenty of time to show remorse, if he so wished. For the time being, he was not contemplating anything of the sort.

In any case, the emperor did not have much time to think about the past. He was busy orchestrating the Hungarian Compromise (Ausgleich). He was willing to accept government in the form of delegations set up to deal with joint affairs, and was more open to the idea of responsible ministries. There was, however, one thing on which he remained as rigid as ever: he refused to surrender control of the army to any form of constitutional arrangement. It would have amounted to a rejection of everything he had ever held dear if he had agreed to share the supreme guarantee of power and the most effective instrument for resolving crises. He remembered that in 1848–49 it had been the army, with a little help from the Russians, which had saved his empire, and ever since it had remained indispensable in resolving domestic problems. Among other things, the army guaranteed order in Hungary. Although the Austrian army lost one war after the other, it proved effective in keeping control over unarmed civilians—its mere presence caused fear and anxiety. Remember that in 1848 Francis Joseph's Christmas present had been the troops, and that in Italy Radetzky had demonstrated that only the army was truly synonymous with order, discipline, and loyalty to the emperor. It was out of the question that the volatility of a majority vote would ever be allowed to have such means at its disposal. The emperor would remain the supreme war lord and that was that.

Deák and his circle were inclined toward bowing to the emperor's will. Although the Hungarian proposal had indeed undergone fundamental changes, the supporters of the Compromise knew very well that Francis Joseph would not voluntarily make concessions on the army. The only way to exact such concessions would be to start the national resistance movement anew, something which they wished to avoid as it would in all likelihood lead to conflict rather than compromise. Furthermore, the reemergence of national resistance would have brought the exiled Kossuth to the fore once more, who was fiercely opposed to Hungary tying itself by a Compromise to an empire which in his opinion was doomed. This must be avoided at all costs.

Now all obstacles were cleared from the path of a Compromise. Francis Joseph appointed a responsible government under the leadership of Count Gyula Andrássy, and at the end of March 1867 the House of Representatives passed a general, then, at the end of May, a more detailed bill concerning joint affairs. On Francis Joseph's part, this was an enormous concession to Hungarian national principles and constitutionalism. Once he had been forced to accept the idea of a responsible government, he at least wanted to retain direct control over it: a resolution of the Council of Ministers made on 17 March 1867 enshrined the emperor's right of "first approval." In other words, in the future all bills had first to be submitted to the emperor for his approval before they were presented in Parliament. This was a particular right of the sovereign, one that was not enshrined in any law, the purpose of which was to retain direct control over—and effectively to restrict—the highest level of executive power. This remained in effect throughout his reign.

But even the Compromise Act—overtly or covertly—contained such absolutist rights as control and command over the army. The same act also stipulated the sovereign's right to decide whenever the two separate delegations responsible for the administration of joint affairs, and elected from members of the Hungarian and Austrian parliaments, failed to reach agreement. (On this point we should recall how much calmer Francis Joseph had become concerning the idea of having two separate delegations). As a result, the delegations would be able to act as a real political counterweight only when both combined against their king and emperor. In every other instance the sovereign had the upper hand. The enforceability of constitutional guarantees was largely dependant on individual attitudes which would develop in Hungary as a consequence of the Compromise. In 1867, however, this still belonged to the future. What seemed certain was that the Compromise would put an end to the illusion of a unified empire, and would extinguish the absolutistic features of the regime at least to a significant extent. This is the compromise with which Francis Joseph had to come to terms.

What the Hungarians knew for certain was that, by its very nature, the Compromise would not resolve all Hungarian national needs since it represented a surrender of the basic prerequisites of an independent state. It was clear that the compromise which Hungary was required to make would be a constant source of political tension within the country, as there would always be some who would give priority to national goals over membership of the empire. However, alongside these certainties, there was also hope that the country would be able to make advance along the road to liberal progress as far as its domestic arrangements were concerned: henceforth, the only thing likely to obstruct this process would be the will of the Hungarians. Hungary and Francis Joseph did find common ground, at least in legislative and political matters. The coronation was the only task which remained, the ceremonial act which was supposed to consummate the unity of king and nation.

Francis Joseph knelt at the top of the steps of the altar of the Church of Our Lady, in front of the archbishop and Count Gyula Andrássy, the prime minister. Francis Joseph had once sentenced Andrássy to death ("the handsome hanged man") when the latter was in exile, so the hanging had had to be postponed indefinitely. Now Andrássy was the prime minister. Francis Joseph would have preferred not to be crowned by the head of a government responsible to an elected parliament, but the Hungarian people had insisted on adherence to the constitution, which demanded that the coronation be performed by the prime minister. Once again, Deák, whom Francis Joseph had once called "perfidious," came to the rescue. According to the law, the palatine was also supposed to be standing by the archbishop during the ceremony, but Hungary had no palatine at this time. Apart from the fact that the Austrian court had ordered him to stay away from Hungary, Stephen had died in February 1867. The palatine's powers had been further reduced by the time of the Compromise (another advantage for absolutism), and the election of a new palatine was postponed—as it turned out, forever. What was to be done? Deák took the view that, in the absence of a palatine, his role should be taken by a public figure selected by the population as a whole. He proposed Andrássy, not as prime minister, but as a private person. This solution catered to everyone's needs. Public opinion would be satisfied that the coronation was to be performed by the prime minister, a constitutional achievement of the 1848 reforms, signifying that the sovereign also accepted the rule of Hungarian law. Francis Joseph, on the other hand, would be able to convince himself that nothing of the sort was taking place and that, since Andrássy had been appointed strictly as a private person, the continuity of feudal ways had not been interrupted.

The coronation was therefore a combination of constitutionalism and absolutism, a compromise which would lead to a deep split in public consciousness later on. The ceremony itself was free of any sign of such a split consciousness, however: the archbishop and Count Andrássy placed the Hungarian Holy Crown on Francis Joseph's head with all due solemnity. The crown fitted him well, as a few days before it had been fitted by court hatmaker Ferenc Pórfi. Since the crown measured 65 cm, while Francis Joseph's head measured only 56 cm, the ingenious hatmaker had lined the crown with cork and cordovan leather to make sure that it would firmly sit on the king's head and neither wobble nor slip down over his eyes. Francis Joseph held the scepter in his right hand, and the orb in his left. Following two greeting shots he placed himself upon the throne. After three vivats, shouted by Andrássy, another salvo was fired and the bells began to toll. Then came the ceremony of anointment: Francis Joseph and Elizabeth were anointed with the consecrated liquid, twice on their right arms and once between their shoulders. The archbishop then held up the Holy Crown, handed to him by the sovereign over Elizabeth's right shoulder. Elizabeth also held the scepter and the orb. The royal couple sat down and the fourth welcoming salvo was fired to the sound of a *Te Deum*. The choice of music—Liszt's *Coronation Mass*—was the result of another "great compromise."

The Hungarian musical community had wanted the composer to conduct his own work, written especially for the occasion. They had sought Elizabeth's support in this, as Liszt's oratorio, entitled *The Legend of Saint Elizabeth,* and composed in 1863 and premiered in

Pest in 1865, was clearly addressed to her. The most Elizabeth could do, however, was to foster a compromise. According to court ceremony, only the court's own orchestra, the Hofkapelle, could play. Another rule was that the orchestra must play a composition by the court conductor. Liszt did not qualify under these rules. The same rules also prevented the fulfillment of the other Hungarian request, that Ede Reményi should play a violin solo by Benedictus. In any case, Reményi was not welcomed by the staunch supporters of absolutism: Reményi was Görgey's favorite violinist and had fought in the War of Liberation of 1848–49, receiving amnesty only in 1860. On the other hand, Reményi was an outstanding musician: in 1854, during his stay in London, he had been appointed the queen's violinist.

By way of a compromise, instead of a piece by the court composer (one Herzbech), Liszt's *Coronation Mass* was to be the coronation music at Matthias Church. On the other hand, Hungarian musicians, particularly Reményi, would not be allowed to perform it. In the event, it was played by the Hofkapelle orchestra and conducted by the court concertmaster, Joseph Helmesberger (although Liszt was invited to the ceremony). The orchestra appeared in church dressed in red and white, the colors of the Habsburg archduke.

The playing of the *Te Deum* was not the end of the coronation ceremony, however, and functions continued at a number of different locations. The coronation procession left the Church of Our Lady slowly and solemnly. Golden and silver coins were thrown into the crowd, while the sovereign knighted a number of dignitaries wearing golden spurs with the sword of Saint Stephen at the Garrison Church. Then the king said his oath in front of the banderia, Members of Parliament, and aristocrats assembled in a circle outside the Inner City Church, promising to obey the laws of the country. The oath included a promise "never to annex or curtail the borders of Hungary and its parts, and whatever belongs to these countries by any right or title, but on the contrary, to increase and expand them as far as possible, and to do everything to fairly serve the public good, fame, and reputation." It was an old custom that the coronation oath repeated the contents of the royal diploma issued by the king prior to his coronation. The royal diploma was more detailed than the coronation oath. A long time had passed between the commencement of Francis Joseph's effective rule and his coronation. As the diploma states:

> We started to rule effectively some time ago, but, as a result of a number of difficulties which arose in the meantime...we were prevented from being crowned as the king of Hungary and its parts. Later, we convened Parliament in 1861 to have ourselves crowned...but this was not to be because of the difficult circumstances existing at the time.

These "difficulties" which had arisen were the events of 1848–49, while the "difficult circumstances" were the period of resistance to absolutism. After making the oath, the king performed a number of strokes with his sword in the square at the head of the Chain Bridge, rode his horse to the top of the hillock erected there, and struck with Saint Stephen's sword towards the four corners of the world, symbolizing that he would protect the country from danger, from whatever quarter.

This time, the ancient rite acquired a special meaning by virtue of the soil from which the coronation hillock was made. The hillock symbolized Hungary, as all of the country's legislative authorities had contributed some soil, the best that they could find in their district. The hillock was covered with a green lawn, and the railings around it were covered with crimson and white velvet. The soil came from every part of the country, including the Mohács Plain, the homeland of Saint Stephen; the place where the Peace of Szatmár was made; the birthplace of Deák; the meadows where the Hungarian tribes who accomplished the Hungarian Conquest had once walked; and, last but not least, from traditionally anti-Habsburg areas committed to national independence. The town of Arad also sent some soil from Világos. With what reluctance Francis Joseph must have stepped onto that soil, given where some of it came from! How far apart were the Habsburg sovereign and traditionally anti-Habsburg national feelings! Although Francis Joseph had become king, could the people forgive him, and could he make them forget about the existence of a "major difficulty" and "difficult circumstances?" How would relations develop between a king and subjects who harbored such feelings? Of course, there are ways to relieve tension: for example, Francis Joseph declared an amnesty for all prisoners and allowed all 1848 emigrants to return, without exception, on condition that they take an oath of allegiance. The nation in its turn gave the king a present on his coronation: the king and his queen received fifty thousand gold coins each. Both declined, however, in order "not only to put an end to the consequences of sad past events, but also to alleviate suffering as far as we can." The royal couple offered the donation "for the benefit of the orphans and widows of ex-servicemen, and the disabled." A fine gesture, indeed, but was it enough? (The nation also presented the royal couple with the Gödöllő Palace with its hunting grounds, a gift they did not decline.)

The people were treated to oxroasting in Vérmező: the king also tasted the meat. There were colorful processions and much pomp. The royal couple viewed the offerings of Pest and Buda from the balcony of the Buda Castle. There was a long procession of flower carts and carriages adorned with fruit baskets. Another sight was a giant cake shaped to symbolize the coronation hillock with Francis Joseph on the top, wearing a crown made from pastry. Fishermen, of course, brought their fish, adorned with the Hungarian tricolor. Someone brought a colt for Rudolf. Another led an ox wearing the colors of the national flag. Elizabeth was dressed in white, while Francis Joseph viewed the procession dressed in his general's uniform. Perhaps the king might recall from which city these fine presents came in such abundance: rebellious Pest or the city which had elected Haynau its honorary citizen? The whole of Hungary attended the coronation, or, to be more precise, all those who mattered. Some were late, as always, including some from more distant counties. It would not be fair to list them here: such failings must be excusable after so many years.

On the other hand, seven Members of Parliament did choose to stay away: Sándor Csanády, István Patay, Imre László, Ödön Kállay, József Madarász, János Vállyi, and János Vidats, who rose early in the morning to go to an inn in Cinkota called the *Cinkotai Nagyicce*. They left the city for the day. They did not want to see the medieval pomp. But however provincial their excursion might seem, it expressed their attitude precisely: they refused to accept Francis Joseph as their king. They were protesting not only against the violation of Hungarian laws, as they saw it, but against much more. They were protesting against the violation of the spirit of 1848, and paying tribute to the memory of the victims of terror and absolutism. But this was also a political protest against the pact between the king and those Hungarians who had helped him consolidate his position. Given the Deák party's parliamentary majority they could do little in the House: they were in the minority, but what they stood for had a clear message, and was shared by many Hungarians. By this time, Kossuth's noted *Cassandra Letter*, which had been written in May, had appeared in the press and subsequently sold in record quantities for the time: 50,000 copies in Hungarian and 10,000 in German. In this letter addressed to Deák, Kossuth writes that the Compromise had

> stripped Hungary of all the higher attributes which make a country into a state; that in the most important affairs it was attached to the strings of others for the promotion of foreign interests, since it could not act freely and independently of foreign interference; that the Hungarian ministry, sunk into subordination, was no longer fully independent; and that under the circumstances of such diminished rights the Hungarian Parliament counted for no more than an inflated county assembly.

Kossuth condemned this surrender of rights, believing it a tragedy for the nation that it had agreed to renounce its right to an independent development at a time when Austria was so weak, and to tie itself, as Kossuth wrote in another place, to a decaying empire. ("Hungary will be the pyre on which the Austrian eagle will be burned" was his vision of the future.) He therefore begged Deák in the name of God, the homeland, and posterity to

> look around, cast the eye of a supreme statesman, and think about the long-term goal towards which you are leading the country, which should live long after we have all turned into ashes: the homeland, which we must love not only for the fleeting present moment, but also for the unchangeable past and the future drawing ever nearer. Don't take this nation beyond the threshold from where it no longer has control over the future!

In all probability the seven Hungarian MPs acted partly under the influence of Kossuth's warning when they chose to spend the day at the inn in Cinkota. Once again the future would decide whether the seven MPs, all wearing Kossuth beards and traditional Hungarian dress adorned with braid, represented the spirit of defiant rebellion or real historical continuity.

There was another absentee from the coronation ceremony: Ferenc Deák himself. He excused himself on the grounds of ill health. He may indeed have felt unwell, but it is difficult to imagine that he would have been unable to attend one of the coronation sites—for example, the square in front of the Inner City Church, or the Chain Bridge, both so close to where he lived. He could surely have sat on a chair for the duration of the ceremony at the Chain Bridge, and watched from a window of the Lloyd Palace, as Elizabeth did. Why then did he choose to stay away from an occasion which would probably never have taken place without him? Possibly he felt uneasy about the attention which would have been directed towards him; he wanted to keep a low profile. Even so, there were other ways to demonstrate modesty and a refusal to inflate one's own importance. For example, he refused to accept the post of prime minister, never accepted medals, and even had the pictures given him by the royal couple removed from their expensive frames, which he returned with many thanks. Was he embarrassed by Kossuth's views? Or had he found out that Francis Joseph had called him "deceitful"? Perhaps. The fact was, however, that when it was necessary, Deák stood up for the Compromise both behind the scenes and on the open stage, despite any personal disapproval, lending the full weight of his personal influence and authority to the cause.

Deák probably cared little what Francis Joseph thought of him, and it was only to be expected that Kossuth would disapprove of the Compromise. Although Deák never answered Kossuth's letter directly, his whole career as a public figure constituted an answer and it is even possible that he was indeed prompted by the former governor's letter to stay away, despite their disagreements on a number of matters. Unlike Kossuth, Deák believed the Compromise and Francis Joseph's coronation to be necessary, but it is not certain that he also thought these should be celebrated. This is probably what lay behind his staying away. A heavy past and a number of small clouds cast a shadow over the great day, 8 June 1867, when Francis Joseph I, God's favored instrument, became Hungary's apostolic king.

ON THE HUNGARIAN ROYAL THRONE: THE LAST 49 YEARS

Schönbrunn, 21 November 1916. The weather was cold and windy. Francis Joseph, now eighty-seven, had spent the day working. Breathing was becoming difficult for him and his gaze started to wander, but he was still at his desk in the afternoon. Those around him knew all too well that he did not have long to live. Members of the press, who wanted to know everything, were waiting for the inevitable. They too were at Schönbrunn, waiting to report the news. For the last two years, readers hungry for details had been pampered by the newspapers. There was no shortage of copy. Perhaps the only criticism that could have been leveled against the press was its monomania, since all the papers covered the same stories. However, given the fact that a bloody war covering a large part of the globe had been raging for over two years, they could not really be blamed. Personal and family tragedies were becoming more and more numerous, and "blissful peace" seemed to be receding ever further into the past. Countless numbers had been killed. And just as there can be a great difference between how people live, so there was in the manner of their death; if not in terms of the how, then at least in terms of the publicity death gives rise to. Needless to say, the death of hundreds of thousands of soldiers in their gray uniforms did not have the same news value as the death of a sovereign.

It was evening. Francis Joseph was dying at Schönbrunn Palace, where he was born. The emperor and king, whose consciousness was clouding over, was attended by his old butler, Ketterle, and his daughter, archduchess Maria Valeria. The doctor, the court chaplain, and the steward of the royal household were all there. Members of the press were waiting in the garden, notwithstanding the cold weather. What did they talk about, if they were talking to each other at all? It is possible that they merely stood there in mournful silence, in anticipation of what was about to happen. Did they praise the old man? Did they remember the decades of peace with nostalgia? Lajos Zilahy, the noted Hungarian writer, attempted to evoke this moment a few decades later in his novel, *The Dukays*.

Pacing among the black coppices and the rain-streaked Greek deities of the Schönbrunn park in the wild wind, a group of newspapermen were discussing the emperor as if he were no longer among the living. There were about ten of them, including three Hungarians and two Germans from Berlin. They were the sort of journalists who are devoted to their craft, and even on such a dark, windy November night they lurked about a source of news. Yet it was not so much news as human interest they were after...

They were discussing the five bloodstained family corpses which sprawled in the memory of the dying old man, now that his past was coming back to take final leave of him. First of all there was his younger brother with the two-tufted blond beard, Maximilian, shot to death while Emperor of Mexico. Then his son, Archduke Rudolf, and the mysterious tragedy of Mayerling. Then his wife Elizabeth— the older newspapermen were well informed about her tremendous, beautiful crown of hair, and the tiny black fan with which she never parted, and her love affairs with Hungarian aristocrats. She was never without the little black fan because her teeth were poor and when she laughed she opened the fan and held it in front of her face. In 1898, as she was about to board ship in the company of her ladies-in-waiting, an Italian anarchist stabbed her through the heart. According to old Bunz, this happened on the 6th of September; according to Őzessy, who parted his blond beard in the middle exactly as Emperor Maximilian had done, the assassination took place on the 10th of September. They made a bet of one hundred Virginias, those long, thin, strong, black cigars rolled on a straw— the favorite smoke of the dying Franz Joseph. Then there was Sarajevo: the murder of the crown prince and princess, which set off the World War. The old gentleman's life had not been exactly enviable.

...One of the newspapermen asserted that Katalin Schratt, former Viennese actress and mistress of the emperor, was kneeling
at the bedside of the dying man. The others rather doubted this.
Lame Karai told the story of another of the emperor's amorous
idyls with a famous and celebrated Hungarian actress, and maintained that he had the story from Madame Sisa herself. It was in
the late Seventies that Madame Sisa, still a raving beauty, was
summoned to the Viennese Chancellery, where one of the higher
officials, a Hungarian aristocrat, delicately invited the *artiste* to
make a certain sacrifice for her Hungarian fatherland. He asked
her, in the name of His Majesty, to appear at the palace at six
o'clock in the afternoon. The lovely woman was led to one of the
smaller French salons in the Burg and left alone. Sitting with her
back erect on a squat and uncomfortable Louis Seize sofa, laced
in an elaborate whalebone corset that was then fashionable and
surrounded by a labyrinth of lacy petticoats, with an ostrich-
plumed hat on her head, she had hardly more than a minute or two
to wait before the great gold and white door swung open and the
forty-seven-year-old emperor stepped in, wearing the uniform of
a general with all his decorations on his chest and a sword at his
side. He clicked his heels and nodded his head ever so slightly,
but said nothing. His cerulean trousers were made of heavy flan-
nel, on which it was difficult to manipulate the buttons. Therefore
the emperor proceeded to unbutton himself only where absolutely necessary. The narrow, short little French sofa did not prove a
comfortable resting place, but this did not disturb the emperor.

According to Madame Sisa's account, the whole thing lasted no
longer than it takes to countersign a parliamentary bill. The
emperor was famous for the fact that he sometimes attended to
affairs of state in a matter of minutes. Afterward he turned to the
wall and carefully buttoned his heavy cerulean flannels. But he
still did not favor the *artiste* with a word, which was understandable enough, since it would have been difficult for an emperor to
find the appropriate word in the given situation. Before leaving he
clicked his heels again and inclined his head. Later the chief of
the Chancellery kissed the actress's hand and bade her farewell
with a mysterious smile of gratitude, quoting the Gospel: "Render
unto Caesar the things which are Caesar's, and unto God the

things that are God's." Everything was satisfactory up to that point, as Madame Sisa said, but several days later she received a crested envelope from the Chancellery with five one-hundred-florin notes inside. This aroused her wrath. She returned the money to the Chancellery at once with the following message: "Tell His Majesty that I am not a prostitute but a patriot."

The newspaper-men mused over the story, the very bluntness of which made it believable. The idyl bore a resemblance to the military terseness of the emperor's speech. According to old Bunz, who also knew Madame Sisa, the incident was credible to the last punctuation mark. In his expert opinion, however, it was impossible to, conceive of five hundred florins which Madame Sisa would return under any circumstances. At most she might think the sum too little.

...Outside the reporters were discussing the number of times—if at all—each of them had seen the emperor at close quarters, spoken to him or shaken his hand. Old Bunz declared that Franz Joseph had once shaken hands with him. A skeptical silence greeted this declaration, for it was common knowledge that the emperor had an abiding hatred for newspapermen, so much so that the representatives of the press were never allowed to cross the military cordon when their sovereign was on parade.

"It was at the horticultural exhibit in Graz," old Bunz began to explain. "I was standing near the entrance, beyond the cordon, when the senior A.D.C. suddenly appeared, opened the cordon, led me straight to His Majesty and introduced me."

Pognár cleared his throat noisily to indicate his conviction that Bunz was lying. Old Bunz continued placidly:

"His Majesty shook my hand and said, 'Ich gratuliere Ihnen... you're the only man in the world of whom there are two exemplars.' The senior A.D.C. turned as red as a poppy. Herr Meyerhoffer, the mayor of Graz, stood behind His Majesty. The A.D.C. had mistaken me for the mayor, for we were really very much alike."

This way the incident seemed more believable. Then Őzessy—the photographer who parted his blond beard in the middle like Maximilian, sometime emperor of Mexico—straightened up from the wall. There was pride and disdain in the wave of his hand as he said:

"Gentlemen, His Majesty once pissed on me!"

The glowing cigarettes turned toward him in the darkness.

"It happened in 1904," began Őzessy's recital, "during the Veszprém maneuvers. You gentlemen may know that His Majesty could not bear to have reporters within a mile of him—and we must concede, as we look at ourselves, that he was entirely right. Nevertheless, I succeeded in concealing myself and my camera in a blackthorn bush, about twenty paces from a little round hillock where I knew the meeting of the general staff would be held. The photograph promised to be wonderful, with a cloudy sky in the background—a beautiful group picture. My camera was so well hidden that only the lens showed through the branches. The generals were already assembled, with the emperor in their midst, but before the meeting began I clearly heard the emperor say: "Verzeihen die Herren....Excuse me, gentlemen"— and he turned on his heel and headed for my blackthorn bush. A moment later a warm, yellow liquid was sprinkling my beard, about as much as would fill a pitcher of beer. Naturally I didn't dare move." The reporters gave credence to this story without comment. Paul Fogoly looked at old Bunz and said, in the tone of an umpire: "That's more than a handshake."

It is clear that there was no love lost between Hungarian journalists and their king. For half a century Francis Joseph had worn the Hungarian crown: wasn't it time to forget about the hangings and the oppression; wasn't it time to try to love him a little? It could be, of course, that the journalists in Zilahy's story were simply malicious— people with an eye only for extremes. The nation, despite all rumors to the contrary, loved its king with an inextinguishable affection—there is plenty of evidence of this. One need only open a contemporary newspaper and look at the articles on Francis Joseph....articles written by people who in private would express themselves quite differently. Deplorable hypocrisy! But hypocrisy of a kind created by the Francis Josephinian era, which was characterized by open loyalty and covert resentment.

Chapter One
THE LIMITS ON FREEDOM OF SPEECH

Those who were not hypocritical, and who resented Francis Joseph and his Compromise of 1867 with their whole being, were conditioned to keep quiet. Those who did not heed the "lesson" meted out to others could meet a tragic end, as the infamous Böszörményi case indicates. László Böszörményi was the editor of the newspaper *Magyar Újság*. This newspaper advocated the ideals of 1848, and so condemned the Compromise. It has written itself into the history of the Hungarian press as the mouthpiece of the opposition in Parliament. Böszörményi was MP for Nagykálló and in this capacity expressed his disapproval of the new era. The 28 August 1867 issue of *Magyar Újság* published Kossuth's famous letter. Kossuth, as was only to be expected, wrote a long pamphlet against the Compromise. Among other things, he expressed the view that "the rule of the Austrian dynasty [is] incompatible with the independence and sovereignty of my homeland." This was the sentence which the public prosecutor used as an excuse to bring a trial against László Böszörményi for incitement. There is no room here to discuss the numerous major or minor infringements of the law committed by the state in the course of the trial. It is an undisputed fact, however, that by a curious interpretation of the Press Act, the editor was sentenced to one-year's imprisonment and a two thousand forint fine. (For the sake of comparison: a minister's annual pay was twelve thousand forints.)

Seemingly, the term of imprisonment was not so bad: one year should have been endurable. In principle perhaps, but not for Böszörményi. It was common knowledge that he was seriously ill with tuberculosis. When in July 1868 he was escorted from his house by four armed bailiffs, he was first taken to the barracks at Soroksár. In November he was transferred to the so-called "Brewery" barracks in Lipót Street, to be locked up in a dark, damp underground cell. What was to be a year's imprisonment turned out to be a death sentence. Böszörményi was subjected to increasing pressure to make him beg for Francis Joseph's pardon, and it was suggested that, if requested, the pardon would most certainly be granted. But Böszörményi would not yield. He had only one soul and one kind of morality. As a result he died in prison on 24 March 1869. His moral fortitude and the infamy of the government's actions were demonstrated by the excuses of the powers-that-be following Böszörményi's death: the reason they had not asked for Böszörményi to be pardoned, in the full knowledge that the sovereign would have granted it, was that Böszörményi would have declined to accept it, and it was not politic to expose the "supreme benevolence" to ridicule. At the funeral, Böszörményi's closest friend, Dániel Irányi, said:

> He was ill and was taken into captivity. He was fatally ill and made a prisoner....Had he begged for mercy, his freedom would have been restored, but he was of the stubborn kind, ready to die rather than bend his knee. He could not be broken, this is why he had to perish.

Böszörményi's ideals and actions were rooted in the spirit of 1848–49 and the period of absolutism which followed. The spirit of the War of Liberation (during which he served in Klapka's army as a captain, subsequently to be pardoned in Komárom) and the horrors of repression instilled in him a strong moral and political commitment to independence and liberalism. In line with this, he never lost sight of the fact that the person now sitting on the Hungarian throne was the same one in whose name the hangings in Arad had been carried out. He had a definite dislike for both king and any compromise with him. Böszörményi's case clearly shows that the open display of one's ill-feeling could have the severest consequences. Considering that all this happened in 1867–68, after the Compromise, that is, it could be interpreted as a warning: Beware! Freedom of the press has its limitations! The other message was, of course, that it was unwise to combine hardline political opposition with moral fortitude: those unwilling to bend could be broken.

It is worth considering how different—more "refined"—the methods of repression had become since the dark 1850s. The editor was not sentenced to death or even to a long prison term. This time the punishment was almost purely symbolic. The paradox of this case is that while such "symbolic" punishment could be fatal, accepting a pardon granted in this way would have morally undermined the person requesting it, and the betrayed ideal would have lost credibility. Consequently, the regime could destroy someone while laying the responsibility at his door. This new world was nothing if not refined: it became increasingly the case in relation to moral dilemmas that even to experience a moral dilemma rendered one in some way "unfit for life." More importantly for our purposes, however, the Böszörményi case signifies that the limits were laid down as early as 1867–68 with regard to the permissible extent of open criticism. Looking at the penal code enacted in 1878—ten years later—it turns out that Böszörményi would have been in an even more perilous position, as under the new act (Section 127.2) his remark would have been considered much worse than an abuse of press freedom, indeed as high treason punishable by detention in a state prison for political offenders for ten to fifteen years. Even more interestingly, high treason was not the only thing which the new act punished severely. (We must add that imprisonment for ten to fifteen years was at the lower end of the scale for treason.) Articles 140 and 141 of Act V of 1878 contained special provisions protecting the king and members of the royal household. They classified all offenses against them not as acts of treason but as "acts of causing offence to the king and members of the royal household." Let us quote two paragraphs.

Article 140: Any person who commits an offensive act against his king shall be punishable with up to two years in prison and banned from holding public office. On the other hand, those guilty of causing such offense by way of disseminating or displaying in public written or printed matter or graphic illustrations, shall be punishable with up to three years in a state prison for political offenders and banned from holding public office.

Article 141: He who commits slander against a member of the royal family, shall be punishable by imprisonment for up to one year, or by detention in a state prison for up to two years if the slander is committed by way of exposure in a document, printed matter, visual portrayal or putting on public display.

The law avoided giving a precise definition of slander. The interpretation always depended on the specifics of the case. The prospect of being sentenced to up to three years in prison for a mere caricature was meant to serve as a deterrent, and suggested that it was best to avoid saying or doing anything that could be interpreted ambiguously. And what could not? Only what was an unambiguous expression of loyalty.

Thereby the law pointed beyond its own wording: it did not only rule out something, but also promoted a certain way of thinking and behavior by suggesting to take up a position of unambiguous loyalty which could not be construed for animosity. The act, which was meant to protect the head and members of the royal family from insults, did not only promote a certain mentality but also carried a clear historical and political message. Historically, Hungarians had developed an intense negative feeling against Francis Joseph over the decades, but publicly could not give expression to their dislike. Now the act went one step even further and intimated that it was not without consequence to express criticism against the Hungarian king even privately, as that too was a punishable offense. Thereby the Hungarians were forced—not for the last time in their national history—to demonstrate their absolute loyalty in the public domain, while it was common knowledge that past experience had taught many to feel quite the opposite for the crowned head of their country.

There was also an important political aspect to consider. According to the wording and the spirit of the Compromise, Francis Joseph was more than a symbol: he was not the kind of king who merely rules but does not govern. On the contrary, he maintained a number of crucial absolutist privileges, and was effectively a powerful political player.

Now this act protected him from any criticism. While it was allowed to openly criticize the government, the Parliament and every political institution, no word of criticism could be said against him who was above the entire political power structure and whose word was all-conclusive! Such mandatory and at the same time absurd ban on criticism played a major role in shaping modern Hungarian political culture. It was a mandatory principle in the sense that it was enshrined in an act of law, and it was absurd because no political criticism could be fair if probably the most important and effective political entities had immunity from it.

Based on the above, it is perhaps not surprising that in the age of Francis Joseph newspapers, political speeches and pamphlets rarely addressed critical remarks to the sovereign. Once again we come back to the sources of split consciousness: any mention of the sovereign in public had to be made in a manner of humble adulation.

At the same time, it is impossible in the emotional, historical, and of course political sense that the country as a whole could have thought as publicly expressed opinion seemed to indicate. There was indeed a split in public consciousness: one could not say what one really thought. In this respect, the situation was little different from the dark period of the 1850s. However, it is perhaps more important to look at what was different from the 1850s. The schizophrenia which characterized the dualist regime, which embraced at least some liberal values, was focused almost exclusively on the king himself. As we have seen, the king was not just a person, he also represented a very strong power concentrated "in one hand," a power which could neither be terminated by a constitution nor subjected to criticism. The result was a situation with only one possible outcome: public consciousness had to split into several consciousnesses. Failure to do so either condemned the individual to the same fate as Böszörményi, or pushed him towards identifying with the regime well beyond what anyone might accept as "pragmatic resignation." Paradoxically, therefore, the easiest thing to do was to adopt a stance of ideological schizophrenia, a stance which became ever more prevalent. What was true on the individual level also characterized the political system as a whole. Schizophrenia offered a sense of relative well-being.

Chapter Two

MÁTYÁS HUNYADI, THE HEROIC LION

The press did everything in its power to persuade
Hungarian public opinion to express unanimous love for its king, and
to identify with him in good times and in bad. The press regularly
reported details of the king's life style, and did so, understandably, in
a tone of absolute loyalty. Reading these reports, readers could gain an
impression of balls, functions, and military exercises, and could even
learn about the king's work schedule. The royal family was subjected
to close scrutiny despite the fact that Francis Joseph clearly disliked
journalists.

Greater freedom of the press notwithstanding, Francis Joseph's
personality was the same as ever. His might and royal throne did not
depend on what public opinion and the press thought: he simply had
no reason to welcome press attention. Nor did he have reason to fear
it, and in any case his entire education had ingrained in him an aversion to seeking popularity. In the event, the newspapers wrote only
favorable notices, and journalists merely tried to surpass each other in
making compliments. All in vain, however, because Francis Joseph's
work schedule left no time for him to browse news reports about himself.

Anniversaries invited the most adulation, and these were numerous, including family and state celebrations. The royal couple celebrated their silver wedding anniversary at the end of the 1870s. The
newspapers *Magyarország* and *Nagyvilág* (20 April 1879) covered the
event as follows:

This week will be memorable for the peoples of Austria and Hungary, and for the royal couple reigning over [them]. This is a royal family occasion, as it is the twenty-fifth anniversary of the day when the royal couple celebrated their wedding; it is also an occasion for celebration for millions throughout the Monarchy.

The Monarchy, and so the royal couple, has faced many vicissitudes through the twenty-fifth years now being remembered. But all these troubles and new sufferings only strengthened the ties between the people and their ruler, the misunderstandings which once stood between the throne and the people are now past, and today Francis Joseph and his sweet wife, our honorable queen, are our beloved royal couple.

What for centuries remained no more than a craving in the nation's bosom is now fulfilled: our king and queen feel as we Hungarians do, and words from the throne are uttered to us in Hungarian, creating a spirit and a feeling which have reunited nation and king after all the troubles and sadness, and which the royal couple have also instilled in their excellent son, His Majesty Rudolf, the crown prince.

Family occasions like this one were used to portray Francis Joseph as a constitutional, well-loved, and truly nationally-minded king. The past was no more than a misunderstanding. Festive occasions simply ignored the sad memories of the past, but the Hungarian people did not forget, a fact which made necessary a constant reinterpretation of the past in a loyal and humane spirit.

The other category of festive events was state occasions: for example, 1892 marked the twenty-fifth anniversary of Francis Joseph's coronation. The capital was richly decorated on 8 June. Main roads were lined with triumphal arches, with inscriptions like "God bless the king!" "The king is the first among Hungarians!" "Our loyalty is unbreak-able!" "Only a blissful country can have a blissful king!" "Hungarians still live, Buda still stands!" and "Ready to give our lives and our blood!" The National Theater staged a dramatic piece to commemorate the coronation. Its writer was Antal Váradi and the title was *Awakening of the Nation*. The story was set at the 1722 session of the Diet in Pozsony and concluded with the line, "Let the nation give its blessing to the Pragmatica Sanctio! Long live the single, indivisible Monarchy!"

Newspapers commemorated the occasion with poetry and adulatory articles. *Magyar Szalon* published an article written in the spirit of Francis Joseph's motto as Hungarian king; "Have faith in the ancient virtue!" by which he must have meant the loyalty of the Hungarian people to their king. The other motto, "Viribus unitis" (With united powers), was also valid, albeit only for the Austrian half of the empire.

The Hungarian people pretended that the Austrian emperor was close to their hearts, but it was impossible to sustain the illusion over the long term, and the moments of truth caused trouble. Not on the anniversary of the coronation, however: the motto of the Hungarian king was devoid of any suggestion of hidden conflict. This motto was even turned into a poem:

> The king is
> the first among Hungarians,
> Every patriot is readily
> At his service.
> Let him rejoice
> In the happiness of his people
> And let his head be crowned
> With deserved Fortune.

And as the king was the first among Hungarians, at least by calling, it logically followed that his anniversaries should be celebrated as national events, as Gyula Rudnyánszky, a poet of the day, suggested in his poem "National Celebration: 8 June 1892." This poem combined national ideals with liberalism, and did not sweep under the carpet the undeniable fact that past actions had tainted Francis Joseph in the eyes of the Hungarian people. To illustrate this, let us quote two passages from the conversation between poet and nation:

> Did you think in times of mourning,
> Among the ruins of great times,
> When earth and sky were blurred
> By the teardrops of your eyes,

Did you think that happiness
Would still come to you in plenty?
And that the same hand which wounded you
Would also place the balm on your wounds
And would take away your need?

With God's blessing a great miracle has happened.
What could not be obtained by your will
Has been given by your benevolent king, the victor,
By his own free will.
Behold! The wasteland has rejuvenated in spring
And your young freedom has sprung
Into a right on the ruins of the past
And has been reinforced by a new temple!

How moving, at least in the official context—particularly the part
about that which could not be obtained by arms being given to the
Hungarians by a benevolent king of his own free will. A great deal had
to be forgotten from the period between 1849 and 1867 before one
could bring oneself to say something like that. But poetry is not a matter of historical objectivity; ideology was much more important—to
portray Francis Joseph as a nationally-minded, liberal, benevolent, and
wise king. And one must not forget what gives leverage to ideology.
Mór Jókai said:

Twenty-five years ago love went hand in hand with a miraculous
sensation: hope in a new, happy, and free era. Today, twenty-five
years of this new era are already behind us, and the homeland has
become happy, mighty, and free in reality and not just in our dreams.

According to prophetic wisdom: "Hungary is not a 'has been' but a
'will be'," or "'Hungary has been, is, and will be!" In other words, everything was fine. A thriving Hungary justified the image of a nationally-
minded, great, and liberal king. The dream of 1848 became reality in
1867, and the credit went to Francis Joseph: Hungary had never been
more radiant than during the reign of this excellent ruler.

The next anniversary, the Millennium of the Hungarian Conquest, celebrated in 1896, was used to broadcast this very message. Nearly all the events in a long series of celebrations, including the Millennium Exhibition, one of the main attractions, and a celebratory opera gala, were used to symbolically suggest the unity of king and nation. In a letter addressed by Francis Joseph to Count Dezső Bánffy, the prime minister, on the closing of the Millennium Exhibition, the king himself emphasized the uplifting effect on Hungary of the unity which existed between the nation and its ruler:

> This nation has shown to the whole world that, after a thousand years of existence, it can boast not only of political achievements, but also of spiritual and material development, and therefore it is deservedly counted among the countries of high culture. This country has also demonstrated its strong patriotism, one of the strongest pillars of statehood, through its pious and exemplary reaction to events which took place, not only in the capital, but throughout the land, [so] demonstrating...its love and affection for my person and dynasty...a nation living in such unity with its king can look to the next millennium with confidence and high hopes.

The coverage of the opera gala paints an even more sublime and convincing picture of an unbreakable unity:

> At center-stage a great genius holds the radiant wreath of eternal glory above the life-size statues of king and queen. The two statues are surrounded by personages symbolizing love, faith, and hope, while at their bases stand representatives of the different social estates within the Hungarian nation—in other words, symbolically, the whole nation: an old farmer, a young peasant woman, a war veteran and a number of serving soldiers, aristocrats, and citizens, each impersonated by a singer of the Opera House. Suddenly, all step forward and solemnly sing the hymn: "God save the Hungarians!"
> At this point the entire distinguished audience rose from their seats, the elegant spectators in the parterre turning away from the stage and bowing to the royal box. The king himself and all the members of the royal family stood up and remained standing, fac-

ing one another, while they listened to the magnificent national anthem, in which the prayers of a whole nation ascend to the father of all peoples, and were moved by it.

This was one of those rare and all the more unforgettable moments when the hearts of king and people, ruler and subjects meet in a single heartbeat, and share the same feeling. The memory of such moments lasts for decades, because nations are not quick to forget.

A moving scene indeed. It is a matter of opinion, of course, whether a nation is quick to forget or not, but it is beyond doubt that the atmosphere of the press report and the celebrations alike were full of the idea of a nationally-minded kingdom.

On the subject of family and state occasions and national anniversaries, all of which expressed essentially the same ideas, one cannot leave unmentioned the celebration which most directly concerns an individual, the king's birthday. On 18 August 1900 Francis Joseph turned seventy. Needless to say, he was greeted in countless poems and celebratory addresses. One of the highest circulation papers of the period, *Vasárnapi Újság*, also commemorated the notable event. One of the celebratory poems, written by Andor Kozma, went as follows:

Heir to Saint Stephen, king of the Hungarians!
Be blessed by a thousand heavenly blessings,
Endowed with strength and wisdom, and
May your glory live forever on the lips of distant peoples!

Be a fortress of Hungarian freedom,
Respected and heeded by the world;
What your people feel,
Let it into your heart,
Let their prayers ascend from your lips to God in heaven.

Command that there be peace, and anyone who disobeys
Should be struck down by your anger like lightning;
Be a heroic lion,
Then merciful,
And may your laurels never wilt on your blessed head!

Hold the Hungarian flag high
For the admiration of the whole world!
Let the nation's prayers
Bring it blessings!
Long live the glorious king of the Hungarians!

This poem contains one new element, namely, the image of the heroic lion. As the lion is the king of the animal kingdom, so Francis Joseph is the king of the Hungarians. Many of the king's subjects would probably have objected to the use of this parallel, but the poem was published by a Hungarian newspaper and so no question could be raised about the inadequacy of the comparison. The newspaper also published a celebratory article:

His Majesty, our king Francis Joseph I, is celebrating his seventieth birthday. This notable day is being enthusiastically celebrated by the peoples of the Monarchy, but by none with greater affection and more sincere devotion than the Hungarian nation. It is no exaggeration to say that there is no other nation in the world today which would surround its ruler with a more deeply felt adulation than the Hungarian nation feels for its crowned apostolic king. And this respect and grateful affection are rooted not only in the conventional feelings which have always characterized this excellent monarchist nation, but also in the belief that, since the reign of the great Mathias Corvinus, there has never been a Hungarian king whose virtues could compare with those with our present king. There are happier and more prosperous countries than Hungary. But if we compare the present state of our homeland and nation with that at the beginning of Francis Joseph's reign, we may safely say that there has not been more rapid or greater improvement and growth in any country during the same period than in Hungary. Others may have risen higher, but the Hungarian people have risen to where we are today from the terrifying depths of suffering, from the verge of a national death which was considered inevitable. And the credit for making this possible goes to a wise, noble-thinking gentleman who now wears the crown of Saint Stephen.

We thank him for all the good that he has done our nation. Let the Omnipotent God keep him for many years and give him strength to accomplish the high office whose heavy duties he has performed with so much diligence during his long reign, full of vicissitudes. The affection of millions of patriots is now united in this prayer-like greeting with which we celebrate our king's birthday.

Francis Joseph was portrayed as comparable only to the last great Hungarian king who was close to the nation's heart: Matthias Hunyadi or Corvinus. At least this is what the contemporary press wrote. After all, belief in something may develop into a conviction—for example, that Francis Joseph really was the most nationally-minded, liberal, courageous, benevolent, and wise king in Europe: a new Matthias Hunyadi. But such a belief could not be absolute. For a start, we know that telling the truth about the king had its legal limitations. Not to mention the fact that between 1849 and 1867 many things had happened to the Hungarian nation which it was unlikely to forget. It is improbable that the dismal memories of the past could so soon have been wiped from the collective memory, despite the fact that from 1867 the country had been governed under the rule of law. Forgetting about the past may also have been hindered by a number of features which persisted in the post-1867 era, one of which was the king himself.

It is advisable to treat official ideology with caution, at least during Francis Joseph's reign. This does not mean, however, that we should not try understand why people should claim what they knew to be untrue.

Chapter Three
WHY TELL LIES?

The coronation consummated the union of Francis Joseph and Hungary as a kind of lawful marriage. But prior to consummating their union, both sides had the opportunity to get to know each other, an experience which called into question the emotional aspect of a traditional marriage before the law. But the everyday reality of a consolidated marriage can make the two parties, if not completely forget, at least play down the events of the past until they ultimately become irrelevant. On the other hand, whenever either party makes a gesture which evokes the bad experiences of the past, what was once forgotten will quickly be recalled. The official Hungarian ideology exemplified the former, claiming that the nation and its king were finally living in absolute harmony. In reality, the situation was far from rosy.

The Compromise had never been fully accepted in Hungary. László Arany, a devoted supporter of the Compromise, wrote as early as 1873:

> Prior to 1867 the choice seemed clear between freedom and glorious death; enthusiasm once again overflowed into extremes; the nation was preparing for a great battle; and desires were so unbridled that people started to formulate bold ideas about freedom which had been talked about since time immemorial: no pragmatic political solution could have satiated their turbulent desires any longer. The post-1867 world of the Compromise therefore left nothing but general disillusionment in people's hearts and emotions. Life has repeated itself: one party continues to play the tune of the same dull grievances, while the other ridicules the loud hopes and the worn-out patriotic phraseology of the first.

By its very nature the Compromise could not answer the great challenge of the nineteenth century, which had released an emotional surge: it was unable to satisfy the desire for absolute national self-determination. It was a logical consequence of national movements that, sooner or later, they culminated in demands for independent statehood. The Compromise of 1867 left Hungarian needs unanswered on this very point. Despite the narrow suffrage, the governing party supporting the Compromise frequently lost elections in all those parts of the country with a predominantly Hungarian population, and so they had to introduce an increasing number of restrictions and to resort to illegal practices to maintain their parliamentary majority. Former Minister of the Interior József Kristóffy said:

> Governments in office [had to] use any means they could in order to maintain the Compromise of 1867 against the nation's will... including the use of force, money, and misuse of authority...everyone knew that the Compromise of 1867, which clearly served the interests of the country as a whole, could not be maintained in any other way. What is more, the more intense the pressure and resistance from the opposition became against the common-law foundations of the Compromise, the more recourse the government had to have to such dubious means, and the more it had to rely on the votes of national-minority electoral districts, as in purely Hungarian populated areas the peasantry would not even hear of pro-Compromise candidates. In areas with a mostly Hungarian population, only those candidates could succeed who built their campaign on the name of "our Father Kossuth" and flaunted Kossuth's flag.

This analysis may be a little oversimplified, but it is an essentially truthful reflection of the situation: in post-1867 Hungary mass support could be obtained by evoking the emotions linked with 1848. Those who supported the Compromise could argue that it was the only pragmatic and realistic solution, but it was not something with which people could emotionally identify, as already explained in connection with Deák's absence from the coronation ceremony. In vain did the apologists of the Compromise portray 1867 as "the ideals of 1848 become reality": this could never be turned into firmly held conviction which would also be accepted emotionally. On the other hand, the absence of such emotional acceptance did not constitute positive rejection. The post-1867 regime did, after a time, produce significant economic growth and a consolidated legal environment. The pluralism of the public sphere also acted as a stabilizing factor, since one could now speak more freely—the Hungarian people were granted the right of *ius murmurandi*, that is, the "right to be disgruntled." "Tolerable" became the key word used to describe the situation—this was not the "real thing," but it was tolerable. Furthermore, political enmities were somewhat abated by freedom of enterprise, economic stability, and the general "calculability" of everyday life. To summarize, while there was a certain frustration resulting from the continuing lack of national self-determination, the situation was not explosive.

The regime of 1867 had another feature relevant to our topic: it inevitably looked for instruments with which to control the national will, and which could impose a conservative interpretation on liberal ideas. When political power must be maintained against national feeling, and yet all attempts to challenge authority remain within the law and do not threaten to start a revolution, the authorities must restrict themselves to legitimate means and the ordinary instruments of government in their attempts to combat them. However, the governing party also had to possess a sufficiently large majority in Parliament firmly committed to maintaining the Compromise and not tempted to support those who challenged it. This had two consequences: on the one hand, it meant coming to terms with the fact that liberalism—and particularly political liberalism—could not be fully implemented or further developed. What was done in this direction did, of course, open up the regime to further criticism which was consistently turned against it at election time. However, this was a lot less damaging than the failure to satisfy national aspirations already mentioned. Giving liberalism a conservative tinge came with the risk of establishing a platform from which the opposition could launch its criticisms. (Of course, in order to be effective such criticisms had to be supported by national grievances, as was the case during the Age of Reform, or more precisely in 1848–49.)

Another argument against the Compromise was that it hindered the creation of a coherent state, not being the product of a desire for national self-determination—in fact, it granted a fair amount of cultural and political independence. On the whole, taking up an oppositional stance against the kind of liberalism which in reality served to conserve the existing regime could not become a mobilizing force of the same magnitude as opposition motivated by national grievances, quite apart from the fact that the chances of uniting the two kinds of criticism were diminishing. On the other hand, those who dreamed of a political career in Hungary had to accept that they would succeed only by taking up this kind of conservative liberalism. As the regime could not be changed within the existing legal framework—among other things, because the restriction of political rights curbed aspirations from "below"— it followed that a successful career could be obtained only with the consent of those "above." In other words, loyalty to the "powers-that-be" was an absolute requirement.

During the period of Dualism there was freedom of the press in Hungary, and although the Penal Code indirectly induced a kind of servility, that in itself could not have led to such widespread duplicity. The real explanation lies in a particular combination of loyalty and split consciousness; in an attempt to reconcile popular national and liberal values with service to a less than fully national-liberal regime. The advocates of the Compromise of 1867 were the main driving force behind this process. Those who pursued a traditional pro-monarchy line had no need of any ideological explanation. For such conservatives the personal qualities of the king were irrelevant: in their view, what was at stake was the God-given world order, in which the sovereign reigns and his subjects obey. According to this view, this had been the way of things since the dawn of time, and that was how it should remain. The main thing was to have a king—it mattered little what he was actually like as long as his rule was legitimate. In such circumstances loyalty was a simple matter: calling into question the monarchic principle could not even be contemplated. In Hungary, on the other hand, national and liberal glory were associated with individuals who did not embrace feudal loyalty: on the contrary, these notions are anti-feudal by their very nature, as they historically and ideologically challenged the privileged few.

The group which represented pragmatic national and liberal values was rather disunited at first, and so it developed a rather curious relationship with the king. Many of this group had come into conflict with Francis Joseph at one time or another: as Kálmán Mikszáth ironically described this group during the 1880s,

> The past of the distinguished gentlemen of this generation were rather unvaried....In 1848 they took part in the Revolution; after 1848 they spent ten years incarcerated in Olmütz or Kufstein; they were released in 1861 and elected to Parliament, where they felt out of place for a while, after which they adopted an oppositional stance, until, having gradually softened up, they rose to the rank of His Excellency, or at least the Upper House, which today looks like an entrance hall to a cemetery.

In the post-1867 world those who had built up their political prestige by supporting the ideals of 1848 and adopting a position of resistance tended to pay the king his due respect, while being careful not to appear servile. Deák's behavior was a classic example of this. He did not ask for rank, and felt uncomfortable even about invitations to court dinners. He insisted on being addressed as *"tekintetes"* (honorable)— a title for which all university graduates were eligible from 1844— having an aversion to the increasingly elaborate titles which were becoming fashionable in the new era. One possible cause of this aversion was the fact that, for instance, the title *"kegyelmes"* (excellency), which had to be used when addressing senior civil servants, was originally used for the court's provincial governors, an office with negative connotations. Many others followed Deák's example. According to the diary of Károly Eötvös, István Bittó—prime minister, 1874–75—"always considered it a mockery to be addressed as *"kegyelmes úr"*—Your Excellency—by his friends, acquaintances, Members of Parliament, and former colleagues in the county administration." Such people had a similar attitude to the awarding of medals by the king. On one well-attended occasion in 1873, for instance, one of the Prussian guests noted that the Hungarians at the gathering, who were wearing tails in accordance with the dress code indicated on the invitation, were not wearing any decorations in contrast to the foreign guests. The Prussian addressed the following question to József Szlávy, the prime minister (this story is also told by Károly Eötvös):

> Your Excellency, is it not customary in Hungary to display orders and medals on such an occasion? Yes it is, [the prime minister replied] and we do wear them—those of us, that is, who have them. Only it is not customary for Hungarians to ask for or to accept decorations.

The truth of this account is amply supported by the case of János Arany, the poet who wrote *The Welsh Bards*. In commemoration of the coronation, Arany was distinguished by Francis Joseph with the Knight's Cross of the Order of Saint Stephen. Arany did everything he could to decline the "honor." He wrote in despair to Baron József Eötvös, minister of culture in the government elected in 1867: "They are hinting at a medal. I wish this 'bitter cup' could be taken from me!" He went on:

> I wish to be a devoted and loyal subject and an obedient servant of the crowned Hungarian king; I do not know what the consequences would be if I were to decline this supreme royal honor; but I have the feeling that in my situation it would be better to face those consequences.

This "situation" was the result of two things: first, Arany felt that to accept the medal would cost him his personal sovereignty, and secondly, he knew that acceptance would bring him into public contempt. Finally, in order to avoid a scandal, he decided to accept:

> I agreed to keep the medal after all, but only on condition that I would neither attend the audience that etiquette demands in such cases nor wear the cross on any occasion. I have kept both my resolutions, and I have excused myself in every way from using the title bestowed on me, which some people have tried hard to use in order to please me, together with the medal.

Tompa summarized the whole medal question as follows: "I carry it, it has stuck to me, although I can help it no more than I can help getting wet in the rain." He concluded with an ironic poem:

His Worships are coming to see me
To hang a medal of honor on me:
Excuse me, Your Worships,
But I don't deserve it.

All that shines
Belongs to literature;
All that is delicate:
Belongs to me alone.

They send me a medal of honor
When I have a stomach ache;
Oh! If I could have a good night's sleep
I would not exchange that for a hundred medals.

The stance of "keeping one's distance" changed slowly but surely over the years. The generation of politicians who derived their public authority from their self-attained sovereignty slowly died out and their places were taken by those who owed their office and political status to the new regime. This was the start of a process of adaptation to one's superiors; when expressions of esteem for the lawful king started to go above and beyond the call of duty, and signs of servility with a view to receiving an honor started to appear. By the 1880s, orders and medals had begun to function as a measure of personal worth: it started to matter who was given what, and what was due to a person on the basis of his social rank or political function. It was as if the experience of 1848 had vanished without trace: noble titles started to increase in value once again. (Francis Joseph, then Charles IV made more than two hundred people aristocrats and ennobled more than four thousand.) There was intense competition for the titles of count and baron, membership of the Upper House, the office of secret councilor, and royal chamberlain. The king, rather than the Hungarian people, was now in a position to bestow prestige and power.

The cost of adapting to one's superiors, and so meeting the requirements of Francis Joseph, was the diminution of one's public dignity. A typical example of this came in 1908, when the Hungarian government was about to commemorate the sixtieth anniversary of Francis Joseph's enthronement as emperor. Plans included erecting a church on the burial site of Árpád, the chieftain who led the Hungarians to the Carpathian Basin. According to official procedure under the Dualist regime, the plan had to be approved by the sovereign. Francis Joseph asked his Prime Minister Sándor Wekerle, whether it really was the burial site of Árpád. Wekerle answered, almost ironically, that "Árpád shall be buried wherever your Majesty orders." Francis Joseph would never have been answered by Ferenc Deák in the same way.

Those in the public sphere and in power politics knew very well that their future prospects depended much more on Francis Joseph than on the "will of the people." Prime ministers and government ministers tended to be removed "from above," and, as the press secretary of one Hungarian prime minister wrote in the early years of the twentieth century, "one must be able to reconcile the responsibilities of a minister with obeying the king's wishes." In other words, anyone who failed to obey the sovereign would be sent packing whatever his merits or whether he was a member of the majority party.

It was a fundamental interest of those who chose to serve the powers-that-be to conceal their servility as far as possible, and to justify their behavior in terms of principles. The conflicts inherent in serving an unpopular regime and ruler in a Hungarian milieu which was proud of its national character and the values of 1848 could be resolved only by claiming that Francis Joseph himself was a nationally-minded and liberal king. The legitimacy of his reign, it was claimed, had been established by his coronation, and so he should be able to count on the loyalty of all law-abiding Hungarian citizens. Needless to say, Francis Joseph was neither nationally-minded nor liberal and, he cared little what people thought of him; but for the promoters of the continuity of the Josephinian regime it was essential to maintain this façade.

This kind of propaganda was intended to satisfy the same need that had existed in the Age of Reform: the need to perceive Habsburgs as Hungarians. The satisfaction of the political and psychological needs of the supporters of the Compromise depended on how effectively they could validate the words "national" and "liberal" in relation to Francis Joseph, notwithstanding the fact that the emperor and his regime had objectively discredited them.

A substantial measure of self-delusion and lies were necessary to achieve this end. The army of so-called "Mamelukes" in the post-Compromise Parliament were described by a contemporary as follows: "In the heart of many an old Mameluke something of the spirit of the Hungarian 1848 still smolders, albeit only in the security of their own home, and within their innermost circle of friends." However, there were also a fair number of social occasions where one could openly insist that, at the bottom of one's heart, one was still committed to 1848. A covert or partially admitted commitment to the spirit of 1848 was very important for the promoters of the Compromise. It allowed them to demonstrate that, personally, they shared popular ideas and only formally supported unpopular measures, under "pressure of circumstances." It allowed them to claim a certain "secret integrity," which was not worth much, but at least established their credentials as "good Hungarians." This was quite different from the rebellious spirit of 1848, and was influenced by the prevalent social mood, which endeavored to express a lack of emotional support for the regime. Expressions of this general mood were increasingly calling into question the national and liberal character of Francis Joseph. The fact that even the supporters of the Compromise harbored, or claimed to harbor, the spirit of 1848 deep inside did not undermine their willingness to serve, though it did further erode an already discredited image of Francis Joseph, which was so necessary from another point of view. Such people hardly believed what they said about the king themselves.

It would be a mistake to think that only the supporters of the Compromise of 1867 had to delude themselves in this way. As we shall see, many of the 1848 generation, or at least those who wanted to make a career, were forced to say and do things in which they did not really believe. The explanation is simple. As the writer Gyula Krúdy noted in retrospect in the early 1930s: "This is what the world was like and little was remembered of a politician's past, with the possible exception of his speeches as recorded in the *Parliamentary Journal*; and only those could be active [in this sphere] whom Francis Joseph deemed fit." In other words, those who wanted to obtain political influence as a member of the 1848 generation had first to demonstrate "infinite devotion" to their beloved king, regardless of what they really thought of him.

Chapter Four

THE GREAT HUNGARIAN
SPLIT CONSCIOUSNESS AND
THE LAMMERGEYER

Francis Joseph did not make life easy for those who
sought to portray him as a nationally-minded and liberal king. As we
have had frequent occasion to mention, it was all the same to him what
his subjects thought of him: his rule was guaranteed by an established
legal framework and political practice. Coerced conformity further
strengthened these guarantees, but the principal form of insurance, the
army under his direct command, would defend his rule even if loyalty
were suddenly to crumble. Although the Compromise changed his
legal status, established political practice and his absolute rights as a
monarch gave him a degree of influence beyond the scope of his
authority strictly speaking, with the result that no one could even contemplate challenging his rule. Francis Joseph had no need to have himself portrayed as nationally-minded and liberal; political changes
notwithstanding, his person and the army under his command continued to assert the unity of the empire. He had no intention of surrendering any of his absolutist rights: for instance, he insisted that all bills
be previously approved by him before being debated in Parliament.
Francis Joseph's actions were always dictated by his own interests,
while Hungarians had no choice but to conform and to resolve their
problems as best they could. All Francis Joseph cared about was that
his subjects obeyed his will, and although he did from time to time
make gestures which boosted national enthusiasm, whenever he wanted to carry through something important he enforced his will in com-

plete and open contempt of national feelings. In this way he frequently confounded the army of servile place seekers who already suffered
from a split consciousness.

The symbols of his reign—the black-and-yellow flag and *Gott
erhalte*—both symbolized absolutism and absolute ignorance of national
rights to the Hungarian mind. They meant a lot to Francis Joseph in a
political sense, symbolizing a unified empire, the goal which he had so
consistently pursued until 1867, and which he did not abandon completely, even after the Compromise. Francis Joseph insisted on both the
flag and the imperial anthem even on occasions linked specifically to
some national event or to some public function of the Hungarian king,
such as the opening of Parliament.

Francis Joseph did not go to the Hungarian Parliament (a liberal
gesture indeed!): instead, MPs had to go to the Buda Castle to attend
the opening and closing of Parliament. Francis Joseph flew the black-
and-yellow flag over the Castle for the occasion, leading to protests
from pro-independence MPs, who argued that the black-and-yellow
flag was the private flag of the Habsburg dynasty, while the Castle was
a public institution. Consequently: down with the black-and-yellow
and up with the red-white-and-green Hungarian tricolor! After first
arising in 1865, the problem emerged once again for the first government of the Compromise, appointed in 1869. Prime Minister Andrássy
noted that the Buda Castle was not a public building, but the private
residence of the king, and so the black-and-yellow, the private flag of
the head of the Habsburg dynasty, was justifiably flown over it, signifying no more than that the head of the Habsburg dynasty, who was
both king of Hungary and Austrian emperor, was in residence in Buda.
Everyone is entitled to display their coat-of-arms and flag at their place
of residence. Deák once again sought a compromise; on the one hand,
he accepted that the king could fly the black-and-yellow flag over his
own house, but on the other he suggested that, at least on the opening
of Parliament, the Hungarian national tricolor should be displayed
next to it. Those who were not satisfied even by this arrangement
could simply stay away.

The use of the imperial flag, which was bound to injure national
feelings, was a constantly recurring problem during the period of dual-

ism; pro-independence MPs registered their protests with their absence from official functions, among other things. As Deák's argument signals, the advocates of the Compromise accepted the use of the Habsburg flag, although they were not happy about it. It stirred up national feeling and recalled particular memories of the sovereign's past conduct which markedly contradicted the national image which pro-Compromisers sought to promote. But there was nothing to be done: Francis Joseph was adamant.

The situation with *Gott erhalte* was similar. Hungarian ears were deeply offended by it, yet on every festive occasion they were expected to listen reverently to the imperial hymn. The following story well illustrates the kind of emotional reaction it could provoke. Ironically, the writer, Géza Gárdonyi (a good musician), came from an assimilated German family. The occasion was the opening ceremony of the Millennium Exhibition on 2 May 1896:

> It was the first day of summer clothes and the maybeetle. The day of the opening of the Millennium Exhibition. I must admit, I was not dressed in tails. I watched with disgust as "my German family" accepted homage from "my Hungary." The king—a "lammergeyer"—was wearing a crimson lambskin hat and a white cloak. The queen was all in black. Some of Árpád's progeny were dressed in Hungarian winter fur cloaks, while others were dressed for the summer. I also sighted top-hats and tails. Those dressed in the ceremonial attire of Hungarian noblemen were mostly traders, although there were also a number of counts and magnates.
>
> The king's speech and *Gott erhalte* played in honor of the Millennium made me sick. After lunch I went to bed feeling ill.

But the story does not end there. In the evening, a thirty-three-year-old journalist paid a visit to the Hungarian Prime Minister Dezső Bánffy:

> We were discussing how the king was humiliating the nation at that time. Bánffy suddenly was unable to speak. Tears gathered in his eyes. The same happened to me. When I was finally able to remove my handkerchief from my eyes, I cried out: "The Austrian

scoundrel!" I had thought to myself, "I don't care even if they hang
me for it, I will say it out loud for once." I could see that Bánffy
had stood up and was looking out of the window as if he had not
heard what I had said. I bowed and left.

The story tells us a great deal. Reading his diary it would appear
that Gárdonyi had not read any of the indulgent articles published in
Hungarian newspapers about the prevalent Hungarian national character in connection with the Millennium celebrations. Or perhaps he had
read them, but the words had left him unmoved? Or perhaps he simply
did not like the music of the imperial hymn—perhaps he did not like
Haydn. And what about Bánffy? Why the shedding of tears? He was
the prime minister after all! If anyone, he was duty bound to love his
king.
     The story has many lessons for us, but based on what we already
know it is not at all surprising, but merely provides a further illustra-
tion of the prevailing atmosphere. On the one hand, it demonstrates
that all the stories told about the king were no more than self-delusion
and an attempt to distort national consciousness, but also that the king
himself prevented this self-delusion from working at even a basic level
by insisting on the playing of *Gott erhalte*. The veil of loyalty could no
longer hide a strong dislike which did not leave even the prime minister unaffected, at least deep in his heart, despite the fact that he was
required to display the opposite to the outside world, particularly during the Millennium celebrations. He was a good example of what we
have called the "Great Hungarian Split Consciousness."
     Francis Joseph, on the other hand, persisted in using these seem-
ingly harmless symbols because he had never renounced his past
actions. Never during his long reign did he find an occasion to reha-
bilitate any of the Arad Thirteen, for example. The furthest he went
was not to forbid the recovery of their remains. Officially, however, he
never gave any sign of having regretted the executions. Probably the
exercise of self-criticism would have come into conflict with the concept of ruling by the grace of God, a justification of his legitimacy
which he never abandoned. He could, of course, have elected to demonstrate regret discretely, by small gestures, but he never did so. He never

gave up awarding medals on 6 October, the anniversary of the executions, considering it as just another day. He did donate his coronation present to the disabled soldiers of the Hungarian army and the orphans of soldiers who did not survive, it is true, but he never did justice in the political or moral sense to those who were executed. At the same time, nothing forced him to do so, and many of those who had turned against him in 1848–49 went on to adulate him after 1867. Francis Joseph from his own point of view consistently and naturally continued to assume that he should reward those who had fought on his side during those difficult times. He was willing to face further confrontations with the Hungarian nation because he wanted to use the past as a deterrent. He therefore pursued continuity with what the Hungarian people had rejected in 1848–49.

Few people knew that the bedroom of the emperor and king in the Burg was adorned with several paintings showing battle scenes involving the imperial and Hungarian armies. One of these paintings shows Alnoch about to make an—unsuccessful—attempt to blow up the Chain Bridge in Budapest, while another depicts Hentzi, mortally wounded defending Buda from the Hungarian troops trying to reoccupy it. Francis Joseph never parted with his favorite paintings, even after he was crowned Hungarian king in 1867. At the same time, the interior of the king's bedroom had nothing to do with the nation; it was the king's private affair. However, Francis Joseph went further and imposed his private attachments on the nation, erecting a memorial to Hentzi in the Buda Castle during his visit to Hungary in 1852, while doing nothing to commemorate those who had fallen defending their homeland. The statue of Hentzi was the subject of constant protests from the Hungarians, to which Francis Joseph and his army paid no attention. What is more, the cult of Hentzi went so far that on 21 May 1889, on the anniversary of the reoccupation of Buda by the Hungarians and of Hentzi's death, General Ludwig Jansky laid a wreath at the memorial. The laying of this wreath caused a wave of protests. Kálmán Tisza, then prime minister, said that Jansky had been thoroughly insensitive, but Archduke Albrecht, superintendent of the Austrian army, came to Jansky's defense. He could not, however, stop new waves of Hungarian protests and riots, when more than seven hundred demonstrators were arrested. The king reacted by promoting Jansky and retired General Baron Lipót Edelsheim-Gyulai, commander of the army corps, whom Tisza had consulted before his speech condemning Jansky's action. Finally, the king issued a insipid statement in which he expressed his commitment to promoting the army's positive image.

The Hungarian Prime Minister Kálmán Tisza was once again taught a lesson about the limitations of the king's "national feelings" and also about how the army stood above the law. The latter he knew anyway, since the Compromise itself had granted the king exclusive control over the army. For a unified army, dualism was meaningless; only the sovereign's will mattered. The Hungarian government had to bite the bullet, as everything Francis Joseph did was perfectly legal: it is not against the law to conspicuously ignore national sensitivities. In 1880, two officers seriously assaulted the editor of a Kolozsvár (Cluj) newspaper, Miklós Bartha, when he reported that army officers customarily addressed new recruits as "Hungarian dogs." These "heroic" soldiers left the unarmed editor bleeding from twenty-four wounds and maimed on one hand. The two officers were sentenced to thirty days house arrest, after which one of them was promoted and the other was hired for personal service by Archduke Albrecht. Ignoring all the protests and leaving the government feeling more than uncomfortable, Francis Joseph once again trampled on national sensitivities.

Francis Joseph was always particularly unbending when it came to the army. He never changed his position acquired at a young age, that the army was the only reliable support of a sovereign's rule, and that to that end the army must be united. Francis Joseph saw himself as the guarantee of that unity. It is not surprising that any Hungarian national demands which might resurface from time to time—the question of Hungarian command, for instance, were firmly rejected; Francis Joseph did not want the Hungarian people to realize that the army as an institution representing the unity of the monarchy meant more to him than Hungarian national demands. The army amply demonstrated how far Francis Joseph was from the ideal of a national king. Conflicts of this nature did, of course, put the ruling parliamentary party in a very difficult situation, as they had to support a whole array of anti-national bills and measures, which were at the same time based on the sovereign's legitimate rights.

There are many examples, probably the best known of which was the debate on the National Defense Force Bill in 1889 during which opinions clashed most strikingly in connection with Articles 14 and 25. Article 14 basically proposed limiting the right of the Hungarian Parliament to recruit as many soldiers as it saw fit. From our point of view, this bill is not crucial, particularly given the fact that, in the event, the bill was amended in accordance with opposition demands, leaving the wording as it was in the old bill. Article 25 of the bill, which did become law, was more injurious to national feeling. Given that the language of the army was German, this article stipulated that reserve officers had to demonstrate their German-language skills: in other words, only German speakers could become reserve officers. This article therefore reinforced the concept of a unified Austria and Germanization, and as a counter-reaction only served to fuel centuries-old anti-Habsburg feelings. Having said that, the bill did make sense; it did not stipulate anything that was not a logical consequence of the Compromise. Nevertheless, it was met by a wave of nationwide protests. The king, and thus the governing party, insisted on the enactment of the bill. Finally, the governing party voted to accept the contested passage, but no doubt at the cost of intense unease. Francis Joseph once again demonstrated that he cared nothing for the glory of being a national king.

The story of Kálmán Tisza, who pushed the National Defense Force Act through Parliament, amply demonstrates the two-faced nature of loyalty to the king. After fifteen years in government, Tisza had completely eroded his political capital and, as befitting a true politician, staged his own fall: he even managed to walk away from being the prime minister of the 1867 regime with the reputation of being one of the 1848 generation, to the great annoyance of Francis Joseph and the great delight of Hungarian public opinion. He achieved all this by standing up in support of Francis Joseph's most resolute Hungarian adversary, Lajos Kossuth, then living in emigration. Act 50 of 1879—enacted during Tisza's time as head of government—stipulated that Hungarian citizens living abroad for more than ten years and failing during that time to report to an Austro-Hungarian consulate were to lose their Hungarian citizenship. Needless to say, this included Lajos Kossuth. Faithful to the role he played in 1848–49 and later, Kossuth, then living in Turin, stated in an open letter dated 20 December 1889: "I have never considered myself even for a moment as a subject of Francis Joseph, Austrian emperor and Hungarian king. This is my position."

Kossuth's position did not come as a surprise. Even before this letter was issued, Tisza had declared that, as the honorary citizen of several Hungarian towns, Kossuth would be automatically allowed to retain his Hungarian citizenship. If Francis Joseph did not make the lives of his ministers easier by repeatedly violating national sensitivities, Kossuth did not make their lives easier either. In another letter, which was also published, he stated that the prime minister's declaration was legally ineffective, unless the act itself was amended accordingly. Of course, Tisza did not have to listen to Kossuth, but, as if he had suddenly broken with his former self, the prime minister declared, without preliminary consultation, that he was willing to amend the Citizenship Act as Kossuth requested. Neither the panicking ministers, nor the meeting of the Council of Ministers chaired by Francis Joseph agreed with Tisza. In response, Tisza resigned as prime minister, and in the twenty-third year of Francis Joseph's reign as Hungarian king, Lajos Kossuth lost his Hungarian citizenship.

As this story illustrates, national feeling and the sovereign's will could come into open conflict. What Tisza did was to play on the split in the Hungarian political consciousness: he knew that by taking a position on Kossuth's side he was bound to upset Francis Joseph, upon whom his position depended; on the other hand, he knew equally well that this was his only chance to redeem himself in the eyes of the Hungarian people.

The past could never go away. Whatever happened was somehow connected with the past, making it impossible to forget or to accept the official ideology. It was not simply that from time to time scandals arose to stir up trouble, but rather that such scandals were inherent in the mechanism of the Compromise between the king and the Hungarian nation. The Compromise was a process, as we have already seen, which forced the Hungarian political elite to attempt to do two contradictory things at the same time: on the one hand they had to create an image of Francis Joseph which everyone knew was false, and on the other they constantly had to deal with its real-world consequences. Everything that Francis Joseph did was legitimate and within the scope of his powers, partly due to the willingness of Hungarian politicians to give in—and that was enough to keep the past alive.

Here are two examples from the 1890s which demonstrate the extent to which this tendency was inherent in the regime, and the kind of relationship which existed between the king and his nation. It is important to keep in mind that as time went on, there were, naturally enough, fewer and fewer people still living from the generation who were mature adults during the events of 1848–49 and the severest period of absolutist repression.

The first example is related to the twenty-fifth anniversary of Francis Joseph's coronation and the statue of Hentzi. This time the story is not about Francis Joseph himself, but the chairman of the Hungarian Union of National Army Associations, a certain Imre Ivánka, a former army officer turned governing party representative. (Ivánka's favorite catchphrase was "Trust appearances!," which was picked up by others and became a political slogan.) In 1892, Ivánka had a brilliant idea: when he found out about plans to unveil a statue to the soldiers of the Hungarian National (Honvéd) Army in the Buda Castle in November, he proposed taking a wreath to the statue of Hentzi—whom the National Army had fought against—also in the Buda Castle, at the time of the unveiling. Ivánka proposed that the Hungarian Hymn should be played at the memorial to the National Army, and *Gott erhalte* at the memorial to Hentzi, both accompanied by a ceremonial salute of cannons. Ivánka put his plan to the prime minister, who reported it to the king. Francis Joseph was delighted—at last he thought that the Hungarian people had come to accept the Austrian general (whom he referred to as a modern Leonidas) as their own hero. But another representative of the governing party, Antal Tibád, who just a couple of years previously had been a state secretary to the minister of the interior, indignantly informed the pro-independence opposition of the loyalist plan (another example of split consciousness). In so doing he exploded a veritable "bomb." The opposition press was full of the "vilification of the Hungarian nation," while in the House of Representatives Károly Eötvös campaigned against the plan. Finally, the Committee of National Army Associations voted against Ivánka's suggestion, and so it was dropped. "Nationally-minded king" and "hero of the nation" were mutually exclusive. (Passions against Hentzi grew so high that an attempt was made to blow up the statue by an outraged journalist who tried to explode a tin of sardines filled with gunpowder. All this great Hungarian terrorist could achieve was to cause an indistinct pop. In 1898 it was decided, with Francis Joseph's consent, to relocate the statue of Hentzi. The Hungarian people argued that the space was needed to erect the statue of Queen Elizabeth—who had been assassinated in the meantime—at the finest spot in the Buda Castle or nearby. Francis Joseph conceded the argument: Elizabeth could not be compared with a mere general. However, the new location of the Hentzi statue signaled that it had lost none of its symbolic significance: it was to be erected in the park of the Cadet School in Hüvösvölgy, Budapest. The Cadet School was not open to the general public, but the statue's placement here signaled the kind of role model that the king of Hungary wanted to put before the future officers of the Hungarian army. The statue's troubled life finally came to an end in November 1918, when it was toppled and smashed during the Democratic Revolution. It was not alone in meeting such a fate: the statue of Francis Joseph erected in 1908 as part of the Millennium Monument was also destroyed as a result of "public outrage." After the revolutions of the early twentieth century, no new statue of Hentzi was made, but Francis Joseph's figure was recreated: his statue was restored (this time cloaked in the coronation mantle, in contrast with the general's uniform which had previously adorned him).

The question arises: if there was such a great discrepancy between how Francis Joseph and the Hungarian people interpreted the past, how could they reach a compromise? The honest answer is that they could not, and this is why lies had to be told continuously, at least regarding the official portrayal of the king. Any attempt to find a compromise could only breed more schizophrenia. The second story we shall use to illustrate our theme concerns an attempt during the late

1890s to make 1848 a common festive occasion for both king and nation.

The year 1898 was a double anniversary: the fiftieth anniversary of the events of 1848, and the fiftieth anniversary of Francis Joseph's ascent to power, at that time still against Hungarian laws and the national will. Let us forget about the second anniversary for the moment and leave it to the Hungarian government of the day to worry about. And worries they had a plenty, as they had to celebrate as best they could a "festive occasion" which the Hungarian people simply refused to acknowledge. The members of the government had enough experience prior to 1898 to make them realize that it was impossible to square the circle. Instead, let us examine the kind of compromise which could be made, between the emotionally positively perceived Hungarian 1848 and the now lawful Hungarian king.

The government decided—naturally, with the king's consent— that 11 April, when the laws of 1848 were sanctified, should be selected for a national holiday. The reader will probably remember that Francis Joseph had attended the Diet in Pozsony, the view of the time being that his presence on that day had lent it an air of legality. However, 11 April had far less of an emotional charge from the Hungarian perspective. The national consensus was that 15 March was the right day on which to commemorate the achievements of 1848. This was, however, unacceptable to Francis Joseph, who had only bad memories of the events which started the March Revolution within the Monarchy; and in any case he could hardly be expected to agree to a national holiday being instituted in commemoration of what he saw as the unlawful riots of a people he despised the aim of which had been to curb the powers of the Habsburg dynasty.

Hungarian politicians—very tactfully—wanted no more than to pick up the very narrow thread which alone among the series of events of 1848–49 could establish a link between Francis Joseph and the Hungarian people. That link was 11 April, the only day on which the reigning monarch, Ferdinand V, his heir Francis Joseph, and the representatives of the Hungarian Diet, including Kossuth, Batthyány, and many others, had gathered together in a lawful manner. Every other day had been spent in an atmosphere of confrontation. The only problem was that the other party to the Compromise, the Hungarian people, had no emotional attachment to that day. Finally, 1848 was commemorated, but the spirit of 1848 was nowhere to be found. What the Hungarian people got was a national holiday which was not recognized by the state, and a state holiday which they never felt was their own.

Chapter Five

AN EVEN GREATER SPLIT
IN HUNGARIAN CONSCIOUS-
NESS AND THE NAKED KING

It is unlikely that Francis Joseph failed to notice this strange "harmony" which so frequently manifested itself. He must have been aware of the adverse emotions and even passions which lay below the surface, while he encountered only reverent words and loyalty from governing Hungarian politicians. Francis Joseph could never have deluded himself that the Hungarians would change their attitudes to him so entirely, simply as a result of his coronation, and forget everything that had once made them rise up against him, including a number of grievances which remained unsatisfied even after 1867. What is more, at the beginning of his reign as king he had had to learn the hard way that the spirit of rebellion, which he hated so much, still lingered in the minds of Hungarians. This developed into something of a phobia in Francis Joseph, who could not free himself from it even in relation to Deák, whom he considered deceitful. Constantly recurring incidents made sure that his suspicions did not go away, even in the post-1867 period. Francis Joseph must have known about the cult of Kossuth, for instance, which reached incredible proportions. This was not reverence enforced on people by any authority or power, but sincere devotion shown by their own free will. Kossuth continued to incite the Hungarian people against Francis Joseph not only in 1849 and during the years of absolutism—many others did the same—but even after 1867, right up until his death in 1894. Few others dared to oppose Francis Joseph so openly, both as a person and for what he stood for in the post-Compromise period. The people simply called him "Father Kossuth," a paternal privilege which would ordinarily go to the person of the king. Kossuth remained intransigent—albeit outside the Austro-Hungarian Empire—and was elevated to a hero of Hungarian political mythology. Francis Joseph discovered that, although he ruled Hungary, he could not break Kossuth or to eliminate his cult.

Francis Joseph was never particularly interested in what people really thought of him. To him, they were merely subjects, whose duty it was to obey the laws drafted with the consent of the king and not to violate the written and unwritten code of loyalty to the monarchy, or at least to give the impression of loyalty to the outside world. Should the Hungarian people ever choose to deviate from this, then they must be broken in. The king cannot be removed from office, whether by means of the ballot box or anything else. In any case, Francis Joseph saw himself as a great deal more than a symbol of royalty: he saw himself as a very real player in the world of power politics, and one with wide ranging authority.

The strongest opposition force was the 48-er Party of Independence, but even it did not challenge the legitimacy of Francis Joseph's rule, which is why Kossuth would not identify himself with them. Even so, the party was able to dominate in those parts of Hungary with a majority Hungarian population, and on that basis was able to keep on putting forward demands—for example, concerning the army or an independent Hungarian national bank—which in one way or another challenged the viability of the Compromise. The party rejected the Compromise of 1867 and only acknowledged personal union between Austria and Hungary. The problem was that even the personal loyalty which members of this party were willing to show had as its object a king who was far from willing to serve as a link between the two halves of his empire. Indeed, he used all his—formal and informal—influence to achieve the very opposite. What could the politically active supporters of 1848 do in such a situation? They had the emotional support of a whole nation, providing a far larger base than the number of those eligible to vote, but their political program made it impossible for them to come to power unless the lawful king was first "displaced," a scenario which usually comes about in the form of a revolution. The absolutism of the "long 1850s" made sure that, under the Compromise, the same kind of united interest which had existed in 1848–49 could not be recreated. This was, therefore, far from being a revolutionary situation! What, then, remained? The law. But the law could not help the opposition attain power. Consequently, sooner or later they too had to adapt to the existing regime, their patriotic expostulations notwithstanding. They had to learn to live with the bitter fact that, as one opposition politician saw it in the 1880s: "In Hungary one can pose as a member of the opposition, but opposition principles must not be allowed to prevail!" Ferenc Herczeg, a writer and pro-government party MP, wrote a few decades later: "Under the reign of Francis Joseph one can talk in a hundred different ways, but one may govern in only one way."

This did not apply to all: for individuals, opportunities existed for some form of resistance, as long as one was content to remain an eternal member of the opposition. But within the "prison house of the law" even "eternal members of the opposition" had to give the king his due. This paradoxical situation is well illustrated by a vignette by Károly Eötvös, the hero of which is a leading figure of the pro-independence opposition, József Madarász (who died in 1915 at the age of 101). Madarász was a political veteran, a member of the pro-independence party, and an MP from the very beginning. The following is a very precise account of what it meant to hold opposition views while accepting the legitimacy of the king's rule:

> Over several years I and my good friend Otto Herman, poor Count Gábor Károly, and a number of other friends set up a new pro-independence party, and elected József Madarász as chairman. We could not have chosen a better man. Of course, we had to elaborate our program.
>
> Our old friend József was a fierce opponent of *Pragmatica Sanctio*, somewhat like a "kuruc" [named after an uprising against the Habsburgs in the first decade of the eighteenth century]. He would not base a program on acceptance of the *Pragmatica Sanctio*. According to him, the Habsburg dynasty might one day die out, in which case the Hungarian people might want to elect...not a

new king, but a president of the republic. Their right to do so must
not be waived; such a possibility must be foreseen by the party's
program well in advance.

Then one of us remarked: "But József, the dynasty has seventy-
seven members still alive, and they will not die out in five hundred years." "Well, that is true. In that case, our program shall be
for five hundred years." Gábor Károly, God rest his soul, suddenly sprang to his feet: "I will not sign a program for five hundred
years. How can I keep to it?"

Madarász would not back down. But as he was an amicable
man, in the end we agreed on a program for a hundred-and-fifty
years for the sake of party unity. Our old friend József is still
backing it. And so am I.

Acceptance of the existing legal order made it extremely unlikely
that those dedicated to a pro-1848 program would achieve rapid success. Something had to be done, but whatever course they chose, they
had to demonstrate their loyalty to the king. What is more, when formulating national demands, one was always supposed to argue that
their satisfaction was basically in the king's interests: the fiction had to
be maintained that the Hungarian king's objectives were identical with
Hungarian national demands. At the same time, no one could seriously believe that Francis Joseph's dream was an independent Hungary.

It is a fact that most of the pro-1848 generation gained in real
terms from the existing political set-up: by the 1880s and 1890s many
opposition politicians were reaping the benefits of the regime in much
the same way as members of the governing party. Their critical voices
did not abate, but their motivation for genuine change weakened. They
became increasingly willing to help operate the power mechanism of
the Hungarian kingdom as dictated by Francis Joseph. In this way they
restricted their room to maneuver to the freedom to express themselves
in a "hundred different ways." But the irresolvable gap between what
could be said, unconditional loyalty to the king, commitment to the
law, and political and personal welfare was not diminished. The behavior of the opposition was therefore extremely inconsistent. They could
"puff up" their own role, but in reality it had no bite. They could be
won over with little difficulty. As little as they liked their king, they

knew that they could not avoid adapting to his regime if they wanted to attain power and influence, at least until such time as the dynasty died a natural death.

One must, of course, make a clear distinction between the final outcome and the process which led up to it. The pro-independence opposition was a "broad church": its members were divided into those who took a shorter or longer time to come to the same conclusion, and the few who would not tolerate the hypocrisy, the inconsistency, and the dishonesty which resulted from the existing situation, and chose to quit in order to remain true to the national interest and the will of the Hungarian people.

All in all, the pro-1848 opposition was diluted, if not in its rhetoric, certainly in its position and interests. This weakening of the opposition gave Francis Joseph an opportunity to show whether he was at least a liberal, even if he was not pro-national. As we have seen, the "official" image of Francis Joseph partly emphasized his liberalism. He was usually referred to as the "most constitutional king," but his constitutionalism was rather lop-sided, given his retention of strong absolutist powers, although one possible interpretation of constitutionalism is as the protection of the rights enshrined by law, including the rights of an absolutist king. It was an ambivalent situation. Francis Joseph had a well-documented past linked with absolutism, reinforced by the continuity of his absolutist rights beyond the end of the absolutist regime. At the same time, in post-1867 Hungary many laws were passed in the spirit of liberalism during the reign of Francis Joseph.

The 1890s marked a breakthrough regarding one of the cornerstones of liberal politics throughout Europe: by the last decade of the nineteenth century the separation of church and state was accomplished in Hungary, and the institution of secular marriage was introduced. Francis Joseph's religious piety was common knowledge, and so it was very difficult for him both emotionally and morally to accept the new religious laws. Few people knew that the separation of church and state was delayed until the mid-1890s because Francis Joseph himself held it back as long as he could. Finally, he had to give in to the modern European spirit, and he reluctantly sanctified the laws. This submission reinforced the view that he was a liberal, in the sense that he had demonstrated his ability to subordinate his own principles to the national will. In any case, in Hungary one could freely express one's political opinions: freedom of the press, freedom of association, and a number of other freedoms could be exercised in accordance with contemporary liberal norms.

At the same time, as we have seen, while one could speak in a hundred different ways, there was only one way to govern.

Why did it take Francis Joseph so long to come to a decision on the separation of church and state? Deák, leader of the parliamentary majority at the time, had called for separation, which he thought essential, as early as the early 1870s (despite being a Catholic, like Francis Joseph).

The lessons of the 1890s, a period characterized by tough political bargaining, reveal other blemishes on Francis Joseph's liberal constitutional reputation. We must also bear in mind that a liberal solution to the political situation could not be coupled with the transformation of the power-political structure or the dualist regime and royal legislative powers. The separation of church and state was a liberal measure, and one which could have been taken much earlier, if the king had indeed been a liberal. Needless to say that was far from being the case. Indeed, Francis Joseph never claimed to be a liberal by conviction. He was willing to make particular, however belated, liberal concessions, but only as long as they did not challenge the status quo. He delayed such measures as long as he could, up to the point of risking open conflict with the Hungarian parliament, which otherwise readily submitted to his will. Francis Joseph did not want to risk a challenge to his rule.

The real trial of Francis Joseph's liberal principles came when proposed liberal measures threatened the existing political power structure. In the early 1900s, both Francis Joseph and his Hungarian opposition were forced to reveal their true colors. There were signs that Francis Joseph would chose absolutism rather than liberalism, provided that the Hungarian people could not be dissuaded from some of their demands. We have frequently made the point that Francis Joseph stubbornly maintained control over the military, as he was entitled to do under the Compromise. This demonstrated the continuity between past and present most vividly. In 1903, the opposition raised new, more explicit demands for the dualistic transformation of the single Austrian–Hungarian army. In simple terms, they wanted to divide the army into a Hungarian and an Austrian army. The former would legally remain part of the single army, but take an oath to the Hungarian constitution and use Hungarian state symbols. Hungarian would be the language of army command and the Hungarian army would be stationed exclusively in Hungary. As regards external symbols (flags and insignia), even some governing-party members sympathized with opposition demands. Francis Joseph made his position absolutely clear when in September he issued a military order at Chlopy in Galicia. He declared, among other things, that the

> army shall remain single and united, as it is now, and a strong power serving to defend the Austro-Hungarian Monarchy against its enemies. My entire armed force shall take an oath to proceed along the path of the serious discharging of its duty, and be permeated by a spirit of concord, which respects all particular national features, but resolves all discord and turns the particular strengths of each ethnic group to the advantage of the greater whole.

In this way the Hungarian king made it absolutely clear that he would not allow the army to be altered. Furthermore, he was empowered to do so by Article 11 of the Compromise. Public opinion was offended by the expression "each ethnic group": how could the Hungarian people be deemed to stand at the same political level as their ethnic minorities? How could Francis Joseph, the Hungarian king, refer to his people as an "ethnic group" at all? Under the Compromise, Hungary was one of two politically equal parts of the monarchy, but the expression "each ethnic group" seemed a reversion to the absolutist spirit of the 1850s and its ideology of the single unified empire. What did Francis Joseph mean? Did he still consider himself emperor of a single Austria?

Francis Joseph regretted the confusion he had created, and that his words could be interpreted as a violation of the Hungarian constitution or as a manifestation of his intention to curb Hungary's legal rights. He insisted that nothing could be further from the truth. However, Francis

Joseph's words, which had been intended to temper the public mood, could not conceal what Francis Joseph meant in earnest. Even if the outbreak of disappointment was dampened in 1903, in 1905 it broke out once again with full force, when the opposition, headed by the Independence Party, won the election. The winners' program incorporated the same demands which had led to the issuing of the Chlopy military order in 1903.

What did liberalism dictate in such cases? The recipe was clear enough: the parliamentary majority may appoint the government, whether others like its program or not. The program can be debated later on. Should this debate prove inconclusive, the different parties being irreconcilable, new elections must be held, after which the emerging majority party can select its government, and so on. Furthermore, if the victorious party consistently challenges the sovereign, the latter must give way.

It is no secret that nothing happened in accordance with the above scenario. Shortly after the elections, the Hungarian king received one of the leaders of the triumphant opposition. Ironically, the name of this pro-independence leader was Kossuth—Ferenc, not Lajos. He was in fact the son of the former governor, but as a politician he was but a faint shadow of his father, so mirroring the opposition as a whole at the turn of the twentieth century. But on one level at least the past seemed to be repeating itself—Francis Joseph was once again facing a Kossuth.

By way of illustrating the balance of power, Francis Joseph told the Hungarian delegation ordered to the Burg that the "so-called Independence Party" must cease its campaigns. The delegation of the Hungarian people, as the representatives styled themselves, voluntarily prolonged their brief visit by hanging around in front of a window niche for another half-hour after leaving the king's chambers: they wanted the journalists to believe that they were in the middle of very important and tough negotiations. They wanted to give the impression to the outside world that the king was devoting a long time to them. In reality, the king, dressed in his general's uniform, had done nothing more than dismiss them with a terse command.

The illusion could not be maintained for long: Francis Joseph did not appoint his new government from the party with the parliamentary majority, but instead entrusted the commander of his Trabant Guards, Géza Fejérváry, with the task. This new government therefore lacked the most important attribute of liberal legitimacy: a parliamentary majority. There was an open division between liberalism and the national will as expressed in the election on the one hand, and the Hungarian king on the other. Francis Joseph acted in accordance with his absolutist upbringing, putting himself above the constitution.

But we should try not to get tied up by the politico-historical details of this crisis: it suffices to mention only the most obvious features. Some time later the king received another delegation of opposition-party members. This audience, in September, lasted no more than four and a half minutes. Francis Joseph simply read out, point by point, to the Hungarian politicians standing in front of him that he would not accept their demands; that he was not prepared to allow the unity of the Compromise and the military to be disturbed. On this occasion, it made no sense to try to create the impression of having had a long discussion.

In another incident four and a half months later—February 1906— the king used military force to dissolve parliament and to close the fine new Parliament building on the bank of the Danube.

In the meantime, another—this time secret—plan was unfolding for the military occupation of Hungary in order to suppress the "cold Hungarian revolution." The plan was officially entitled "Resolving the Hungarian Crisis by Force of Arms." This military operation—code-named "U"—calculated that on the Hungarian side there were 282 battalions, 146 cavalry units, and 78 batteries of artillery, while the imperial army comprised 654 battalions, 239 cavalry units, and 166 batteries. The imperial army would attack from four different directions, aiming to strike the heaviest blow on Budapest. For a while it must have seemed to Francis Joseph that he had traveled back in time more than half a century—indeed, that it was 1848 all over again. However, as posterity generally discovers, a parody can never compare with the original.

On the other side, a number of "patriots" began to wear badges featuring a tulip, indicating a boycott of Austrian products. (Ironically, the badges were made in Vienna.) As another example of resistance, in Debrecen a raging crowd beat unconscious the lord lieutenant of the unlawfully appointed government.

At the same time, Francis Joseph finally agreed to support the extension of voting rights, on the urging of the Fejérváry government and after showing some reluctance, despite the fact that in Hungary dualism would be even more difficult to maintain under conditions of nearly general suffrage; pro-1867 politicians were not concerned by reform of the electoral system, and for good reason. Francis Joseph decided that he would address any crisis when it actually manifested itself. For the time being, he had to combat, at whatever cost, current troubles.

Lengthy preparations were finally drawing to an end: in April 1906 the coalition surrendered and abandoned its demands for an independent army and economy. In fact, virtually all its demands were relinquished. Francis Joseph met coalition leaders on 6 April 1906, including the son of Kossuth (who could never be appeased), and the son of Andrássy (who on one occasion was). At the end of the audience Francis Joseph shook hands with Kossuth. Francis Joseph was 76 at the time, Ferenc Kossuth 65, and Andrássy 46. Francis Joseph had won.

And with what ease! It appeared with the utmost clarity during this crisis as at no time since 1867 that the king was neither nationally-minded nor a liberal. In other words: the king had no clothes! At the level of appearances he was very finely dressed, meaning that he could behave as if he were nationally-minded and liberal—he could sublimate hardnosed politics into a kind of wisdom. Of course, he could not have done so without a choir of Hungarian politicians repeating the appropriate phrases over and over again, using this façade to justify their own actions. Public opinion was also willing to give in to appearances: people did not want to face the fact that they had wasted their votes, and had demonstrated and protested in vain. It therefore served a very real purpose to portray the lack of substance as virtue, and the government basically continued in the same vein as its predecessors, perhaps with a little more national flair or "*rothweiss-grün*." Francis Joseph could rest on his laurels: the former opposition now come to power would do nothing against his will. His prejudice was also reinforced, in terms of well-sounding patriotic phrases, that the Hungarians lacked moral stature: their actions were at variance with their words.

They were playing the role of the revolutionary "kuruc" while being nothing but "labanc"collaborators. More precisely, they were pretending to be "labanc" while feeling themselves to be "kuruc." Whatever was the case, the most important thing was to retain their loyalty.

The Great Hungarian Split Consciousness showed no sign of healing; on the contrary, it seemed to be deepening. As for Francis Joseph, he was the same as ever: the firm hand on the tiller of the ship of state, the wise statesman. Wise indeed, if he could win even while naked.

Chapter Six

THE NON-EXISTENT "MAGIC SPELL": THE KING'S PERSONALITY

An attractive personality can be a strong counterweight to political ambivalence. There are many documented cases of politically motivated surges of emotion being tamed by an influential personality. Such personalities held the unconditional—and intrinsic—respect of even their political adversaries. (For instance, the Compromise was greatly promoted by the more or less universal regard for Deák's honesty, morals, and personal influence, regardless of party sympathies.) The king was another example: his personality and human character meant a lot, even if his personality was not untainted by his politics: after all, no clean-cut separation is possible between the political and the personal ego. But it was precisely the character and quality of the difference in this respect between Deák and Francis Joseph which would determine whether the politically and historically motivated and already deep-seated split in Hungarian national consciousness would diminish or remain unchanged.

The ordinary person could see a great deal, and there was a lot more besides which he could not have known, or might only suspect, about his king. When a nation and a sovereign live side-by-side for such a long time, as the Hungarian people and Francis Joseph did, then the parties inevitably get to know one another fairly well. The press certainly did its level best to ensure that its readers were served with credible stories and not merely unverified gossip. Festive occasions always offered a good opportunity to show the king as a "private person." Short sketches about him were a popular genre, demonstrating what a courageous, wise, humane, and good-tempered man the king was, with a good sense of humor and a capacity for empathy. They also gave a detailed account of personal aspects of the king's official functions: what he said to whom during his official visits; what he had wanted to know; and whom he had honored with his attention. What is more, as Francis Joseph became older and plagued by illness, detailed reports began to appear about the state of his health.

On the pages of the 3 May 1914 issue of the newspaper *Alkotmány*, for instance, readers could find out the following:

> The sovereign was in a good mood and very vigorous all yesterday; he showed no ill effects as a result of the bad weather, and the doctors were very satisfied with their evening examination. Shortly after eight o'clock the king retired to bed and fell asleep straightaway. His condition seemed so favorable that his physician decided not to stay in the room next to the bedroom, as had been his wont during the first phase of the illness, but retired to his quarters, as he had done on a number of occasions lately. The king was woken up shortly after midnight for the first time by an irritation in his throat, making him want to cough, and the recurrent urge to cough and the discharge of mucus continued to disturb his dreams from time to time until the morning. Nevertheless, the king woke up at the usual time and ate his breakfast...with good appetite, and was constantly engaged with matters of state in his study. The disturbing of his night's rest did of course mean that he was not as fresh as he had been for the last couple of days, but this is no cause for alarm and it is hoped that the coughing irritation at night will not stay with him long: the doctors concluded that the easing of the catarrh and the retreat of the symptoms of the illness are fully under way. The following statement has been issued concerning the state of his Majesty's health: "'His night's rest was disturbed from time to time. Generally feeling quite well."

It went on like this day after day. Everyone knew precisely how His Majesty's catarrh was doing, providing an opportunity to worry about His sick Majesty and to discuss the state of his health with the neighbors.

All this was meant to highlight the fact that everything about the king was common knowledge: whether he was ill, or in good health, in which case even his diet would be discussed. His subjects could rest assured, as was constantly made clear to them, that the dutifulness of their king made him the first among the civil servants of the Monarchy. Newspapers also discussed his life-style, and the diligent reader could learn every possible detail. Even today, we know little more about Francis Joseph than contemporary readers.

Francis Joseph would get up at four o'clock in the morning in summer, and slightly later, at five o'clock, in winter. If we were to glance inside his bedchamber, we would discover that the king slept on an iron bedstead used by army officers and washed himself in an ordinary army basin. He shaved himself and started the day with a very modest breakfast, usually just a glass of milk. (He would also take a couple of spoonfuls of sour milk a day: his father had taught him that it was one of the secrets of a long life.) After breakfast, he would sit down at his desk and work by himself. He would spend the quiet of the morning on private correspondence and then turn his attention to matters which he had not been able to finish on the previous day for one reason or another. At seven o'clock in the morning he would be handed, in a large, locked briefcase, the documents of the Cabinet Office. What did the locked briefcase contain: what were the affairs which came under the authority of the Cabinet Office but required the very highest approval? The Cabinet Office had charge of the affairs of civil government, including all the Hungarian and Austrian ministries and the ministries of joint affairs. The armed forces were a case apart. These ministries constituted separate organizational entities, but all court-related matters came under the authority of the Cabinet Office, court finances included. After seven o'clock the sovereign would be handed the reports of the Military Bureau, another executive branch. The official language was German, and in this connection the sovereign's direct apparatus was governed by the principle of unity rather than dualism. The king would finish his paper work by ten o'clock at the latest, and would then receive his adjutant general, the heads of the Military Bureau and the Cabinet Office, the Hungarian referent, and sometimes the lord steward and his ministers. The king would usually take his lunch some time between midday and 1 P.M. in his study. The writer Gyula Krúdy swore that Francis Joseph ate sausages with horseradish and drank a glass of brown ale. We know about the ale for certain, and the sausages with horseradish cannot be excluded, but they would surely have become rather boring after a couple of days. The main thing is that the king liked a simple lunch. He would usually go for a half-hour walk after his meal through the garden exclusively reserved for him. Upon returning to his study, he would list through the semi-official journal of the Foreign Ministry and the selected press review, which of course included articles published in Hungarian newspapers. The afternoon would be devoted to wording the highest-level resolutions, writing announcements, and dealing with urgent matters and requests. Dinner was served around six o'clock.

He ate at a set table, not simply from a tray. When Elizabeth was at home, they ate together; when she was away, he usually ate alone. (Apart from his wife, Francis Joseph liked to have his younger daughter, Maria Valeria, by his side.) He preferred to keep his menu simple, although the gourmand Gyula Krúdy insisted that the so-called Viennese beef on the bone had been popularized by Francis Joseph. His meals were such that they almost called for being taken alone. As Krúdy said:

> Beef (like fish) tastes best when eaten alone, and company is required only with poultry, roast game, and the master creations of culinary art, such as spring snipe, when it feels so good to discuss the quality of the dish with someone....There is nothing to discuss about beef: its flavor, which comes from a foreign land, has to stand up for itself.

(Had the king eaten Hungarian beef on the bone, he would probably have done grave injury to the principle of dualism.) The king hardly ever had soup, so the stock in which the meat was cooked was enjoyed by the domestic staff. After meals, Francis Joseph would light a cigar—not the expensive cabanos popular throughout the Monarchy, but the cheaper Virginia. He seldom indulged himself with a more expensive treat. Towards the end of his life, he swapped Virginia for

Regalia Media, and, in addition, allowed himself one expensive Corona cigar a day. He would usually not receive anyone after lunch, and would make an exception only if it was an urgent matter which could not be delayed, in which case he would not hesitate to do his duty. He usually went to bed at eight or nine o'clock in winter. Former Cabinet Secretary István Pápay recalled that Francis Joseph ordered that he be woken up during the night if an appeal for a pardon was dispatched by wire regarding an execution to be carried out next morning. The wired message would be returned to the officer in charge without delay, and would contain either a zero, crossed out, meaning that the king approved the death sentence or the words "pardon to be issued immediately."

This is how the Hungarian king spent the average day. To remind the reader of only one detail: Francis Joseph's working attire was his general's uniform. Several versions of this existed: according to contemporary gossip, his wardrobe contained more than three hundred. Certainly, paintings, photographs, and even film recordings confirm that the general's uniform was Francis Joseph's choice from the age of thirteen. Indeed, the king was seldom seen in civilian dress, despite the fact that he spent most of his time as one of the busiest officials in the Monarchy. This never-changing style of dress was a true reflection of Francis Joseph's character, the embodiment of absolutism, the two main instruments of which were the bureau and the bayonet.

These two instruments had played an important part in his education: Radetzky taught him about the importance of the uniform and the military, as did, from the 1850s, Francis Joseph's great uncle, Archduke Albrecht, while Metternich and Schwarzenberg stressed the importance of the bureau. Most importantly, Francis Joseph's own experience confirmed these beliefs; his own world view rested on the same pillars. Francis Joseph aimed at attaining the ideal of the official-cum-soldier; after all, both have in common the concept of service and the discharging of duty. From the standpoint of the individual, this had two consequences. On the one hand, it inevitably called for a puritanical lifestyle, and on the other, it required a certain insensitivity to others, reducing human relationships to a matter of control and subordination. All this fitted very well with the essentially feudal image of the king.

However attractive the image of a puritanical and dutiful king might be, the rigidity of the insensitive soldier–bureaucrat forever issuing orders could be repulsive.

Adherence to rigid rules was another common feature of the values of the soldier, the bureaucrat, and the sovereign. The depository of the supreme will behaved with his subjects in accordance with the rules of Spanish etiquette. For instance, the sovereign could be addressed only when he had given his expressed permission. This attitude probably differed little from that of a senior army officer or bureaucrat.

Francis Joseph never doubted that he was doing the right thing. Those who met him were left in no doubt that he fully identified with his role. And he met many people. Senior government officials of the Monarchy met the sovereign while discharging their official duties. In the course of brief audiences they had to remain standing, but might be invited to sit down for more detailed discussion of particular issues. At meetings chaired by Francis Joseph, everyone was entitled to give his opinion: the emperor and king was willing to listen to views which conflicted with his own. However, if he chose to make his own point, that was the end of the discussion, and speakers had to conclude as soon as Francis Joseph signaled that the audience was over.

The so-called "public audiences" held on Mondays and Thursdays (from 9:45 A.M. to 1 or 2 P.M.) were particularly formal, not to say rigid. Such audiences were by invitation only, and only those likely to obtain a favorable decision or who were coming to thank the king for their appointment or a medal—provided that they belonged to salary-category six or above—had much chance of getting on the list. According to the unwritten rule, secret counselors, chamberlains, and members of the Upper House had to attend an audience once a year to pay their respects. It has been calculated that Francis Joseph held over four thousand audiences, each attended on average by a hundred people. What could he do in the three or four hours available for each meeting? A little arithmetic tells us that he would have been able to devote only around two minutes to each person. This rapid pace could be kept up only if Francis Joseph met the visitor standing, signaled when he was ready to listen to him, and cut the visitor off mid-sentence as soon as he had reached the designated two minutes, at which point the visitor would back out of the audience chamber, bowing. Standard procedures had to be followed. There were no "extraordinary" incidents—no one ever physically threatened Francis Joseph—yet there were some who did not have a clear understanding of what good behavior was. Some thought that when addressing the king they had to say his full title, beginning with emperor of Austria and ending with lord of the Wendish frontier-earldom. Others became so overwhelmed that they forgot to present their petition, and one lady fell over her long dress as she was trying to back out of the audience chamber. Francis Joseph never lost his nerve, however, and showed majestic understanding in such cases, at least according to the disseminators of such stories. But what else could he do with such oddities? Invitees dressed in accordance with a strict dress code. Women as a rule wore a black silk dress, gentlemen of a civil occupation either tails or, in Budapest, the Hungarian ceremonial attire. Everything was all sparkle and glitter and absolutely formal.

Public audiences dazzled visitors with the superficial pomp of the ruler's power, but they did not really reveal Francis Joseph's personality. The most they indicated was that the emperor and king was a lover of form. The meetings of senior politicians with His Majesty were more revealing of Francis Joseph the individual, however.

Those who wished to speak in Hungarian were free to do so, as were those who attended public audiences. Yet Hungarian politicians tended to speak German (with Ferenc Kossuth, the king initially spoke in Italian and French, then Kossuth switched to Hungarian and Francis Joseph to German, so that the dialogue was conducted on the principle of parity.) Not all senior Hungarian officials spoke good German. Francis Joseph even suggested to Dezső Bánffy that he speak in Hungarian: Bánffy replied, probably as a gesture of politeness: "Don't worry, Your Highness. It will be good for me to practice my German."

The manner of one's speech was also meaningful. As a rule one was expected to address Francis Joseph with humility. Dezső Szilágyi, the notedly hot-headed parliamentary debater and politician, who could easily destroy the arguments of his adversaries, visited the king on several occasions in his capacity as minister of justice. He could not always control his temper. Francis Joseph is known to have complained that he had the feeling that Szilágyi treated him in an off-hand manner! But this was not what caused the minister's downfall.

When not openly challenged, Francis Joseph treated the heads of his government according to their usefulness. (To remind readers, in 1866 Francis Joseph contemplated what use he could possibly make of Deák.) As long as government officials discharged their duties as he wished, even the likes of Kossuth's own son could become a minister. On the other hand, Francis Joseph had no qualms about getting rid of someone as soon as they became superfluous. It is typical that of all his Hungarian ministers Francis Joseph attended the funeral of Tivadar Pauler alone. Kálmán Tisza was not considered worthy of the same honor, and he did not get further than the bier of Andrássy. As both formalities and the king's behavior suggested, politicians were treated like senior subjects rather than as partners.

However, Francis Joseph did make a great impression as a private individual on those who had a feudal outlook and behaved accordingly. Among Hungarian politicians, Count Károly Khuen-Hédervári — the ban of Croatia since the 1880s, prime minister in 1903, and minister responsible for the king's person in 1904–1905 — was one of those who had a personal liking for the king. At the same time, Khuen was noted by Hungarian politicians for his narrow-minded authoritarianism and was unanimously disliked, even in his own party. Khuen was awarded the Golden Fleece and the Saint Stephen medal, and he deserved them, so diligently did he guard his king's interests against his own compatriots, who demanded an independent national bank and that Hungarian be the language of army command. At one session in the House of Representatives, Ferenc Rigó said something rude to the Hungarian prime minister concerning his mother and himself as a newborn baby. Newspapers reported laconically that the comment was not suitable for publication. Francis Joseph asked his faithful servant what Rigó had said. Khuen beat around the bush and only alluded to the nature of the slur. Francis Joseph replied in all seriousness: "You see! The Hungarian people always demand the impossible!" As minister of the interior in 1905, József Kristóffy said that "constitutional order has never managed to become rooted in Francis Joseph's soul." This was a matter not only of political principles, but also of human behavior.

The large-scale military exercises which were held several times a year were a real delight to Francis Joseph, bringing variety to his everyday routine. Francis Joseph rode his horse regularly until the age of eighty-four, and habitually exhausted up to three horses during a single military maneuver. On such occasions the emperor and king was in his element: although he tended to lose the wars waged during his reign, he nevertheless loved the army and military exercises offered him the comfort of feeling himself close to the main pillar of his empire. It is also interesting that he was willing from time to time to make short speeches to his soldiers in their mother tongue. As the reader will remember, in autumn 1848 Francis Joseph had addressed the Hungarian regiment fighting on the side of the Habsburgs in the Hungarian language. Francis Joseph was aware that his Hungarian soldiers understood enough German to grasp military commands, but they did not speak the language fluently; if he wanted to communicate something to them, he had to speak their mother tongue. It was a different proposition with officers, who all spoke German.

Officers had to take military exercises very seriously indeed: they could be punished by early retirement if they made a mistake during a maneuver. Francis Joseph's strength was not the knowledge of how to win wars but formal discipline, something which is probably partly explained by his incomplete education. Any officer whose soldiers appeared in a disorderly fashion or whose uniforms were not impeccable would be reprimanded. Hungarians had less affinity with the Josephinian ideal of a unified army, which was more of a source of conflict than of harmony.

If his personality had had any attractive aspects they would have best been demonstrated outside the political sphere, mostly on social occasions and at entertainments. Francis Joseph's favorite pastime since his youth was hunting: he owned one of the finest hunting grounds in the country, a present to him from the Hungarian people. Throughout his long life Francis Joseph made many kills, and his favorite was big game: he shot many chamois and deer. When he was hunting, Francis Joseph underwent a complete transformation, at least in his looks. He threw away his beloved uniform and put on a pair of short leather breeches (down to his knees) and a gray hunter's jacket.

He would put his hunter's hat on, and according to contemporary eye witnesses, would stalk the game with an almost childlike joy. He preferred stalking to more mechanical hunting with a pack. When stalking, at least he could feel that he was getting the game himself. It is interesting to read Ferenc Molnár's stories about Francis Joseph the hunter and to consider how he internalized this experience and whether or not it affected his personality. These stories are also a good barometer of the general mood regarding Francis Joseph.

I would like to describe here...in quite an objective way two anecdotes which a kind elderly man, who happened to be Francis Joseph's royal head keeper, told me some fifteen years ago. These anecdotes are to be valued for their rarity, because there are hardly any anecdotes about Francis Joseph in circulation. [This in itself expresses as much of a value judgment as any good anecdote—A. G.] For several decades this elderly man accompanied Francis Joseph on hunts across the extensive forests of Gödöllő. He was a loveable old Hungarian man with snow-white hair. No one knew the royal forest and its game stock better than he did.

The first story goes as follows: The hunting party was getting ready to set off. A two-horse open carriage had stopped outside the castle gates, waiting for the king. The old head keeper stood by the side of the carriage, his hat in his hand. His Majesty was on time. The head keeper bowed his head. His Majesty raised his hand to his hat, and sat inside the carriage. This was the signal that the head keeper had been waiting for and when the king was already comfortably seated, the head keeper placed his right foot on the hub of the front wheel in order to climb on the coach-box, next to the carriage driver. As soon as he had set his foot securely on the hub of the wheel, and his left foot had just been raised from the ground, leaving him hanging between earth and sky, His Majesty's voice rang out: "Why don't you come and sit with me?" The elderly gentleman got down, thanked Francis Joseph for the invitation, and got inside the carriage, facing the king on the jump seat. It went on like this year after year....so that the movements of the head keeper (stepping up on the hub of the wheel and stretching out his hand towards the carriage driver) became a mere formality, and these movements were always followed by the ceremonial invitation:" Why don't you come and sit with me?" As a natural consequence of this habit, the movements of the elderly head keeper lost some of their concentration, not to say sincerity and enthusiasm, as the years went by. A keen observer would have noticed that the head keeper only pretended that he was going to sit by the side of the carriage driver.

One day the following happened: The king got inside the carriage and Mr. R. played out the comic role of wanting to get on the coachbox, but his performance was not good enough. (Perhaps he was out of sorts that day.) In any case, although he had already placed his right foot on the hub of the wheel, he failed to align his left foot as quickly as he should have done and instead paused in that position for a second and waited for the invitation. Francis Joseph noticed. It was an uneasy thirty seconds: Francis Joseph did not utter a word. The head keeper began to sweat, feeling that he had lost the king's favor. As the invitation was not forthcoming, he finally decided to raise his left foot in the air, but it was already too late and the king remained silent. Mr. R. sat down next to the carriage driver and the carriage set off. After this incident, the head keeper was never invited to sit in the king's carriage again.

The other anecdote goes like this: His Majesty was going boar hunting, accompanied by his head keeper. There were just the two of them. The wild boar had their own established paths around Gödöllő. Fodder was always put out for them in the same place and at the same time, and thus they were taught to appear at these "feed stalls" with the regularity of a train service. Feeding stalls were placed not too far from each other. His Majesty would not start boar-hunting before the game had already been drilled and the head keeper had a reliable timetable at his disposal: indeed, the boar were referred to as the "3:20" boar, the "4:40" boar, and so on, indicating the likely time of their appearance.

So the king and his head keeper set off, and the poor "3:20" boar appeared by a bush precisely on schedule. The king fired a shot at him, but only wounded him. The wild boar stopped for a second and decided to charge at the king ferociously. It was a dangerous moment. The king's life was in danger. Mr. R. concluded his story by remarking: "I swear, we were close to having a new occupant of the throne!"—Recognizing the importance of the moment, the head keeper lifted his gun—faster than His Majesty could have fired another shot—and finished off the boar with a single well-directed shot. This was followed by a short silence: the head keeper sighed with relief and waited to be thanked. However, His Majesty, who had raised his gun to fire it, now slowly lowered it once again. He gave the head keeper a sharp look and said to him, clearly articulating every word: "Is it you or I who is being entertained here?"

The only lesson of this anecdote is that it is easier to change clothes than to change one's character. A king will remain the king even during hunting, even when he is dressed in short trousers.

Naturally, Francis Joseph was even more formal and identified with his role even more fully when he moved in court circles and participated in the entertainments that life at court could offer. The rigid formality of lunches at court was the result of a curious mix of etiquette and the king's own personality. As soon as the emperor and king finished his meal, the butlers would remove the plates from everyone else, too. And Francis Joseph was noted for eating quickly, not to say vigorously. He cared little about anyone else—perhaps this is not surprising given his penchant for eating alone. What is more, Francis Joseph was not a gourmand. Guests at these lunches more often than not stayed hungry, despite the lavish spread. The politician Béla Barabás, who attended such meals on a number of occasions, wrote: "The ceremonial feast would end at eight o'clock in the evening, and, having returned home from a pompous court lunch, I would enjoy my own dinner." The ceremonial nature of court lunches was designed to reinforce in participants a sense of being privileged, but not even that could bring them closer to their sovereign.

After lunch it was time for the usual "cercle": when the king stood up from table, guests moved to another room, where the king circulated among his guests, distinguishing those present with a remark or question. As a rule, he spent between one and five minutes with each person, along the following lines (as reported by Barabás): " 'Where are you from?' The answer: "Nagyvárad" (Oradea). The king's reply: 'What a busy city! I have heard so many good things about it'." That was more or less what the "cercle" amounted to.

The "cercle" was what made court balls worth attending: they gave people the opportunity to get closer to the sovereign as a private individual. But we must first make a distinction between a "court ball" and a "ball at the court": Francis Joseph was always careful to do so. Moreover, the Hungarian court was not even a court in the true sense of the word. It was a recurrent request—sometimes put more tentatively, sometimes more strongly—that a genuine Hungarian royal court be finally established, but Francis Joseph always rejected such requests. He probably thought that setting up a separate court for the Hungarian king would underline the principle of dualism within the Monarchy. His decision was certainly not motivated by the desire to save money: the Hungarian Parliament was more than generous, spending four times as much on their king per annum as on the Parliament (which consisted of over four hundred MPs), not to mention the Upper House. But the nation's generosity was in vain: Francis Joseph did not want a Hungarian court. Instead, he appointed to Budapest a number of court officials who officially reported to the steward of the royal household in Vienna. Around the time of the Millennium, a Hungarian lord chamberlain's office was created, headed by Court Counselor Aladár Szegedy-Maszák, but it never achieved the status of the Viennese steward of the royal household.

Francis Joseph considerably extended and improved the Buda Castle, but he did not want a separate court there. From a strictly legal point of view, the balls held at the Castle were given by the Hungarian king, under the auspices of the imperial lord chamberlain's office. Invitees to these balls, on the other hand, were not the kind of people who would vehemently protest against such details. A "court ball" was for a more select audience than a "ball at the court." Balls usually started at 8:00 P.M. and lasted until midnight. The king (and the royal family) would be present from 9:00 P.M. to 11:15 P.M. at the latest. The king would not omit the usual "cercle," and sometimes he even danced. In any case, he never talked very much. As already remarked upon, his utterances and questions were fairly standard: both types of ball were quite formal and did not strive to make guests feel relaxed. The same may be said about so-called "court festivities," the only difference being that the latter did not include dancing. Court festivities were meant to provide an opportunity for making an appearance, creating an imposing visual impression, and had little to do with creating a relaxed atmosphere: we might mention the archers of the Hungarian king—the arciere—the Trabant Guards, butlers, festive lights, the glittering crowd of finely dressed people. The list could be continued. In sum, none of these occasions was really suitable for getting close to the king as a private individual: balls were held for the sake of social display, and in that sense they served their purpose well: everything was as rigid and precise as the king himself.

The king was much the same in all situations, whether he was working or enjoying himself: he was not charming or given to delivering "bons mots." He had neither the personality nor the charm with which to ease the ambivalent feelings which the Hungarian people had towards him. Even so, he managed to "get along" somehow. The external manifestations of his rule, the feeling of social exclusivity which went with being associated with him, and his political actions created enough leverage with Hungarian politicians to persuade them to obey Francis Joseph's will. Besides, as we have seen, Francis Joseph never sought popularity; he was not the kind of person who valued social attention. All he wanted was to rule and that he did; he did not need to be a "personality." His acquired values were at odds with any notion of impressing his subjects with his personal aura. He believed that if the throne shone brightly the sovereign would be a remarkable man by virtue of that alone. Had he not been so rigidly formal and ceremonial, Francis Joseph would have been a modern king rather than the traditional king he was, a relic of a previous age. Under these circumstances, it is not surprising that he was such an uneasy talker, and that he did not know how to be ironic or sarcastic. In his world there was no room for a conversation between equals, and nothing could be more dangerous than sarcasm likely to undermine one's authority.

Francis Joseph remained true to himself, and did everything, at work and at play, with incredible energy and perseverance. He attended so many functions and had to exchange remarks with his subjects on so many occasions that it is not surprising Francis Joseph mostly expressed himself in stereotypes that sounded over-formal to the average ear and sometimes even made the aging king look somewhat simple-minded. To illustrate, here is a story from 1896 about the Millennium celebrations. The king was visiting the Millennium Exhibition, which featured, among other things, a model village representing Hungary's various regions and peoples in order to show the visitor how multifaceted the country was. The king was accompanied by Baron Ernő Dániel, the minister of trade. When they caught sight of the village, Francis Joseph asked his minister: "Is this a village?" "Yes, Your Highness." The king continued, "Well, let's see it." The village huts came complete with peasants dressed in the traditional style of the region they represented, who greeted visitors as live exhibits. Francis Joseph turned to one of them: "Are you from these parts?" to which the peasant replied, "I am, but thank God, Your Highness, only while the Millennium (celebrations) last, and then I can go home".

Another Millennium story was reported by *Fővárosi Lapok*. On 6 June, Francis Joseph ceremonially laid the foundation stone of the extension to the Royal Palace. The foundation stone incorporates a document written on parchment and signed by Francis Joseph himself, an act for which the inkpot was held by Alajos Hauszmann, the architect of the new palace wing.

Then the king walked up to the architectural committee and a group of builders, addressing Nándor Holtzspach first: "Am I right in assuming that you started building the palace from the bottom up?" He replied: "Yes, Your Highness." In response to which the king remarked: "Well, I'm sure it must have been hard work."

Clichéd questions and clichéd answers. Similar remarks, which received great publicity via the press, inspired Jenő Heltai to write a poem. Heltai simply recalled Francis Joseph's utterances during his visit to the Millennium Exhibition, particularly in the pavilion demonstrating the development of the printing industry. The poem is entitled "The King's Visit to the Hall of Poetry."

As the king entered through the big gate,
Dr. Miksa Falk made a fine speech,
He declared in raptures,
That this was a hall of poetry.

"Nice, nice, very nice"—His Highness said—
"That we now have a pavilion for this at last.
You do make poetry here, don't you?"
"Let's ask someone," Falk said.

"You mean all those people sitting over there looking so gloomy?"
"They are poets, Your Highness, if you please."
"And who inspires them?"
"The Muse, Your Highness," Falk told him.

How delighted the Muse was, oh, how delighted!
His Highness had gracefully smiled on her
And asked: "Has this factory been here long?
Have you exported anything yet?"

These lines, characterized by a particular brazenness, contain a fair amount of covert criticism of Francis Joseph's insensitivity to the arts. He was noted for his preference for bucolic idylls and military scenes, and, as already mentioned, he had difficulty appreciating Shakespeare's dramas. For Francis Joseph, his character, values, and rank formed an integral whole. Consequently, he had difficulty relating to the outside world on anything like equal terms. He could not accept alternative ways of thinking, and he did not even try. Instead, Francis Joseph tried to impose his own vision on the world. Whenever he was forced to come face to face with private and historical modes of thinking different from his own, he experienced it as a crisis. Only very strong external pressure could make him accept—though never understand—differences, whether about politics, the family, or his relationships with other people. Even when such differences did not really matter, Francis Joseph usually did not see the comic side of the situation and was therefore unable to help the other person relax. Here is another story to illustrate this point.

Ever since the 1848 Revolution, Francis Joseph had been extremely irritated by demonstrations and unrest. Whenever he was informed of such demonstrations, he usually took an exaggerated interest in the problem. Francis Joseph assumed that his own way of thinking—or unstated expectations—were shared by others. The Secretary to the

Budapest City Council Ferenc Harrer reports an incident in 1906 which involved István Bárczy, whom he knew quite well:

> During one of the king's visits, a famous incident happened with Bárczy, who welcomed Francis Joseph in his capacity as deputy mayor. The king's visit to Budapest coincided with a workers' protest. When, a few days later, the king arrived at the railway station, on his way back to Vienna, the first question he addressed to Bárczy, who was seeing him off was: "Has it broken up yet?"
>
> At first, Bárczy did not understand the question, and, as it was December, he assumed that the question related to the thawing of the ice, and so he replied: "Not yet, Your Highness." Obviously bewildered, the king left him. It was only then that Bárczy realized that the king's question must have referred to the workers' demonstration.

Only a sense of humor could have eased the tension of such situations, but Francis Joseph did not have one. Instead, he had an almost pathological urge to express himself in terms of clichés, which sometimes made him look narrow-minded. We must therefore be careful not to trust appearances entirely: Francis Joseph was no fool, but he did find it difficult to free himself from the constraints of his own character. Furthermore, the somewhat absurd harmony—at least from the contemporary point of view—of Francis Joseph's character was a very strange, even obsolete reflection of the historical status quo. Francis Joseph, if he had ever somehow come to see himself as an exhibit, would probably have remarked, as he usually did on such occasions: "Everything is very nice; everything is very good; and I like everything."

Chapter Seven

OUR FATHER KOSSUTH, PRINCE REZSŐ, "FERENC JÓSKA" AND ELIZABETH OF BAVARIA

Francis Joseph's personality was totally unsuited to resolve the politically and historically motivated ambivalence of the Hungarian people. The king was viewed as a man of average intellect combined with an extraordinary sense of duty, discipline, and ambition, a rigid personality devoid of humor or charm, and cursed with poor conversational skills. His personal deficiencies were compounded for Hungarians by memories of an unpleasant past and the fact that they would have to put up with him until the day he died.

Was there any possibility of resolving this situation? And if so, by what means?

Ever since the awakening of their national consciousness during the Age of Reform, the Hungarian people had subconsciously sought a patron in the Habsburg dynasty as some form of alliance with it seemed ever more inevitable. The reader will probably remember that in 1847 Francis Joseph and Palatine Stephen had "competed" for recognition as pro-Hungarians, or had at least created that impression. But it quickly turned out that the concept of a pro-Hungarian Habsburg was no more than an illusion. From the mid-1860s, Queen Elizabeth gradually came to take on the psychological role which, with the death of Palatine Joseph, had been left unfilled.

In order to appreciate this psychological need fully, the traditional loyalty of the peasantry to the sovereign on the basis of the belief

In order to appreciate this psychological need fully, the traditional loyalty of the peasantry to the sovereign on the basis of the belief that he was their chief patron and protector against the nobility must be understood. The events of 1848–49, the Compromise, and the combination of national with social grievances did great damage to this native faith but did not altogether remove the yearning for a father figure.

In the popular consciousness, Lajos Kossuth came to replace the king as the father with a strict but fair hand. This was not altered by the fact that, after 1849, Governor Kossuth had no effective political influence over the lives of the peasantry; he continued to be known as "our Father Kossuth" until the end of his long life and even afterwards. It is a fair assumption that this yearning for a father figure would have faded had Hungary's history taken a more democratic turn, if, in other words, the events of 1848–49 had come to a successful conclusion. If Kossuth's political program had been implemented, there would have been no need for a Kossuth myth to comfort a defeated nation. That Hungary took a very different course can partly be blamed on Francis Joseph.

At the same time, faith in the king continued to a limited extent, partly as a matter of tradition and partly in view of the fact that the sovereign legitimately enjoyed considerable powers. Legitimacy was an important consideration, given that the Hungarian intelligentsia, which had controlled the consciousness of the masses, had founded its entire political program upon legitimacy and the rule of law (they even called the events of 1848–49 a war of self-defense). In light of this, the sovereign could not be banished form the national consciousness merely because of any personal deficiencies he might have or because he constituted a foreign power.

It is a commonly recognized phenomenon in mass psychology that in societies where the top of the social and political hierarchy is beyond the reach of the ordinary citizen, the latter seeks somehow to bridge the gap. In Hungary the masses projected certain habits, views, and attitudes of their own onto the figure of the sovereign and then onto Kossuth, who was generally accepted as leader of the nation. The perception of a resemblance, however illusory, between the common people and their leader has a reassuring effect, indicating that the latter is as human as we are; in turn, we must somehow resemble our superior, and on this basis have good reason to consider ourselves higher up the ladder than we really are. In this way the masses can approach what otherwise would be entirely inaccessible to them. This phenomenon is also exploited by authoritarian regimes: an otherwise comprehensively repressed society is furnished with self-esteem with no risk of rebellion.

With this in mind we should find it easier to disentangle the complex threads of social and political philosophy which underlay the acceptance or rejection of Francis Joseph.

Francis Joseph's personality and political image were out of step with the world view of the Hungarian peasantry, among whom the Kossuth myth flourished. Although the image created for him by official propaganda resembled that of Matthias Corvinus, Hungary's renaissance king, famous for his sense of justice and concern for the lower orders, there is no indication that a Francis Joseph cult ever got off the ground. Nevertheless, József Kristóffy insisted in 1905:

> After the lesson of 1849 this nation will never again rise against Your Royal Highness or your successors....The Hungarian peasant cannot be incited [to fight against the king] because in his eyes the king is the supreme "overseer" whose assistance he in needs greatly: the king is there to keep an eye on state officials and to protect [the peasant] against their depredations, should it prove necessary.

Kristóffy's appeal to the people's faith in the king notwithstanding, by the time it was written Francis Joseph was no longer perceived as the nation's all-powerful protector. Nevertheless, the desire for a Habsburg ruler possessing Hungarian national feeling and a Hungarian temperament remained.

If the object of this desire was not Francis Joseph, who was it to be? The choice fell on Archduke Rudolf, whose image was transformed into that of a folk hero. Lajos Kiss, the renowned ethnographer, includes the following Rudolf legend in his Hódmezővásárhely collection:

> I was an eight-year-old schoolboy when Rudolf died. Coming from a poor family, I heard many legends about him both at home

and elsewhere, about his death, life, disappearance, and wander-
ings. Of the more typical stories I recall the following:

As soon as news of Rudolf's death spread throughout the country, rumor had it that his father had killed him because of
[Rudolf's] great love for the Hungarian people—Rudolf was
every inch a true Hungarian. When he wished to amuse himself
he would order a gypsy to play Hungarian music for him on the violin. His favorite songs were: "I Had a Mother Once" and "Lajos
Kossuth's Message Reads" [a popular song among Hungarian rev-
olutionaries in their fight against the Austrians (!)]. He could also
see through his father's ministers.

One day, Rudolf led a very fat horse out of the stable and when
his father asked why, he answered: "This is how fat your ministers
are." Then a horse which was all skin and bones was dragged
before them. "And this is your poor nation." Finally, a blind horse
was led out. "And this is you, father, because you have no eyes for
the nation's misery and for the fact that the great ones are parasites
on your people." These are the kinds of things that made his father
angry with him.

Rudolf was perceived as the ideal prince: social justice and national feeling personified. And he was a Habsburg, which legitimized him
both nationally and socially. For all these reasons Francis Joseph had
him assassinated. What popular opinion could not find in its king, it
had to find somewhere else.

It is, of course, not true that Francis Joseph had his son murdered:
we know that in 1889 Rudolf committed suicide. But it was common
knowledge that he and his father did not get along: Francis Joseph's
insensitivity and rigid adherence to the law of matrimony (Rudolf
wanted a divorce) did not help to resolve their conflicts. The
Hungarian people's dislike of Francis Joseph naturally led them to an
affinity for Rudolf, regardless of his personal merits. It is significant
that the news of Rudolf's death was not believed for a long time. The
following is another story from Hódmezővásárhely:

During the First World War Rudolf again became the subject of
much talk. Even those who at first listened with suspicion later

came to the conclusion that he was alive. Some even claimed to know where he was:

Of course, Rudolf has been wandering ever since his mother died, and he has been wandering in America. He did not tell his father how he was getting on or where he was, but as soon as the war broke out he telegraphed: "Do you need me?" His father replied: "Since we have managed without you until now, no doubt we will get through this by our own efforts. But if you want to, you may come."

In the nation's imagination, the good prince had either to die or go wandering—and all because of his father's malevolence. The king could not endure Rudolf's genuine Hungarian spirit, love of the Hungarian people, and good heart. This was partly in praise of Rudolf and partly a criticism of Francis Joseph. Prince Rezső (as Rudolf's name was Hungarianized), the heir to the throne, and his father were considered polar opposites; from which comparison Francis Joseph came off very much second best.

But how can this be reconciled with the familiar patriarchal Hungarian name, Ferenc Jóska, which was widely used in reference to Francis Joseph: surely this nickname indicates some degree of affection for him? The name Ferenc Jóska is partly of folk origin—it figures in the songs of regular soldiers in the Austro-Hungarian Army, but in a particular context. The following lines come from the literary periodical *Magyar Szalon*, in 1892:

In Ferenc Jóska's courtyard there is a pond
A Hungarian hussar fell into it on his horse
The horse's leg is being looked after by the chief vet
But the poor hussar is not lamented by anyone.

Or:

When Ferenc Jóska mounts his horse
He remembers the times when he was a recruit
He wipes the tears from his eyes
But how much does a hussar have to suffer?

He freezes in a riding school in the winter
And he gets soaking wet in the camp in the summer.

It would be difficult to discover a trace of warmth in these passages, even with the help of the most ingenious methods of textual
analysis. The name is adapted to fit comfortably in a patriarchal peasant's world view, but its bearer is associated with feelings of suffering
and defenselessness, and a world in which a horse receives more care
and attention than a human being who frequently risks his life for his
king. At the same time, other army songs—faithful to the spirit of the
joint army—feature Francis Joseph as the king and emperor. What
could be the relationship between a Hungarian peasant boy and the
emperor, one might ask?

While the name "Ferenc Jóska" is undoubtedly familiar it does not
express the Hungarian people's willingness to accept its bearer. On the
contrary, these songs express the incommensurable distance between
the regular soldier and his supreme commander. The familiar patriarchal name could only attempt to bridge this distance, it could not
reduce it.

"Ferenc Jóska" was much in use among the middle classes. It did
not refer to the king himself, but designated a kind of *jacket de rigueur*
for distinguished social occasions. Wearing the "ferencjóska" meant
being presentable in "good society." This was a peculiar form of
adjustment to the manners of the higher social classes: by wearing the
frockcoat or "ferencjóska" a Hungarian gentleman set himself apart
from his inferiors and claimed kinship with those above him. Such kinship was an illusion. In the Imperial Court the frockcoat would not
have been considered presentable at all (in such elevated circles tails
or festive hussar dress were the norm). My point is that the clothes one
wears are one way of laying claim to a particular social status. Because
the claimed status was in this case entirely imaginary it was sufficient
that the name of the relevant garment had some connection, however
tenuous, with the king. Most of those who proudly donned the "ferencjóska" could not expect much more: apart from the fact that they
could not afford tails or festive hussar dress, they were never invited
to social occasions where they would have been required. By this "turn

of phrase" the king is presented as a member of the petty bourgeoisie, someone who uses Jewish jargon, plays cards for small stakes and who reads the same newspapers as his fellows. No one seemed to care that this illusion had little in common with reality. On the contrary: even the highest political circles were not averse to circulating such obvious nonsense for the simple reason that in this way the king at least emerged as a flesh and blood creature.

The petty bourgeoisie was the social stratum where, if anywhere, patriarchal feelings for the king could be found. For members of this class it was vital to keep well informed about everything concerning the sovereign, including a catarrh and anything else that which might point to similarities between the great lord and his faithful vassals. It appears to be a thrilling experience for some to discover that even the greatest and most powerful of men are vulnerable human beings. Béla Barabás, an independent MP not devoid of petty-bourgeois sentiments himself, counted it among the most touching memories of his life when the sovereign called Elizabeth of Bavaria "a feleségem" (Hungarian for "my wife") in his presence. It meant that a wife was only a wife even in the royal family.

As we have seen some social classes tended to mold the king in their own image: the peasantry rejected him and transformed his son into a folk hero, while the petty bourgeoisie found relief in making the king into the very model of a philistine.

The gentry was more ambivalent; for them, the king was the object of both total loyalty and total rejection. When a party of "gentlemen" had had a few too many one of them would always ask the gypsy violinist to play a "bawdy" song in the spirit of the extract below:

Oh, the German is a crafty one
Why doesn't the devil eat
His lungs and liver
As well as his rib [Hungarian slang term for "wife"].

Nevertheless, another member of the party would almost certainly invite his fellows to drink to the king's health as soon as the song had finished and everyone would join in shouting "Long live the king!"

The bourgeoisie seemed to have a double consciousness: one minute they would pose as the champions of Hungarian national resistance, and the next they would stick out their chests in the front row of a delegation welcoming their foreign overlord. For many there appeared no contradiction in hanging the portraits of both Francis Joseph and Lajos Kossuth next to each other. They declared their loyalty to the king of Hungary, but were unwilling to give up the 1848 spirit of resistance. When there was a political crisis, nothing was simpler than to utter the "magic words"—as was often done among parties of friends as described by Miklós Bánffy's portrait of the period entitled *Megszámláltattál* [the title is a quotation from the Bible, literally: "to have been measured and found too light"]—"The old executioner must be sacked from the Castle, and have done with it!" Too many words seldom result in action. But even this kind of patriotism consolidated the emotional rejection of the sovereign; those who set the tone had to find someone else onto whom what the king lacked could be projected.

The choice eventually fell upon Elizabeth of Bavaria, a royal figure with a history as the protector of the Hungarian people during the years of absolutism. Her role in bringing about the Compromise was also emphasized and much made of her supposed love for Hungary. Elizabeth already had her own political and psychological cult before Rudolf came to be blessed in the same manner. To an attitude fundamentally oriented towards the past it seemed quite obvious to return again and again to something that had already been widely circulated in newspaper articles and oral tradition and so to heighten further the nation's sympathy for Elizabeth. And Elizabeth was sensitive enough to seek to confirm such expectations by subtle signs of favor. After the Compromise she continued to appear grateful for Hungary's regard for her. Probably one of her most frequently quoted remarks was addressed to the writer Mór Jókai in 1873, words the Hungarian press ensured would go down in history: "Here [in Hungary] one feels eternally free."

Those gazing through red-white-and-green spectacles and dreaming of a dynasty with Hungarian sympathies were entirely won over, discovering in this sentence infallible proof that Elizabeth adored

Hungary, the Hungarian people and, unlike her husband the king, would not keep her sentiments a secret. Unfortunately, a letter written by the queen to her mother from Gödöllő in Hungary reveals a more prosaic reality: "Here, far away from relatives and free from harassment, one is so free, whereas there [in Vienna] one is surrounded by the whole imperial family. Here no one disturbs me, as if I were living in a village where I can come and go as I please."

But the Hungarian people were not looking to understand Elizabeth; their sole desire was to integrate her in their own world view. Indeed, as time went on the Hungarian people professed to discover ever more similarities between their own plight and that of the queen. Elizabeth was unable to break her alliance with her husband any more than the Hungarian nation could. At the same time, she, like the Hungarian people, would not simply abandon him. But Elizabeth's increasingly frequent travels without her husband and her separate agenda seemed to indicate that, again like the Hungarian people, she would leave him if she could. On top of everything else Elizabeth was a beautiful woman, ever the potential object of tender feelings. National feeling combined loyalty, chivalry, and admiration directed at Elizabeth and rejection of Francis Joseph. Elizabeth surrounded herself with Hungarian maids and minded not at all being known in Western Europe as the "Hungarian woman." But her true love was less the Hungarian people than her independence; less Hungarian soil as such than Gödöllő, where she could "come and go as she pleased" and indulge her passion for horseriding. Sándor Márki, the queen's biographer, calculated that Elizabeth spent not much more than seven years in Hungary (114 days before 1867 and the remainder in the period between 1867 and her death in 1898). In the 44 years of her married life the queen was to be found six times as often outside Hungary as within it, though between 1868 and 1897 not a year went by without her visiting Hungary at least once. Perhaps more significant is the fact that all but sixty-nine days of her time in Hungary were spent in Gödöllő and Budapest. Márki wrote:

> She spent five weeks in Mehádia (1887) and four and a half weeks in Bártfa (1895); she once visited Zagreb and Fiume, but

otherwise never entertained herself in Hungary [outside Gödöllő and Budapest], the natural beauty of which interested her so little that she traveled through Transylvania for the first time on a night express train (on 17 April 1887) and passed by the High Tatra Mountains in such bad weather (on 23 July 1895) that she could not see a thing. She never made the visit to Balatonfüred [a lake resort] which she had always planned nor to Kovászna.

Elizabeth, an enthusiastic traveler, was little interested in Hungary. Public duty summoned her to Budapest on several occasions, but she felt at home only at her palace in Gödöllő, a gift from the Hungarian people. Elizabeth's memory still survives there. In many stories Elizabeth inspires sympathy because of her unfair treatment at the hands of her husband. Cecília Szekeres's 1987 collection includes the following anecdote told by an eighty-year-old peasant:

> And Francis Joseph was a great villain, you know. "Jóska," as the old man called him, would sneak out every night while they were staying here to visit a peasant maid. He was such a greedy man. The queen could not complain about this, though maybe she was glad he left her alone....

(Whatever credence might be given to this story, it nevertheless hints at the real relationship of the king and queen.) Elizabeth emerged as a role model for the Hungarian gentry having done almost nothing to deserve the honor.

In what follows we would like to single out two minor details to illustrate the extent to which the Elizabeth cult became a mass psychological phenomenon.

In 1889, the Lower House of Parliament was in turmoil over the new defense act. The opposition had organized a twenty-thousand-strong demonstration against the proposal to make the rank of army officer dependent upon the possession of a language certificate in German. Many banners bore the inscription: "Long live Lajos Kossuth!" while the masses shouted "Long live the king!" at the same time demanding that the relevant passage of the act—included at the king's express wish—be withdrawn. The demonstration culminated at Francis

Joseph Square, in front of the Lloyd Building which housed the governing party's club. The journalist Mór Szatmári, an eyewitness, described the events as follows:

> The crowd turned to face the Royal Palace and thousands of hats were waved in the air. The king was hailed. Then the human river moved onto the Corso [a promenade by the Danube], every flag was lowered towards the Royal Buda Palace and the words were taken up by everyone: "Long live the king!
> I wonder whether Francis Joseph I was watching? I doubt it. But whether he was or not this was the climax of the whole demonstration as the protesting masses paid tribute to the Hungarian king. All eyes were fixed on the palace windows: will any of them open? Is there someone behind them?
> Suddenly a murmur began to circulate in the crowd: a white female hand had been seen waving a white handkerchief from one of the windows. There was no doubt that both hand and handkerchief belonged to Queen Elizabeth. Hundreds confirmed aloud that they too had seen the white handkerchief. In fact, no one had seen anything. Patriotic fantasies and the crowd's auto-suggestion were at play. But the legend grew and so did the number of those who believed in it.

The myth undisturbed by facts continued to live and thrive. In 1894, Kossuth died and his ashes were laid to rest in Hungarian soil. A crowd of a hundred thousand paid their last respects to Francis Joseph's great antagonist. The government was not officially represented at the funeral: the Prime Minister Dezső Bánffy, claimed to have urgent matters to attend to. Ordinary Hungarians naturally sought to satisfy both sides of their split consciousness. They wished to find similarities between Kossuth's funeral and that of Ferenc Deák eighteen years before. At Deák's funeral, though the king had excused himself, Elizabeth paid her respects at the catafalque and Kossuth, then in exile, sent cypress boughs to the funeral of his former comrade and the godfather of his eldest son, their conflicting views on the Compromise notwithstanding. The fact that the king and the government had chosen not to pay their respects while the whole nation mourned their

"Father" might have had serious consequences had the story not got around that among the many thousands of wreathes lay one dispatched in secret by Queen Elizabeth, who—in defiance of her husband—positively admired Kossuth, the hero of the Hungarian Revolution and War of Liberation, who had emerged as its symbol. Elizabeth's wreath served as clear proof that it was possible both to serve Francis Joseph and to feel an affinity with Kossuth, at least symbolically.

The fact is that Queen Elizabeth had not sent a wreath, nor had she waved a white handkerchief. But this is beside the point. The cult of Queen Elizabeth was needed to reconcile the deep-seated ambivalence inevitably brought into being by historical conditions and it must be said that she "played her role" well as the personification of qualities that, in reality, she lacked quite as much as her husband.

Just as the peasant consciousness had framed Rudolf's suicide to its own liking, so the consciousness of the gentry presented the death of Elizabeth, suggesting she had been murdered. Two years after the queen's death Gyula Gábel published a book in her honor, including the memories of members of the Habsburg dynasty and outstanding Hungarian public figures which clearly reveal the extent of the mythology surrounding the queen's person. Some of these stories could not have been openly discussed before, not because it was forbidden but because while Elizabeth was alive the facts of her life too obviously belied them.

The pearl of the writings dedicated to the national cult of Queen Elizabeth was a poem by Lajos Pósa entitled "The Queen's Dream" [A királyné álma], of which the following is an extract:

What was the dream, our good queen,
That you saw in your crypt in Vienna?
"I dreamt I was back at home
In my beautiful Hungary.

I dreamt there was heavy rainfall:
Not from the drizzly skies,
But from the sad eyes
Of my faithful Hungarian people."

In accordance with Habsburg custom Elizabeth was buried in Vienna. Later in the poem the tears of the sad Hungarian people grow into a sea which penetrates the crypt, lifts up the coffin, and carries it back to Hungary to rest, for which in the last line of the poem the poet asks the blessing of God.

After her death Hungary became Elizabeth's undisputed homeland, and it appears to be grateful for the privilege: a number of posthumous memorials and statues were erected to Elizabeth. (The first, in Felsőmuzsa, dates back to 1899.) In 1932, after many vicissitudes, the Elizabeth Memorial was finally completed from donations that started to come in soon after her murder. "If her tomb must be in Vienna, she must at least have her statue in Budapest, the city that she so dearly loved," wrote *Vasárnapi Újság* eight days after the assassination. (Today the statue—by György Zala—stands at the Buda head of the Danube bridge named after her.)

Elizabeth's undoubtedly attractive person became the object of a national cult largely because of the ambivalent relationship between Francis Joseph and the Hungarian people, which still cherishes her memory and the faith it has invested in her to the present day.

Prince Rezső, Ferenc Jóska, Elizabeth, "our Father Kossuth": these were the nation's solutions to the ambivalence aroused by Francis Joseph.

Chapter Eight
"FRANCIS JOSEPH HAS SENT WORD..."

National consciousness successfully sought out the character traits it needed for the resolution of its inner tensions (and in people whose real personalities were in fact quite different). But was there, during Francis Joseph's long reign, even one moment when king and nation fully identified with one another? In other words, did the Hungarian people ever manage to strike an emotional chord with its king in the political sphere?

Concord of this kind is created when a king does something to satisfy a general national desire. In the case of Francis Joseph there was bound to be something alarming about this: as we have seen, Francis Joseph by his very nature was incapable of becoming a nationally-minded king. However, those seeking to heal the split in the Hungarian national consciousness were excited by the possibility that the king might be able to do something to encourage the nation to attach itself to the Hungarian monarch. If the king were to satisfy some national aspiration or other, the result might be that exaggerated enthusiasm and acceptance would become universal and unchallengeable. On the other hand, if he failed in this respect the result might be an exaggerated negative reaction. On the basis of both scenarios the danger existed that national interests would be lost sight of, as people mistook a part for the whole. Some sort of emotional identification between king and subjects, however tenuous, was at best bound to end in disappointment, but might also turn into tragedy.

The basic tone of Hungarian national feeling had been set by the events of 1848–49, in terms of both positive and negative emotions, although the intellectual elite of the nobility during the Age of Reform also had some influence: their formulations acquired substance in 1848–49, but with a far wider social impact.

Anti-Russian attitudes were axiomatic for progressive thinking during the Hungarian Age of Reform. This was not inspired by a dislike of the Russian people or of Russian culture, but by the recognition that tsarist Russia was an enemy of liberal progress and that Russian expansion directly threatened Hungary. Hungarian liberals supported the anti-Russian Polish uprising in the early 1830s. Kölcsey, Deák, and Kossuth all believed that Russia, "the northern colossus," threatened Europe with its chains and that so many Poles had been killed that a bridge could be built from their bodies long enough to connect with the more civilized parts of Europe. Russia was feared as it "extended the iron rod of its autocracy over one-sixth of the known world." But the liberal position was not the only available alternative: national conservative politicians were also worried by Russia. As the liberal politician Pál Felsőbüki Nagy put it: "we are watching our frontiers with due concern: along three-quarters of our border a new power has suddenly made an appearance, which some years ago we knew only from afar."

The worries of the Hungarian people were not without foundation. In 1831 Russia had sent its troops against Poland, and the general who occupied Warsaw was Paskevich, whose name Hungarians were to learn in 1849. And although the Russians did not subjugate the object of their 1849 occupation, turning it into a province, their intervention brought about the collapse of everything that the Hungarian people had been fighting for. Anti-Russian feeling grew out of the real-political recognition of a narrow circle and into a basic emotion of a whole people.

After 1867 the concerns of pro-Compromise Hungarian politicians were reinforced by a new development: they were concerned that Russia would assume the role of powerful protector of Hungary's Slav minorities and would assist them in breaking up historical Hungary. Recognition of the Pan-Slav danger headed by Russia was another acute cause of anti-Russian feelings. Count Gyula Andrássy, the Hungarian politician who rose to the position of foreign minister of the empire, never gave up hope of uniting the empire in the anti-

Russian cause. This finally took place in 1878. The Russian–Turkish war broke out in 1877, and by the following year the Russians had advanced as far as the gates of Constantinople. The English navy was called into action since it was a basic British interest that Russia be prevented from taking control of the Dardanelles. Russian victory in the Balkans heralded the danger of Slav nationalist movements which could have unforeseeable consequences for the Austro-Hungarian Monarchy, among others. Andrássy suggested war with Russia. He thought that with assistance from Europe, the Monarchy could resolve its problems with the Slavs. It was a unique opportunity. However, Andrássy's proposal was supported only by Kálmán Tisza, the Hungarian prime minister.

Tisza knew that in Hungary a pro-Turkish, i. e., anti-Russian position would arouse unanimous and enthusiastic support. University students in Budapest had held large-scale demonstrations in support of the Turks as early as 1876, during the Serbian–Turkish (indirectly a Russian–Turkish) conflict. On 5 October 1876, twelve thousand people went onto the streets. Students presented a decorative sword to the head of the Turkish army, Abdul Kerim. They even made up a song: "Abdul Kerim has sent word." By way of thanks, the Turkish sultan returned part of the Corvina library to the Hungarian nation. (Ironically, the codices were returned to Vienna.) Ignác Szabadi-Frank composed a pro-Turkish march which was played on every suitable occasion. A delegation of Hungarian students to Constantinople was reciprocated by the visit of a Turkish delegation. Kossuth wrote polemical letters against Russian expansion. In turn, negative responses to the Hungarian demonstrations included pro-Russian demonstrations in Zagreb to the accompaniment of the Russian national anthem.

Tisza could see that this represented a unique opportunity to turn public opinion towards support for the Monarchy and Francis Joseph, provided that the king accepted Andrássy's proposal. The crisis was resolved when, Russia was forced to back off by diplomatic pressure, and the Monarchy occupied Bosnia-Herzegovina. This step was extremely unpopular in Hungary, where protests were held, against it, and the fallen Hungarian troops were commemorated. Occupation—the result of an agreement between the Great Powers—could well become annexation one day, the legal basis for which was provided by the Hungarian Crown. Bosnia-Herzegovina was brought under the authority of the joint Austro-Hungarian Ministry of Finance by right of the Hungarian Crown and the coronation oath.

Consequently, the great reconciliation of Hungarian king and Hungarian people did not take place in 1877–78, thus delaying the great disappointment which would probably have followed.

What did not happen in 1877–78 was finally accomplished in 1914. In Sarajevo, the capital of the annexed province, a Serb student assassinated the heir to the Austrian throne, Francis Ferdinand, and his wife Sofia. Hungarian public opinion had little use for the archduke, who wanted to reorganize the Monarchy counter to Hungarian interests and made no secret of his anti-Hungarian feelings. The archduke also disliked Francis Joseph, as the emperor and king had excluded Ferdinand's children from succession to the throne—Ferdinand had married below his rank—under the rules of *Pragmatica Sanctio*, which he enforced mercilessly.

The Monarchy declared war on Serbia, which amounted to declaring war on Russia, Serbia's ally. In Hungary, enthusiasm was abundant. Pro-government and opposition politicians, peasants and their masters all shared the same joy. All of a sudden, everything looked so simple. The nation was in raptures about its king, who was suddenly discovered to be growing old. Since an old man cannot be left to face trouble alone, at last the nation felt that their king would have to seek their assistance. Legitimacy, loyalty to the king, and the human reaction of not wanting to leave an old man in the lurch were all combined with the help of anti-Serbian and anti-Russian attitudes. Ordinary people had no idea what war was all about, however. The last time the Monarchy had been involved in major military action was in 1866, and time had dulled memories. The Bosnian occupation had taken place thirty-six years previously, and had not required large numbers of soldiers. It was generally believed that the military action would amount to little more than a military exercise during which the Serbians and the Russians would be taught a lesson by the Hungarian hussars. The king, a kind and wise old man, after all, knew what he was doing; he had thought everything out carefully. Nothing could dampen the enthusiasm.

In such a situation, with feelings running so high, it was possible to use a particular segment of national feeling to create an entire national ethos. While in 1848 the song had been "Lajos Kossuth Has Sent Word," and in 1878, for want of a better person and to considerably fewer people, it was "Abdul Kerim Has Sent Word." Now, in 1914, it was "Francis Joseph Has Sent Word."

This was also the title of a play by Árpád Pásztor, staged in the autumn of 1914. The play was written in a new style and expressed sincere zeal for war in the form of enthusiastic verse and songs. One was dedicated to István Tisza, prime minister of the country about to enter the universal conflagration:

> Until now Count Tisza was always met with cries of "Down with him!"
> "Down with him!" was the response to the spirits tax.
> To everything that was black-and-yellow,
> And to the Hungarian referent.

In contrast, today:

> "Long live Count Tisza" resounds throughout the land,
> "Long live the army," "long live the Austrian people!"
> What a miracle has happened,
> This is war, *das ist der Krieg*.

Another song was dedicated to Francis Joseph expressing true affection and filial devotion:

> Ferenc Jóska stayed away from the ball,
> He is an old man and his feet are not as light as they were,
> It does not matter even if he cannot dance,
> We will make the Serb dance!

And:

> Ferenc Jóska wrote a letter this morning,
> Saying that the army should go marching,

Don't you go marching, our good old king,
You just watch
What we will do for you.

The dramatis personae includes an old soldier who had fought in
1848. He is dying, and he decides to return for the last time to the battlefield of Segesvár. He knocks on the door of a peasant house and
declares straightaway:

"I am looking for the hoof-print of the horse of Father Bem, and
the ringing of Petőfi's verse on this plain. I wanted to see once more
the land where the flame of Hungarian freedom was extinguished." At
this point in the play there is the sound of thunder and lightning. A
shepherd nearby comments: "This flash was caused by the steel hoof
of Bem's horse, and the thunder was Petőfi's verse." The Hungarian
national anthem starts playing in the distance. The old hero of 1848
breaks out in the following words: "'It is as if the seas had started
moving, as if the hills and forests were advancing like armies from
these houses, in never ending rows. The world has become too small
for the human race. Evil is on its way to tread down truth, but we shall
stand in its way and we shall either crush it or perish. My muscles feel
young, my steps feel hard as steel once again...my coat is too tight...let
me cast it off. My hair is as black as ebony, just as it was a long time
ago." He tears off his coat, revealing a field-gray army coat under-
neath, and he brushes away his gray wig and beard. "Listen! "The
scene goes dark, the sound of the howling wind carrying the song "'Be
Faithful to Your Homeland' is heard. Still in the dark, the old soldier
puts on an army cap which he picks up from a pile of things on a
wooden case; he also dons a belt and takes a weapon in his hand. "It
feels as if I have lived for a thousand years; as if I have come in search
of Chieftain Árpád; as if I have been beating at the gates of Constantinople
with Botond....My flag was flying in Italy together with Louis the
Great. I was one of Thököly's *hajdús*; one of Rákóczi's *kurucs*; one of
Father Bem's artillerymen; and now I am one of Ferenc Jóska's soldiers....Every fighting Hungarian man is my brother, and every
Hungarian parent is my parent." He calls out: "'Good bye, father!" "Now
men are stepping out of every hut and tiled house. We have become one

now that we have to die. There are no masters, no peasants, no rich, no poor any more. There is only one thing left: the homeland! We all live for the homeland, and the homeland is for all of us." Behind the stage a row of peasants in army caps and reservists line up carrying kitbags on their shoulders, saying: "'Good bye! We are going to war! Serbs look out!" At the same time, the band plays the Prince Eugen March.

The play attempts to bring everything together: the homeland, a thousand years of history, 1848, the field-gray uniform—and Francis Joseph. The figure of Petőfi, murdered by Cossacks, is now directly associated with that of Francis Joseph, who had instigated the Russian intervention in the first place.

Another play written at the same time and with much the same purpose was *We All Have to Go*, written by Gyula Hegedűs and Jenő Faragó. The play was written in celebration of 18 August, Francis Joseph's birthday, 1914. The ending is set fifty years on, on 18 August 1964. The scene is the National Museum. Flags and military trophies hang on the walls, confiscated from Russian and Serb soldiers by the Hungarian army in 1914. In the middle of the hall there are two enormous glass cases, one holding the crown of the Serbian prince, the other the crown of the Tsar of All the Russias. Above the glass cases, on the wall, hang the portraits of the two victorious allies, Francis Joseph and William II, the emperor of Germany. It is a fine summer's day, and there is a constant stream of visitors:

Woman: And has Russia become a republic then?
Man: Yes, it is the happiest of republics. We Hungarians liberated them all: Poles, Jews, Bessarabians, and Romanians.
Woman: Oh yes, I was taught that at the high school for girls. When we reclaimed our country, we dictated the terms of the Warsaw peace. And the Russian people made the Romanovs flee.

Now an old grandfather enters the scene with his grandson, Pistike. The sight of military trophies evokes nostalgic recollections:

Lajos, the grandfather: It was a victory a day: the Germans were cutting down the French like...carrots: Lüttich, Namour, Brussels, Paris...

Pistike, the grandson: And was Paris held by the French then?

Listening to the visitors, the portraits of Francis Joseph and Emperor William II start to speak:

William II: See how happy the Hungarian people are? This is your doing!
Francis Joseph: And happy is the world because you wanted it so, my friend!
William II: So we did not live in vain.
Francis Joseph: We have given them eternal peace!
[Curtain]

But the real world and the end of the First World War bore little resemblance to the scenario of the play. The Hungarian people failed to liberate Russia, and the visitor would have looked in vain for the crown of the Russian tsar in the Hungarian National Museum. Further-more, Paris remained in the hands of the French! As far as the future happiness of the Hungarian people was concerned, that was far from certain.

Indeed, it did not take long for the dreams of 1914 to begin to look a little shop-soiled. By the end of the year it started to become clear that what Hungary had undertaken was unlikely to be a victory march and certainly would not end as quickly as expected. The play was cancelled.

As the war dragged on, people began to realize that it served no Hungarian national interest to cover the battlefields of Russia or Italy with the bodies of Hungarian soldiers. Enthusiasm and the feeling of unity quickly evaporated and their place was taken by disappointment and a sense of national tragedy. Francis Joseph did not live to see the final outcome, but the nation did.

The relationship between a king and his subjects is in many ways like a marriage: lies and deception have to be paid for in the end. But that is only one possible conclusion; the other is to insist that every-thing is all right, and that that is how they will remain.

* * *

EPILOGUE

Schönbrunn, 21 November 1916. It is cold and windy. The journalists in Zilahy's novel are shivering with cold as they wait outside, talking. Inside the end is near.

Upstairs in the dying man's room Maria Valeria brought her tearful face closer to the emperor's large-lobed, wrinkled ear, once brick-red but now the color of spoiled meat.

"Would you like some more water, Papa?"

The emperor did not answer his daughter's question, nor did he open his eyes. The court physician leaned over the bed and felt for the pulse on the emperor's left hand, which lay motionlessly on the camel's-hair robe. A few seconds later his eyes swept above the kneeling group and sought the Duke de Montenuovo. Someone passed his glance along into the adjoining room, and the Lord Chamberlain entered with the court chaplain, who immediately leaned over the emperor and administered extreme unction. A warm fragrance of melting wax emanated from the candles. All the people from the anteroom came in, lackeys and archdukes, and the room filled with kneelers. The chaplain began the prayer for the dead, in a voice which seemed to come from the depths of bygone centuries, and the kneelers echoed him with a murmur that was like the intermittent patter of rain: "Subvenite sanctos..."

Now and then a woman's sobbing rose above the monotonous murmur. The physician had still not taken the tip of his thumb from the emperor's artery, nor his glance from the white face of his watch. At the close of the prayer he cautiously returned the emperor's hand to the camel's-hair robe, slid his watch into a waistcoat pocket and turned toward Crown Prince Charles with a salutation which no human voice had ever addressed to the arch-duke before:

"Your Majesty! I beg to report that His Imperial Majesty has quietly mounted to the bosom of the Lord."

The newspapermen sensed something from the shadows darting behind the lighted windows, and they hurried to the main en-trance of the palace. In less than a minute a young colonel appeared on the uppermost steps, the wind tossing his blond hair:

"Gentlemen, His Majesty died at five and a half minutes past nine."

In a matter of moments the news filled the imperial city, like an explosion in a hollow cave. Everyone knew it was coming, every-one had expected the report for days, but it still rang sharp and clear, solemn and frightening, like an incredibly long, subdued cannonade, which is very similar to the pervasive, rumble of an earthquake. It took but a few minutes for the sound to pass along the sky, through forests and mountains, over battlefields and oceans. Everyone felt that only a rusty, vast iron gate could make such a thunderous noise, at the mouth of some huge, timeless tomb.

BIBLIOGRAPHY

As I noted in the Preface, the aim of this book is by no means to provide a rounded biography of Francis Joseph. Instead, I wanted to analyze the relationship between Francis Joseph and the Hungarian nation: I selected my sources accordingly. In order to make the book a relatively easy read, I did not include footnotes, incorporating references to my sources in the main text. This Bibliography includes the general historical material which I found useful.

Apart from the relevant historical literature, I relied mostly on memoirs, contemporary pamphlets, and the press. Given that the perception of Francis Joseph contains some folkloristic elements, I also considered anecdotes and popular beliefs reflected in literary sources to be of equal reference value. The authors of these works are given in the main text.

Another crucial source of information are Francis Joseph's letters, many of which have been published: letters to his mother—covering the period 1838–72—were published in 1930, those to Elizabeth (1854–98) in 1966, and those to Katalin Schratt in 1949 (reprinted in 1992). A random selection of this correspondence was published in Hungarian translation in 1924, entitled *Francis Joseph's Hand-Written Confidential Correspondence and Secret Orders*. The latest selection of correspondence in Hungarian was published by Mária Tolnainé Kiss, entitled *Dear Ida!—Letters from Queen Elizabeth, Francis Joseph, Gyula Andrássy, and Katalin Schratt to Ida Ferenczi* (Budapest, 1992).

Francis Joseph has always attracted at times intense interest, resulting in an extremely high number of publications, the quality of which is sometimes below standard.

A basic text on the subject is J. Redlich's *Kaiser Franz Josef von Österreich* (Wien-Leipzig-München, 1924). The latest reliable study on the subject, with a very different point of view, is a book by Steven Beller, *Francis Joseph* (London, Longman, 1996). Redlich and Beller have also published a number of important monographs. As a rule, the most difficult problem is to distinguish between the emperor's personal biography and the history of the empire under his rule. The most personal account is the 3-volume monograph by E. C. Corti, the third volume of which was finished by Hans Hugo Sokol after the author's death: Volume I: *Vom Kind zum Kaiser: Kindheit und erste Jugend Kaiser Franz Josef I. und seiner Geschwister* (Graz, 1950); Volume II: *Mensch und Herrscher: Wege und Schicksale Kaiser Franz Josef I. zwischen Thronbesteigung und Berliner Kongress* (Graz, 1952); and Volume III (co-authored by Sokol): *Der Alte kaiser: Kaiser Franz Josef I. vom Berliner Kongress bis zu seinem Tode* (Graz, 1955).

At around the same time as Corti's last volume a general historical analysis appeared, written by Alexander Novotny, *Kaiser Franz Josef und seine Zeit*...(Wien, 1954). Interest continued throughout the 1960s and 1970s. Otto von Habsburg also wrote a book entitled *Kaiser Franz Josef* (Wien, 1966). Important works published in the UK and the USA include Murad's *Francis Joseph I and His Empire* (New York, 1968); Zbynek A. B. Zeman's *Twilight of the Habsburgs. The Collapse of the Austro-Hungarian Empire* (London, 1971); and Lavender Cassels' *Clash of Generations. A Habsburg Family Drama in the Nineteenth Century* (London, 1973). *Kaiser Franz Josef und sein Hof* (Hamburg, 1984) focuses on Francis Joseph's personality.

Among works by German authors the following deserve mention: Franz Herre: *Kaiser Franz Josef von Österreich* (Köln, 1978), and Erich Kielmansegg, *Kaiserhaus. Staatsmänner und Politiker* (Wien, 1966).

In the 1980s a large number of events and publications were devoted to Francis Joseph and his reign: large-scale exhibitions were held in Schloss-Graffeneggben (Austria) in 1984 and in 1987. The first exhibition covered the period from 1848 to 1880, and the second 1880 to 1916. The catalogues of these exhibitions were published in two volumes, entitled *Das Zeitalter Kaiser Franz Josefs*.

In the 1990s two important new publications appeared: Jean-Paul

Bled's *Franz Joseph* (Oxford, 1992), and Allan W. Palmer: *Twilight of the Habsburgs: The Life and Times of Emperor Francis Joseph* (London, 1994). Their merits notwithstanding, neither book contain anything substantially new.

In the late 1970s, alternative approaches—anthropological, semantic—started to appear. It was around this time that Robert J. Evans published *The Making of the Habsburg Monarchy 1550–1700: An Interpretation* (Oxford, 1979). (Before him Claudio Magris had addressed the question of myths about the Habsburgs, but from a different viewpoint. In 1988, part of Magris's lengthy, and somewhat diffuse, work written in the early 1960s was published in Hungarian translation, entitled *A Habsburg-mítosz az osztrák irodalomban* [The Habsburg myth in Austrian literature]. Most recently, Marie Tanner has analyzed the image and self-image of the Habsburg dynasty in *The Last Descendant of Aeneas: The Habsburgs and the Mythic Image of the Emperor* (New Haven, 1993). The topic of image and self-image is continued by Andrew Wheatcroft in *The Habsburgs. Embodying Empire* (London, 1995).

As already pointed out, most biographical writings concentrate on issues of general history, as Francis Joseph was an important decision-maker for decades. The most widely regarded synthesis is Robert A. Kann's *A History of the Habsburg Empire, 1526–1918* (Berkeley, 1977). Two earlier publications enjoy almost identical recognition, namely A. J. P. Taylor: *The Habsburg Monarchy 1809–1918* (New York, 1948), and A. J. May: *The Habsburg Monarchy 1867–1914* (Cambridge, 1951). Another widely used reference is C. A. McCartney: *The Habsburg Empire 1790–1918* (London, 1969). Two Hungarian authors have attained similar recognition: one is Oszkár Jászi, whose book *The Dissolution of the Habsburg Monarchy* was published in 1929 in English, and printed in Hungary only in 1982; the other is François Fejtő, whose *Requiem pour un empire defunt. Histoire de la destruction de l'Autriche-Hongrie* (Paris, 1988), appeared in Hungarian in 1990.

Mention must also be made of an Austrian publication, the work of several authors. This a thematic analysis of the history of the Monarchy, edited by Adam Wandruszka and Peter Urbanitsch. Six volumes have been published in the *Die Habsburger Monarchie 1818–1918* series (Vienna, 1973–) so far.

Aspects of Hungarian history have received relatively little attention in the international reference literature: Francis Joseph is perceived by the world at large mostly as an emperor rather than as an emperor and king. Naturally, one of the main reasons for this is that most scholars researching the Austro-Hungarian Monarchy, and/or Francis Joseph, do not speak Hungarian, and consequently do not have access to a wealth of Hungarian source material. Another cause, no less important, is that for a long time Hungarian historiography and publishing gave little stimulus or inspiration to the outside world. More specifically, for a long time Hungarian historiography hardly dealt with Francis Joseph at all. The first noteworthy monograph was published in 1907, written by Sándor Márki and entitled *Francis Joseph I. King of Hungary*. One serious drawback of this otherwise very informative book is that it was produced while Francis Joseph was still alive, thus loyalty takes precedence over objective analysis. Under the Horthy regime a biography of Francis Joseph was written by István Perlaky (in 1938), but its quality is questionable.

The first serious work on the subject in Hungarian is credited to Dávid Angyal, who analyzed the initial stages of Francis Joseph's life. This monograph, entitled *The Young Francis Joseph*, appeared in 1942, and still affords fascinating reading.

After that no monograph was written about Francis Joseph for a long time, despite the fact that a number of excellent shorter works appeared. In Volume VI/1 of *The History of Hungary* (1979) György Szabad paints a very good portrait of the Hungarian king (pp. 447–550). Although it should be pointed out that Francis Joseph did feature in a number of general works, Gusztáv Beksics mentions him in *Hungarian Stories About the Millennium* only apologetically, whereas Gusztáv Gratz and Gyula Szekfű wrote hardly anything of substance about him. In 1980, Péter Hanák wrote an excellent short essay entitled *Francis Joseph's Bedroom*, which appeared in the 4 October issue of the periodical *Élet és Irodalom*. Hanák's essay and shorter studies about Francis Joseph's era are available in the 1998 winter issue of *Budapesti Negyed*, edited by Andrea Pető.

A number of more comprehensive analyses, written from a variety of viewpoints, appeared in the late 1980s. The first Hungarian edition of the present volume was published in 1988, and Éva Somogyi's book *Francis Joseph* appeared in 1989.

The subject continued to be neglected despite the fact that enthusiastic interest in the Habsburg dynasty never ceased in Hungary. Imre Gonda and Emil Niederhauser wrote a book entitled *The Habsburgs* (Budapest, 1977), which naturally covers Francis Joseph among others. (A new edition was published in 1998.) Péter Hanák continued to write about the Monarchy and in issue 1984/2–3 of the Hungarian periodical *Medvetánc* he gave the first deep analysis of the conflict-stricken relationship between Hungarians and Francis Joseph's world view. This study, entitled "1898: The Head-On Clash of National- and State-Patriotic Values in the Monarchy," signaled that there was still much research to be done on this topic. In issue 1986/3 of the periodical *Valóság*, John T. Salvendy writes, among other things, about Francis Joseph's psychopathology.

In the 1990s, many books appeared which were related to Francis Joseph in one way or another. These were mostly translations from other languages. One of these was the *Habsburg Encyclopedia* (Budapest, 1990) edited by Brigitte Hamann. Hamann has written another book about Rudolf and Elizabeth. Writings about the world view of the petite bourgeoisie deal with Francis Joseph only marginally. It should be emphasized that in Hungary attention has been concentrated mostly on Queen Elizabeth.

Sándor Márki was the first Hungarian historian to devote a book to Queen Elizabeth, *Elizabeth, Queen of Hungary: 1867–1898* (Budapest, 1899). The essential ideology had been already formulated (by Sándor Márki in "'Queen Elizabeth. Memorial Speech Held at the Ceremonial General Assembly of the Francis Joseph Hungarian Royal University, Kolozsvár, 19 November 1898"). A contemporary publication cited in the text is *Elizabeth: In Memory of a Great Hungarian Queen*, edited by Gyula Gábel (Budapest, 1900). A new and more decorative edition of the same appeared in 1906.

Commemorations of Elizabeth were held also at a local level, but one has the impression that publications produced on such occasions were meant to commemorate the organizers rather than Elizabeth. (Such publications include: *The Szepesség Mourns. Memorial Album to Queen Elizabeth*, edited and published by Gyula Telléry (Budapest, 1899), and memorial cards related to the unveiling of the statue of Queen Elizabeth "of glorious memory," Bártfafürdő, 16 August 1903, edited by Dezső Arányi (Bártfa, 1903).

Between the two World Wars Elizabeth became the heroine of a number of novels: one example is a book by a fashionable female writer of the period, Julianna Zsigray, who wrote *Elizabeth, the Hungarian Queen* (Budapest, 1937). Indirect, but constant interest in the subject is amply demonstrated by an auction held on 5 December 1935, at which Elizabeth's books and personal belongings were auctioned. For a description, see the auction catalogue: *Artifacts, Books of Artistic Value and Other Works of Art from the Heirlooms of Queen Elizabeth* (Budapest, 1935).

Most recently, Emil Niederhauser has written a book about Elizabeth, or more precisely, about her assassination: *The Assassination of Queen Elizabeth* (Budapest, 1985). Continuity of interest is also indicated by the appearance of a number of new publications dealing with Elizabeth (among other topics) directly or indirectly. A reprint appeared in 1989 of Egon Caesar Corti's biography of Elizabeth (1935), and Brigitte Hamann's *Queen Elizabeth* (1988) was published in Hungarian translation. Another publication deals with *The Relics of Three Generations at the Hungarian National Museum (1823–1875)* (Budapest, 1988).

The 150th anniversary of Queen Elizabeth's birth was commemorated in Hungary by exhibitions in Szeged and Gödöllő. In Szeged, an exhibition guide was published, while in Gödöllő a highly informative booklet appeared *Exhibition of the Gödöllő Local History Collection Commemorating the 150th Anniversary of Queen Elizabeth's Birth* (Gödöllő, 1987). Issue 87/10 of the periodical *Gödöllői Mindenes* contains a modern ethnographic collection about Elizabeth, to which I have referred, entitled *Memories of the Queen*.

The exhibition held by the National Museum of Hungary entitled *The Hungarian Compromise, 1867* featured a large number of relics related to Elizabeth (the exhibition was organized and the catalog written by Katalin Körmöczi).

In 1991, the Museum of Austrian Culture (Eisenstadt) dedicated an exhibition to her memory, entitled *Sissy: Elizabeth, Queen of the Hungarian People*, which used mostly Hungarian material.

In 1992, the Hungarian National Museum held an exhibition about Elizabeth, which was arranged by Katalin F. Dózsa. The Museum also published an exhibition catalogue entitled *Elizabeth, Queen of the Hungarian People*, which contains several studies on the subject.

The 100th Anniversary of Elizabeth's assassination was remembered in Gödöllő by a symposium. At the same time a reprint edition of Géza Ripka's book *Gödöllő: Home Town of the Royal Family* was published.

Recently, a number of publications by American scholars have appeared in Hungarian which give more insight into the character of Francis Joseph and his era, although he is not their principal subject. These include: István Deák: *Beyond Nationalism. A Social and Political History of the Habsburg Officer Corps, 1848–1914* (New York, 1992), and Carl E. Schorske: *Fin-de-Siècle in Vienna: Politics and Culture* (New York, 1981).

As I have already mentioned, contemporary publications assisted me greatly with the writing of this book. These may be classified as sources rather than reference literature, given that in the public domain loyalty was a mandatory requirement. No criticism was possible: apart from anything else it was prohibited by the Penal Code. The tone of contemporary assessments is best illustrated by a specific example, such as *A Reseda Branch for the Grave of Our Unforgettable King* by the Hermit of Hanvay [Zoltán Hanvay] (Rimaszombat?, 1917); or *From the Life of a Wise King* (Budapest, 1911). Nevertheless, even writings like this, which may be found in large numbers, have their reference value in that they reflect contemporary views and the factual information contained in them often cannot be found anywhere else (as is the case with Falk-Dux's *Coronation. A Memorial Album* (Pest, 1867).

I also quote from József Kristóffy's memoirs, *Hungary's Calvary. The Road to Collapse. Political Memoirs. 1890–1926* (Budapest, 1927) and from those of Béla Barabás, *(Memoirs. 1850–1929* (Arad?, 1929). The author of the ethnographic collection concerning Rudolf is Lajos

Kiss, *Vásárhelyi Kistükör* (Budapest, 1964). Other quotations were taken from Mór Szatmári's historically valuable book *Twenty Years of Storm in Parliament* (Budapest, 1928). The names of István Pápay, István Kray, Jenő Szontagh, and Ferenc Herczeg must also be mentioned. Another crucial source was *Struggle, Failure, Repression* (Budapest, 1978), and the collection of memoirs entitled *The Earth Has Turned Gray* (Budapest, 1985).

Among literary authors Miklós Bánffy, Kálmán Mikszáth, János Arany, László Arany, Joseph Roth, Robert Musil, Karl Kraus, Árpád Pásztor, Gyula Hegedűs, Géza Gárdonyi, Ferenc Móra, Gyula Krúdy, Ferenc Molnár, and Lajos Zilahy were indispensable sources of reference.

Last but not least, I would like to mention a text which proved very useful in terms of understanding the milieu and interpreting the period in general. Somewhat eclectic, but nevertheless very informative is László Tarr, *A Country of Mirages* (Budapest, 1976), and also *The Millennium* (Budapest, 1979). I edited a selection of press publications related to the Millennium entitled *Budapest 1896* (Budapesti Negyed, 1996/10-11). Together with Katalin Jalsovszky and Emőke Tomsics, I also produced *Once Upon a Time There Was a Hungary* (Budapest, 1996). Katalin Jalsovszky and Emőke Tomsics have also edited *Imperial Vienna, Royal Budapest* (Budapest, 1996).

In my opinion two books by Péter Hanák are essential for developing an adequate conceptual framework for interpretation: *Hungary in the Monarchy* (Budapest, 1975), and *The Garden and the Workshop: Essays on the Cultural History of Vienna and Budapest* (Princeton, 1999).

* * *

I owe special thanks to András Arató, without whose support this book could not be published. I also owe many thanks to a number of people who helped me write the original version of this book, particularly now that it is being published in an English edition.

INDEX

ABOUT THE AUTHOR

ANDRÁS GERŐ is professor of history and chairman of the Department of Social History at Eötvös Loránd University, Budapest, and professor of history at Central European University. He has also been a visiting professor at the University of Pennsylvania, Utrecht, Amsterdam, and Columbia University. He has published widely in English and German as well as Hungarian, and is editor in chief of the *Budapest Quaterly,* a historical journal. His most recent publications are: *Unfinished Socialism* (Budapest: Central European University Press, 1999), co-authored with Iván Pető, and *The Hungarian Parliament (1867–1918). A Mirage of Power* (Boulder, CO: Social Science Monographs, 1997).